lonely planet

HAWAII

TOP SIGHTS, AUTHENTIC EXPERIENCES

THIS EDITION WRITTEN AND RESEARCHED BY
Amy Balfour, Loren Bell, Greg Benchwick, Sara Benson,
Jade Bremner, Adam Karlin, Craig McLachlan, Adam
Skolnick, Ryan Ver Berkmoes, Luci Yamamoto.

Contents

Plan Your Trip

Hawaii's Top 12 4
Need to Know 16
Hot Spots For 18
Local Life 20
Month by Month 22
Get Inspired 25
Itineraries 26
Family Travel 32

Honolulu   34
...at a glance   36

Chinatown 38
'Iolani Palace 44
Pearl Harbor 46
Bishop Museum 50
Manoa Falls Trail 52
Sights 54
Activities 63
Tours 65
Shopping 66
Eating 67
Drinking & Nightlife 70
Entertainment 71
Getting There 71

Waikiki   72
...at a glance   74

Kuhio Beach Park 76
Surfing 78
Sights 80
Beaches 86
Activities 88
Tours 89
Shopping 89
Eating 91
Drinking & Nightlife 96
Entertainment 98
Getting There 100
Where to Stay 101

Na Pali Coast Wilderness State Park   102
...at a glance   104

Boat Tours of the Na Pali Coast   106
Kalalau Trail 110
Ha'ena State Park ... 114
Sights 118
Activities 119
Shopping 119
Eating & Drinking 119
Getting There 119

Hanalei Bay   120
...at a glance   122

Black Pot Beack Park & Around 124
Beaches 128
Activities 129
Tours 129
Eating 130
Drinking & Nightlife 131
Getting There 131

Waimea Canyon   132
...at a glance   134

Hiking Waimea Canyon 136
Hiking Koke'e State Park 140
Sights 144
Activities 145
Shopping 146
Eating 147
Entertainment 147
Getting There 147

Moloka'i   148
...at a glance   150

Halawa Valley 152
Hiking Kalaupapa Trail 156
Sights 160
Activities 161
Shopping 163
Eating 164
Drinking & Nightlife 165
Getting There 165

Road to Hana   166
...at a glance   168

Pi'ilanihale Heiau 170
Pi'ilani Trail 174
Ke'anae Peninsula ... 176
Waterfalls & Swimming Holes 178
Beaches 180
Sights 180
Tours 180
Activities 181
Shopping 183
Eating 183
Drinking & Nightlife 185
Getting There 185

Kihei & Wailea   186
...at a glance   188

Whale-Watching 190
Best Local Food 192
Beaches 196
Activities 197
Eating 198
Drinking & Nightlife 199
Getting There 199

2

Waikiki
Waikiki is back, baby! Dig in.

Hawaii's most famous beach resort was a haven for tacky plastic lei, coconut-shell bikini tops and motorized, hip-shaking hula dolls. But real aloha and chic-modern style have returned. Beach boys and girls surf legendary waves by day, and after sunset tiki torches light up the sand. Every night hula dancers sway to ancient and modern rhythms – backed by slack key guitars and ukuleles – at oceanfront hotels, open-air bars and even shopping malls.

Right: Waikiki Beach (p78)

3

Na Pali Coast
Rugged adventures on land and sea

The Na Pali Coast should top everyone's to-do list. Make the oceanic journey by sailing a catamaran, or pit your paddle and kayak against the elements. For hikers, Ke'e Beach is the entry point for the rugged, 11-mile-long Kalalau Trail. Hawaii's most famous trek will transport you to a place like no other, where verdant cliffs soar above a sloping valley abundant with fruit trees, waterfalls and solace seekers.

CHASE CLAUSEN/SHUTTERSTOCK ©

MESE BERG/SHUTTERSTOCK ©

Hanalei Bay

Beach life is the best life here

Voted one of the USA's best beaches many times over, this crescent-shaped bay delights lazy sunbathers and active beachgoers alike. Surfers can charge massive (and some beginner) waves while onlookers amble along the golden, sandy shore. Surf lessons go on near the pier, and most afternoons see locals and visitors firing up barbecue grills, cracking open cold brews and humbly watching the daylight fade.

4

Waimea Canyon

Lush, rugged and divine for exploring

Formed by millions of years of erosion and the collapse of the volcano that formed Kaua'i, the 'Grand Canyon of the Pacific' stretches 10 miles long, 1 mile wide and more than 3600ft deep. Reached via a serpentine scenic drive, roadside lookouts provide panoramic views of rugged cliffs, crested buttes and deep valley gorges. Steep hiking trails drop into the canyon floor to survey its interior. It's a bounty of amazing sights.

5

Moloka'i

History and views on the most Hawaiian island

More than 50% of Moloka'i's people have indigenous heritage. Locals favor preservation of land and culture over schemes promoting tourism. Yet there is aloha spirit everywhere and visitors find a genuine welcome. The island is also home to striking Kalaupapa Peninsula and the Halawa Valley, an end-of-the-road place with hundreds of sacred taro patches, ancient temples and waterfalls pounding into swimmable pools.

Road to Hana

Hold on tight for a dramatic drive

A roller coaster of a ride, the Hana Hwy in Maui twists down into jungly valleys and back up towering cliffs, curling around 600 twists and turns along the way. Fifty-four one-lane bridges cross nearly as many waterfalls – some eye-popping torrents, others soothing and gentle. But the ride's only half the thrill. Get out and swim in a Zen-like pool, hike a ginger-scented trail and savor fresh guava and coconuts.

Kihei & Wailea

Golden-sand beaches and pristine resorts

Famed for phenomenal swimming, snorkeling, sunbathing and sunny skies, the beaches are world class. Beyond the beaches, with its tidy golf courses, protective privacy walls and discreet signage, Wailea looks like a members-only country club and is South Maui's most elite haunt. Amenities shine. If you're not staying here, say a loud *mahalo* (thank you) for Hawaii's beach-access laws that allow you to visit these beautiful strands anyway, with dedicated public parking lots.

MONICA AND MICHAEL SWEET/GETTY IMAGES ©

EQROY/SHUTTERSTOCK ©

Haleakalā National Park

Otherworldly beauty from shore to summit

As you hike into the belly of Haleakalā, the first thing you notice is the crumbly, lunar-like landscape. Then you experience the eerie quiet – the only sound is the crunching of volcanic cinders beneath your feet. The path continues through an unearthly world, a tableau of stark lava, rainbow-colored cinder cones and ever-changing clouds. At the coast, waterfalls tumble into brilliant pools, flanked by trails, viewpoints and one amazing bamboo forest.

WESTEND61/GETTY IMAGES ©

PNG STUDIO PHOTOGRAPHY/SHUTTERSTOCK ©

Waipi'o Valley

A stunning and mysterious tropical valley

A mysterious green bowl full of ghosts and legends. A sacred site. A retreat from the outside world. Waipi'o's special distillation of all these makes it irresistible. Many choose to snap a photo from the panoramic overlook, one of the Big Island's most iconic views. Others trek down to the valley floor to stroll a black-sand beach and peer at distant waterfalls. Access is limited beyond that, which only enhances the mystery.

10

Mauna Kea

Gaze at a blanket of stars

Star light, star bright, the first star I see tonight...whoops, scratch that. Up here, the night skies are clearer than almost anywhere on Earth. Stars sear the night white, and choosing the first is near impossible. Not to worry: with free telescopes set up for visitors to browse the celestial glory, you don't have to choose just one. Get here by sunset for a heavenly double feature or show up during meteor showers for all-night star parties.

11

Hawai'i Volcanoes National Park

Fiery sites abound on the Big Island

Set on the sloping hillside of the world's most active volcano, this fantastic park dramatically reminds you that nature is very much alive and in perpetual motion. An incredible network of hiking trails encompasses lava flows and tubes, steam vents and wild beaches.

12

Plan Your Trip
Need to Know

When to Go

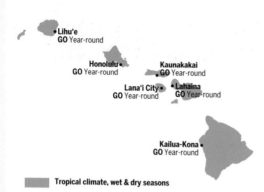

- Lihu'e
  GO Year-round
- Honolulu
  GO Year-round
- Kaunakakai
  GO Year-round
- Lana'i City
  GO Year-round
- Lahaina
  GO Year-round
- Kailua-Kona
  GO Year-round

Tropical climate, wet & dry seasons

High Season (Dec–Apr & Jun–Aug)

○ Accommodations prices up 50–100%.

○ Christmas to New Year's and around Easter are the most expensive and busy.

○ Winter is rainier (but best for whale-watching and surfing), summer slightly hotter.

Shoulder (May & Sep)

○ Crowds and prices drop slightly between schools' spring break and summer vacation.

○ Temperatures mild, with mostly sunny, cloudless days.

Low Season (Oct & Nov)

○ Fewest crowds, airfares to Hawaii at their lowest.

○ Accommodations rates drop – around 50% less than in high season.

○ Weather is typically dry and hot (not ideal for hiking).

Currency
US dollar ($)

Language
English, Hawaiian

Visas
Visitors from Canada, the UK, Australia, New Zealand, Japan and many EU countries don't need visas for stays of less than 90 days. Other nations see http://travel/.state.gov.

Money
ATMs are available in cities and larger towns. Credit cards are widely accepted (except at some lodgings) and are often required for reservations. Tipping is customary.

Cell Phones
Foreign phones that operate on tri- or quad-ban frequencies will work in Hawaii. Or purchase inexpensive cell phones with a pay-as-you-go plan here.

Time
Hawaiian–Aleutian Standard Time (GMT/UMC minus 10 hours)

Daily Costs

Budget: **Less than $100**

- Dorm bed: $25–45
- Local plate lunch: $6–10
- Bus fare (one way): $2–2.50

Midrange: **$100–250**

- Double room with private bath at midrange hotel or B&B: $100–250
- Rental car (excluding insurance and gas) per day/week: from $35/150
- Dinner at casual sit-down restaurant: $20–40

Top End: **More than $250**

- Beach resort hotel room or luxury condo rental: more than $250
- Three-course meal with a cocktail in a top restaurant: $75–125
- Guided outdoor adventure tour: $80–200

Useful Websites

Hawaii Visitors and Convention Bureau (www.gohawaii.com) Official tourism site; comprehensive events calendar and multi-lingual planning guides.
Hawai'i Magazine (www.hawaiimagazine.com) All-island news, features, food and drink, and travel tips.
Lonely Planet (www.lonelyplanet.com/usa/hawaii) Destination information, hotel bookings, traveler forum and more.
Hana Hou! (www.hanahou.com) Hawaiian Airlines' engaging in-flight magazine, with feature stories available free online.

Opening Hours

Banks 8:30am – 4pm Monday to Friday; some to 6pm Friday and 9am – noon or 1pm Saturday.
Bars Noon – midnight; some to 2am Thursday to Saturday.

Government offices 8:30am – 4:30pm Monday to Friday; some post offices open 9am – noon Saturday.
Restaurants Breakfast 6:30am – 10am, lunch 11:30am – 2pm, dinner 5pm – 9:30pm.
Shops 9am – 5pm Monday to Saturday, some noon – 5pm Sunday; shopping malls have extended hours.

Arriving in Hawaii

Honolulu International Airport (HNL) (p313)

Car Most car-rental agencies are on-site. Drive takes 25 to 45 minutes to Waikiki via Hwy 92 (Nimitz Hwy/Ala Moana Blvd) or H-1 (Lunalilo) Fwy.
Taxi Metered, around $40 to $50 to Waikiki, plus 50¢ per bag and 10% to 15% driver's tip.
Door-to-door shuttle Costs $16/30 one way/round trip to Waikiki; operates 24 hours (every 20 to 60 minutes).
Bus TheBus 19 or 20 to Waikiki ($2.50) every 20 to 60 minutes from 5:30am to 11:30pm daily (large baggage prohibited).

Getting Around

Most interisland travel is by plane, while a rental car is best for exploring individual islands.

Air Interisland flights are short, frequent and expensive.

Boat A ferry connects Maui with Lana'i.

Bus Public buses run limited routes on the larger islands and can be time-consuming, except on O'ahu.

Car Rent a car to explore, especially on the Neighbor Islands. Consider a 4WD on Lana'i and Hawai'i, the Big Island.

For more on **getting around**, see p314

Plan Your Trip
Hot Spots For...

Beaches

Thinking of Hawaii instantly conjours images of golden sands backed by tropical palm trees. With hundreds of miles of coastline, you'll be spoiled for choice.

SAM STRICKLER/SHUTTERSTOCK ©

O'ahu
O'ahu has so much going on, especially if you like sun, sand and adventure.

Waikiki (p72)
Learn to surf, then join a sunset cruise.

Maui
The strands are golden on the Valley Isle and prime for sunbathing.

Big Beach (p200)
A mile-long crescent with turquoise waters.

Kaua'i
The beaches attract outdoor adventurers of every skill level.

Hanalei Bay (p120)
For surfers, paddlers, and beach bums alike.

Adventures on Land

Hawaii's islands have as much to offer landlubbers as water babies. Strap yourself into a zipline harness, lace up those hiking boots or climb into the saddle.

INGO70/SHUTTERSTOCK ©

Maui
An ancient footpath encircles the island, passing centuries-old structures.

Pi'ilani Trail (p174)
This coastal footpath crosses 14th-century stepping stones.

The Big Island
Lofty volcanoes offer a range of wild natural sights on hikes for every ability level.

Hawai'i Volcanoes National Park (p250) High, low, there's fire wherever you go.

Moloka'i
History and scenery collide on the most Hawaiian island's striking trails.

Kalaupapa (p156)
Descend to a remote peninsula by foot or by mule.

Scenic Drives

Ready to hit the road? These islands may be small, but you can still take unbelievably beautiful road trips up volcano summits and past high pali (cliffs).

PAUL LAUBACH/SHUTTERSTOCK ©

Maui
Ancient sites, towering waterfalls and intriguing communities are linked by gorgeous drives.

Road to Hana (p166)
Coastal drive featuring waterfalls and 54 stone bridges.

O'ahu
Cosmopolitan, yes. But even the most ardent city denizen needs to let their hair down. In a convertible, perhaps?

Tantalus Round-Top (p62)
Take in the views round this native flora filled route.

The Big Island
Pockets of organized activity dot the volcanic regions, with roads leading to wild adventure.

Chain of Craters Road (p265)
Drop through an active volcanic zone to old lava flows.

Waterfalls & Swimming Holes

Wade through the mud and step over slippery tree roots on jungly trails, all so you can swim in a crystal-clear pool under a rain forest cascade.

FOMINAYAPHOTO/SHUTTERSTOCK ©

Kaua'i
The folds of crinkled Na Pali coastline hide a bounty of waterfalls – not always easy to reach.

Hanakapi'ai Falls (p111)
A hike-earned gem ready for swimmers.

Maui
Head to the Road to Hana and the rain-loving East Side for a gorgeous waterfall lineup.

'Ohe'o Gulch (p210)
Waterfalls tumble into the sea in Haleakalā National Park.

Moloka'i
The mysterious Halawa Valley is a place of ancient history and lush beauty.

Moa'ula & Hipuapua Falls (p155) Hire a local guide to hike to these twin beauties.

Plan Your Trip
Local Life

DEBORAH KOLB/SHUTTERSTOCK ©

Activities

Mark Twain explored Hawaii for the *Sacramento Union* in the 1860s, and he wrote quite vividly about his many adventures. After climbing Haleakalā in 1866, for example, he described the sunrise as 'the sublimest spectacle I ever witnessed.' Today, adventurers might pay the same compliment to the whole state. On the water, kiteboarders skip across swells, surfers ride monster waves and snorkelers float beside green sea turtles. Humpback whales draw sightseers to Maui in winter. On land, hikers climb misty slopes while mountain bikers hurtle through leafy forest. Everyone stops to watch the fiery cauldron on the Big Island. It's all a sublime spectacle indeed.

Shopping

Arts and crafts purchased in Hawaii will likely become treasures for a lifetime – and be proudly displayed in your home. A good place to start your search? Shops and galleries run by local art co-ops which sell members' work. You'll find everything from paintings and photographs to jewelry and furniture. Crafts with historic local roots include woodworking, *lauhala* weaving and the making of *kapa* (pounded-bark cloth) for clothing. You may also find interesting art and jewelry at annual festivals across the islands, which typically have an art fair along with the food and live music.

Entertainment

In tourist enclaves along the coast, you'll find live music – usually a guy or girl on guitar – playing light rock classics and easygoing island favorites, from late afternoon onward. Larger cities like Honolulu and Kahului have performance halls where you may be able to catch slack key and ukulele concerts from well-known musicians. Hawaiian luau combine food, music and hula. For a more enriching experience try to find a luau that focuses on traditional food, dance and hula.

LINDA HUGHES/SHUTTERSTOCK ©

Eating

Hawaii's cuisine is a multicultural flavor explosion, influenced by the Pacific Rim and rooted in the islands' natural bounty. The first Polynesians brought nourishing staples such as *kalo* (taro), *niu* (coconut), chickens and pigs. Later plantation-era immigrants imported rice, *shōyu* (soy sauce), chilies and other Asian and Spanish influences. Over time, all these wildly different flavors became 'local.' Step out of your comfort zone to try local specialties such as *loco moco* (dish of rice, fried egg and hamburger patty topped with gravy or other condiments), Spam *musubi* (rice balls)and shave ice. In many top restaurants, Hawaii regional cuisine is on the menu, with the chef adding a healthy gourmet spin to longtime basics – bringing tasty flair to local fish, beef and produce.

★ Best Plate Lunches

Super J's (p247)

Rainbow Drive-In (p93)

Kilauea Fish Market (p131)

Da Kitchen Express (p198)

Mana'e Goods & Grindz (p164)

Drinking & Nightlife

For the most part, Hawaii is not a late-night kind of place. The sun sets early and things typically quieten down well before the wee hours. You'll find plenty of easy-drinking mai tais and tropical drinks at oceanfront bars, but it's the cocktail bars and upscale restaurants that are really having fun, creating delicious specialty drinks using locally sourced spirits and ingredients. Craft breweries are now firmly established on the larger islands and most have taprooms and offer tours of their production facilities.

From left: Hawaiian dancers fire twirling; *Loco moco*

Plan Your Trip
Month by Month

January

Typically Hawaii's wettest and coolest month, January is when tourist high season gets into full swing.

✿ Chinese New Year

On the second new moon after the winter solstice, usually between late January and mid-February, look for lion dances, firecrackers, street fairs and parades.

February

Peak tourist season continues. Winter storms bring more rainfall and cooler temperatures.

✿ Waimea Town Celebration

Over a week in mid-February, more than 10,000 folks gather in Waimea (Kaua'i) to celebrate with canoe races, a rodeo, lei-making contests and live music (p147).

March

Another busy month, despite lingering rainfall. College students and families take a one- or two-week 'spring break' around Easter, falling in March or April.

✿ Whale & Ocean Arts Festival

Throughout the winter, Maui welcomes migratory humpback whales with an annual whale count and an art show, live entertainment and kids' activities in early March.

✿ Honolulu Festival

In mid-March, this three-day festival is a unique blend of Hawaiian, Asian and Polynesian cultures, with arts-and-crafts, live music and dance performances, culminating in a parade followed by fireworks.

April

Peak tourist season winds down as rainstorms lessen. Resorts are less busy after

Above left: Performers in the Aloha Festivals, Honolulu

Easter, once college students and families finish taking their 'spring break' vacations.

🎋 Merrie Monarch Festival
On Hawai'i (Big Island), Easter Sunday kicks off Hilo's week-long celebration of Hawaiian arts and culture. The Olympics of hula competitions draws top troupes from all islands, the US mainland and abroad.

✕ Waikiki Spam Jam
Residents consume almost seven million cans of Spam annually. Waikiki's wacky one-day street festival in late April is all about *ono kine grinds* (good eats).

May
Crowds thin and prices drop slightly between spring break and summer vacation. Temperatures remain mild, with mostly sunny and cloudless days. Hotels sell out for the Memorial Day holiday weekend in late May.

★ Best Festivals
Aloha Festivals, September

Triple Crown of Surfing, November/ December

Merrie Monarch Festival, March/ April

Koloa Plantation Days Celebration, July

Kona Coffee Cultural Festival, November

June
Arriving before most families start summer vacations, visitors in early June can take advantage of warm, dry weather and hotel and flight discounts.

🎋 Moloka'i Ka Hula Piko
According to Hawaiian oral history, Moloka'i is the birthplace of hula. In early June, this

Above right: Surfer in the Triple Crown of Surfing (p24)

free, three-day hula festival draws huge crowds.

July

Temperatures rise and rain is scarce. School summer vacations and the July 4 holiday make this one of the busiest travel months. Book early and expect high prices.

🎊 Independence Day

Across the islands, Fourth of July celebrations inspire fireworks and fairs.

🎊 Koloa Plantation Days Celebration

On Kaua'i's south shore, this nine-day festival in mid-July is a huge celebration of the island's sugar-plantation and *paniolo* (Hawaiian cowboy) heritage.

August

Families taking summer vacations keep things busy all around the islands. Hot, sunny weather prevails. Statehood Day is a holiday observed on the third Friday of the month.

☆ Hawaiian Slack Key Guitar Festival

On O'ahu, free open-air concerts by ukulele and slack key guitar legends, with food and craft vendors and an arts-and-crafts fair, happen in mid-August.

September

After Labor Day weekend in early September, crowds dwindle as students go back to school. Hot, dry weather continues.

🎊 Aloha Festivals

Begun in 1946, the Aloha Festivals are the state's premier Hawaiian cultural celebration, an almost nonstop series of events on all the main islands during September.

🎊 Kaua'i Mokihana Festival

In mid-September, Kaua'i's week-long contemporary Hawaiian arts and cultural festival includes a three-day hula competition in ancient and modern styles.

October

The slowest month for tourism, October brings travel bargains on hotels and flights. Weather is reliably sunny, but very humid when the trade winds don't blow.

✕ Hawaii Food & Wine Festival

Hawaii's hottest chefs and most lauded artisan farmers gather for this homegrown culinary celebration in mid-October to early November.

🎊 Halloween

On Maui, Lahaina's Halloween carnival is a great street party. Other places to get festive on October 31 include Waikiki on O'ahu.

November

Toward the end of the month, vacationing crowds (and scattered rainfall) return. Thanksgiving on the fourth Thursday is a popular and pricey time to visit.

♥ Kona Coffee Cultural Festival

For 10 days during the harvest season in early November, the Big Island honors Kona brews with a cupping competition, a coffee-picking contest, a recipe cook-off, coffee farm tours, art shows, live music, hula and more.

☆ Triple Crown of Surfing

O'ahu's North Shore hosts pro surfing's ultimate contest, known as the Triple Crown of Surfing. Runs from early November through mid-December, depending on when the surf's up.

December

As winter rainstorms return and temperatures cool slightly, peak tourist season begins in mid-December, making the Christmas to New Year's holiday period extremely busy and expensive.

🏃 Honolulu Marathon

Held on the second Sunday in December, the Honolulu Marathon is Hawaii's biggest and most popular foot race.

Plan Your Trip
Get Inspired

Read

The Maui Coast: Legacy of the King's Highway (Daniel Sullivan; 2015) Vibrant photo book.

The Wave (Susan Casey; 2010) Chronicles Laird Hamilton's big wave riding on Maui.

Hotel Honolulu (Paul Theroux; 2001) Satirical tale about a washed-up writer managing a Waikiki hotel.

Wild Meat and the Bully Burgers (Lois-Ann Yamanaka; 1996) Growing up local in 1970s Hilo, told with raw emotion in pidgin.

Kaua'i: The Separate Kingdom (Edward Joesting; 1988) Strong historic storytelling.

Watch

The Descendants (2011) Contemporary island life, with all of its heartaches and blessings.

50 First Dates (2004) Silly rom-com shot on gorgeous Windward O'ahu beaches.

The North Shore (1987) Glorious cheesy and highly quotable, this movie is bitchin'!

Blue Hawaii (1961) Romp poolside with a ukulele-playing Elvis during Hawaii's tiki-tacky tourism boom.

From Here to Eternity (1953) Classic WWII-era drama leading up to the Pearl Harbor attack.

Listen

E Walea (Kalani Pe'a; 2016) Grammy winner for Best Roots Album, Pe'a is a Hilo-born up-and-comer.

Tell U What (Brittni Paiva; 2012) Ukulele prodigy's latest collection shows off her range.

Legends of Hawaiian Slack Key Guitar: Live from Maui (2007) Won George Kahumoku Jr a Grammy for slack key guitar album of the year.

Facing Forward (Israel Kamakawiwo'ole; 1993) The all-time best-selling album by legendary Hawaiian musician Iz.

Memories of You (Diana Aki; 1990) The 'songbird of Miloli'i' epitomizes the Hawaiian falsetto style.

Above: Tiki carvings, O'ahu.

Plan Your Trip
Five-Day Itineraries

Big Island: Hilo to Kona

Only on Hawai'i can you fully appreciate the power of Pele, goddess of fire and volcanoes. Here, pass stark lava deserts, hike across huge craters and glimpse red-hot molten lava, if you're lucky. Stay in Hilo, Puna or Volcano and reserve one day for Mauna Kea.

Mauna Kea (p230) Explore the summit area attractions then enjoy the stunning sunset and magnificent stargazing.

Hilo (p266) Learn about volcanoes at the 'Imiloa Astronomy Center then picnic at Lili'uokalani Park, where views of Mauna Kea are your backdrop. 🚗 40 mins to Hawai'i Volcanoes National Park

Puna Seek out lava attractions, from tide pools to the newest black sand. 🚗 50 mins to Mauna Kea

Hawai'i Volcanoes National Park (p250) Check out the fiery caldera and other sights on the scenic Crater Rim Drive. Spend another day hiking. 🚗 20 mins to Puna

Maui to Lana'i

You've got time, you've got money and you want outdoor adventures and tranquil relaxation in equal measure. But you're also willing to rough it when the rewards – hidden waterfalls and geological wonders – make it worthwhile.

Lana'i (p200) Hop off the ferry then explore Lana'i City followed by snorkeling at Hulopo'e Beach. 🚢 1 hr to Lahaina, then 🚗 45 mins to Wailea

Kihei (p190) Spend two days snorkeling the coast, lying on the beach, eating local food and learning about humpback whales. 🚗 90 mins to Haleakalā National Park

Haleakalā National Park (p204) Rise early to watch the sunrise - make a reservation! - then hike into the crater. Camp in the park or overnight in Kula. 🚗 1 hr from Kula to Lahaina, then 🚢 1 hr to Lana'i

Wailea (p188) Spend your last day on the beach at a resort then savor a top notch dinner with an ocean view.

Plan Your Trip
10-Day Itinerary

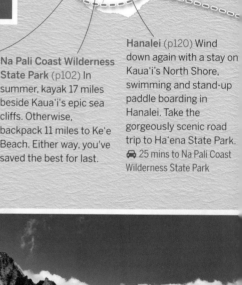

Oʻahu to Kauaʻi

Think of this as your 'town and country' trip to Hawaii. Start off in the breezy streets of Honolulu, sleeping in mod style at the classic beach resort of Waikiki. Then trade the big-city buzz for the small-town scene on verdant Kauaʻi.

Waimea Canyon (p132) Lace up your hiking boots and spend a couple of days hiking the canyon and Kokeʻe State Park.
🚗 2 hrs to Hanalei

Na Pali Coast Wilderness State Park (p102) In summer, kayak 17 miles beside Kauaʻi's epic sea cliffs. Otherwise, backpack 11 miles to Keʻe Beach. Either way, you've saved the best for last.

Hanalei (p120) Wind down again with a stay on Kauaʻi's North Shore, swimming and stand-up paddle boarding in Hanalei. Take the gorgeously scenic road trip to Haʻena State Park.
🚗 25 mins to Na Pali Coast Wilderness State Park

North Shore Wend your way along the Windward Coast, with jungle hiking trials, ancient lava-rock fishponds and captivating offshore islands. Save at least an afternoon for the world-famous beaches of the North Shore. Return to Honolulu.
✈ 40 mins to Lihue, then 🚗 1 hr to Waimea

Waikiki (p72) Laze on the sand, learn to surf and pose for a pic with Duke Kahanamoku. Catch the evening hula and light show at Kuhio Beach Park.
🚗 20 mins to Hanauma Bay

Hanauma Bay Spend a morning snorkeling in the bay, then swim off the beaches of Waimanalo, and surf, kayak, windsurf or kiteboard at Kailua Bay.
🚗 20 mins to Turtle Bay, then 🚗 5 mins to Waimea Bay

Honolulu (p34) Shake off the jet lag and explore the museums and historic sites of the capital city then dive into the fun of Chinatown. 🚗 20 mins to Waikiki Beach

FROM LEFT: PUNG/SHUTTERSTOCK ©; DIRKR/SHUTTERSTOCK ©

Plan Your Trip
One-Week Itinerary

Maui & Hawai'i

Looking for tropical adventures? Hit up Maui for its postcard-perfect honeymoon beaches, serpentine coastal drives and hang-loose surf scene. When you're ready for bigger thrills, jet over to the Big Island, where erupting volcanoes, mysterious valleys and deserted beaches await.

Road to Hana (p166) Start at Huelo. Drive this cliff-hugging road at a leisurely pace, stopping to kick back on the black-sand beach at Wai'anapanapa State Park. 🚗 3 hrs to Hana

Haleakala National Park (p204) Spend a day hiking around an ancient volcano and watching the weather change from the summit. Camp or overnight in Kula. 🚗 35 mins to Road to Hana

Hana (p180) Go horseback riding, order lunch at a food truck and sunbathe on the gorgeous Hamoa Beach. 🚗 2 hrs to Kahului airport, then ✈ 45 mins to Kona airport

Wailea (p188) Get into resort mode by strolling the manicured beaches, getting a seaside massage and dining on Maui-grown beef and produce at your resort. 🚗 1 hr 45 mins to Haleakala National Park

Hilo (p266) Walk along this harborfront city, exploring its historic architecture, eclectic shops and the astronomy center. 🚗 40 mins to Hawai'i Volcanoes National Park

Kona (p245) Base yourself here and take advantage of the great local beaches and farm tours. 🚗 90 mins to Hilo

Hawai'i Volcanoes National Park (p250) Spend a full day here hiking the otherworldly Kilauea Iki Trail; driving Chain of Craters Rd; and hopefully spying some hot lava glowing fiery red after dark.

Plan Your Trip
Family Travel

With its phenomenal natural beauty, Hawaii appeals to families. Instead of hanging out in shopping malls, kids can play on sandy beaches, snorkel amid colorful tropical fish and even watch lava flow. Then get them out of the sun by visiting museums, aquariums and historical attractions.

Hawaii for Kids

There's not too much to worry about when visiting Hawaii with kids, as long as you keep them covered in sunblock. Here, coastal temperatures rarely drop below 65°F (18°C) and driving distances are relatively short. Just don't try to do or see too much, especially if it's your first trip to Hawaii. Slow down and hang loose!

Eating Out

Hawaii is a family-oriented and unfussy place, so most restaurants welcome children; notable exceptions are some high-end dining rooms. Children's menus, booster seats and high chairs are usually available everywhere – but if it's a necessity at every meal, bring a collapsible seat.

If restaurant dining is inconvenient, no problem. Eating outdoors at a beach park is among the simplest and best island pleasures. Pack finger foods for a picnic, pick up fruit from farmers markets, stop for smoothies at roadside stands and order plate lunches at drive-in counters.

Grocery and convenience stores stock national brands. A kid who eats nothing but Cheerios will not go hungry here. But the local diet, with its variety of cuisines, brightly colored fruit and plethora of sweet treats, may tempt kids away from mainland habits.

Entertainment

Commercial luau might seem like cheesy Vegas dinner shows to adults, but many kids love the flashy dances and fire tricks. Children typically get discounted tickets (and sometimes free admission when accompanied by a paying adult).

If parents need a night out to themselves, the easiest and most reliable way to

find a babysitter is to ask a hotel concierge, or else contact **Nannies Hawaii** (☎808-754-4931; http://nannieshawaii.com).

Cultural Activities

Waimea Valley (☎808-638-7766; www.waimea valley.net; 59-864 Kamehameha Hwy; adult/child 4-12yr $16/8; ☉9am-5pm; 👶🍴) Botanical gardens, archaeological sites and waterfall swimming on O'ahu's North Shore, with poi-pounding, lei-making and hula-dancing lessons.

Old Lahaina Luau (☎808-667-1998; www. oldlahainaluau.com; 1251 Front St; adult/child $120/79; ☉5:15-8:15pm Oct-Feb, 5:45-8:45pm Mar-May & Sep, 6:15-9:15pm Jun-Aug; 👶) Hawaii's most authentic, aloha-filled luau comes with music, dancing and an *imu*-cooked whole roasted pig, on Maui.

Pearl Harbor (p46) Squeeze inside a WWII-era submarine; pace a battleship's decks; or become a virtual-reality pilot, on O'ahu.

Kamokila Hawaiian Village (☎808-823-0559; http://villagekauai.com; 5443 Kuamo'o Rd; village admission adult/child 3-12yr $5/3, outrigger

★ Best for Kids

Kuhio Beach (p76), Waikiki

Ko Olina Lagoons, Ko Olina, O'ahu

'Anaeho'omalu Beach, Waikoloa Resort Area, Big Island

Wailea Beach (p196), South Maui

Baby Beach, Po'ipu, Kaua'i

canoe tours adult/child $30/20; ☉9am-5pm; 👶) Outrigger canoe rides, traditional craft demonstrations and replicas of ancient Hawaiian houses, on Kaua'i.

Hawai'i Volcanoes National Park (☎808-985-6000; www.nps.gov/havo; 7-day entry per car $10; 👶) Hike to petroglyph fields or watch traditional *hula kahiko* dancing and chanting on Hawai'i, the Big Island.

From left: Children on the beach at sunset; Performers at Old Lahaina Luau

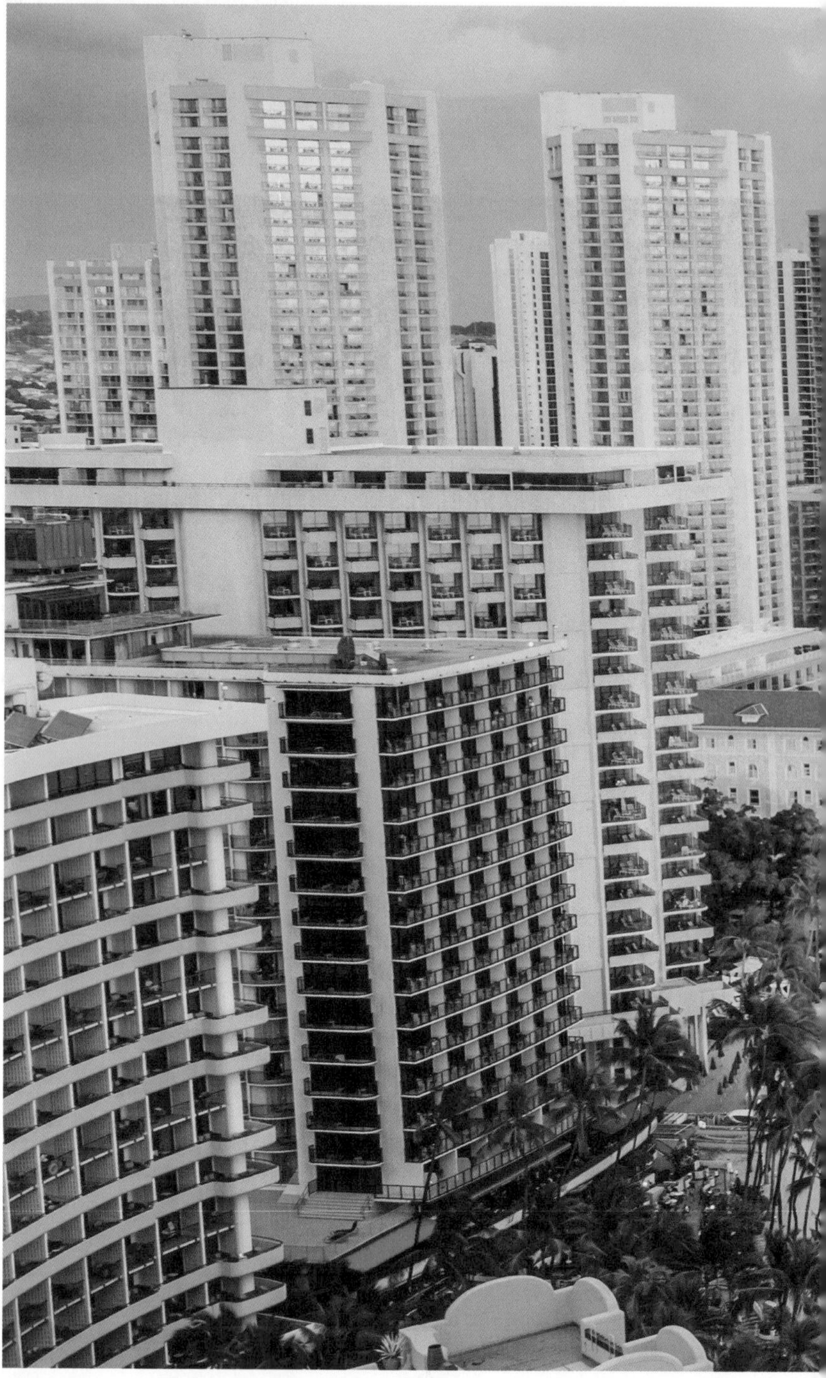

Honolulu skyline over Magic Island (p59)

Arriving in Honolulu

Once you're on O'ahu, getting to Honolulu is easy using either your own rental wheels or TheBus public transportation system. Major car-rental companies are found at Honolulu International Airport and in Waikiki. Just northwest of Waikiki, the Ala Moana Center mall is the central transfer point for TheBus. Several direct bus routes run between Waikiki and Honolulu's other neighborhoods.

Sleeping

Honolulu doesn't have much in the way of accommodations. Most visitors sleep by the beach at Waikiki, where there are many options. Waikiki is so close that it's easy to get to the sights of Honolulu, either by car or bus. There are a few places to stay out near the airport (not recommended), plus a couple of spots around Ala Moana Center.

Hawaii Theater (p41)

1000 WORDS/SHUTTERSTOCK ©

Chinatown

The scent of burning incense still wafts through Chinatown's buzzing markets, fire-breathing dragons spiral up the columns of buildings and steaming dim sum awakens even the sleepiest of appetites.

Great For...

☑ Don't Miss

Blooming orchids at Foster Botanical Garden – they are entered on the National Register of Historic Places.

The location of this mercantile district is no accident. Between Honolulu's busy trading port and what was once the countryside, enterprises selling goods to city folks and visiting ships' crews sprang up in the 19th century. Many of these shops were established by Chinese laborers who had completed their sugarcane-plantation contracts. The most successful entrepreneurial families have long since moved out, making room for newer waves of immigrants, mostly from Southeast Asia.

Chinatown Markets

The commercial heart of Chinatown (www.chinatownnow.com; ⊗8am-6pm) revolves around its markets and food shops. Noodle factories, pastry shops and produce stalls line the narrow sidewalks, always

Statue at Kuan Yin Temple (p40)

LEIGH ANNE MEEKS/SHUTTERSTOCK ©

crowded with cart-pushing grandmothers and errand-running families. An institution since 1904, the **Oʻahu Market** sells everything a Chinese cook needs: ginger root, fresh octopus, quail eggs, jasmine rice, slabs of tuna, long beans and salted jellyfish. You owe yourself a bubble tea if you spot a pig's head among the stalls.

At the start of the nearby pedestrian mall is the newer, but equally vibrant, **Kekaulike Market**. At the top end of the pedestrian mall is **Maunakea Marketplace**, with its popular food court.

Dr Sun Yat-sen Statue

Known as the 'Father of the Nation' in the Republic of China and the 'forerunner of democratic revolution' in the People's Republic of China, Sun Yat-sen traveled to

ⓘ Need to Know

There are pay parking garages scattered across the neighborhood.

✕ Take a Break

Enjoy Vietnamese fusion at the **Pig & the Lady** (p68).

★ Top Tip

Chinatown's art galleries provide a free map of the neighborhood's two dozen galleries.

Hawaii in 1879 and was educated at 'Iolani School and O'ahu College (later to become Punahou School and have Barack Obama as a student). Sun Yat-sen learned the ideals of the French and American revolutions and became President of the Republic of China (effectively now Taiwan) in 1912.

Foster Botanical Garden

Tropical plants you've only ever read about can be spotted in all their glory at this **botanic garden** (☎808-522-7066; www. honolulu.gov/parks/hbg.html; 180 N Vineyard Blvd; adult/child $5/1; ⏰9am-4pm, guided tours usually 1pm Mon-Sat; ⓟ) ✿, which took root in 1850. Among its rarest specimens are the Hawaiian *loulu* palm and the East African *Gigasiphon macrosiphon,* both thought to be extinct in the wild. Several of the

towering trees are the largest of their kind in the USA.

Oddities include the cannonball tree, the sausage tree and the double coconut palm capable of producing a 50lb nut – watch your head! Follow your nose past fragrant vanilla vines and cinnamon trees in the spice and herb gardens, then pick your way among the poisonous and dye plants. A free self-guided tour map is available at the garden entrance.

Kuan Yin Temple

With its green ceramic-tile roof and bright red columns, this ornate Chinese Buddhist temple is Honolulu's oldest. The richly carved interior is filled with the sweet, pervasive smell of burning incense. The temple is dedicated to Kuan Yin, bodhisattva of mercy,

Grocers in Chinatown

JA-IMAGES/SHUTTERSTOCK ©

whose statue is the largest in the interior prayer hall. Devotees burn paper 'money' for prosperity and good luck, while offerings of fresh flowers and fruit are placed at the altar. Respectful visitors welcome.

Hawaii Theater

This neoclassical landmark first opened in 1922, when silent films were played to the tunes of a pipe organ. Dubbed the 'Pride of the Pacific,' the theater ran continuous shows during WWII, but the development of Waikiki cinemas in the 1960s finally brought down the curtain. After multi-million-dollar restorations, this nationally registered historic site held its grand reopening in 1996.

Izumo Taishakyo Mission

This Shintō shrine was built by Japanese immigrants in 1906. It was confiscated during WWII by the city and wasn't returned to the community until the early 1960s. Ringing the bell at the shrine entrance is considered an act of purification for those who come to pray. Thousands of good-luck amulets are sold here, especially on January 1, when the temple heaves with people who come seeking New Year's blessings. The original Izumo Taisha is in Shimane Prefecture, Japan.

Masked performer in Chinese New Year parade, Chinatown

NAGEL PHOTOGRAPHY/SHUTTERSTOCK ©

Chinatown Walking Tour

Honolulu's most foot-trafficked neighborhood, Chinatown is also its most historic. Soak up the atmosphere with this walk through the colourful streets.

Start Dr Sun Yat-sen Memorial Park
Distance 1 mile
Duration 1-2 hours

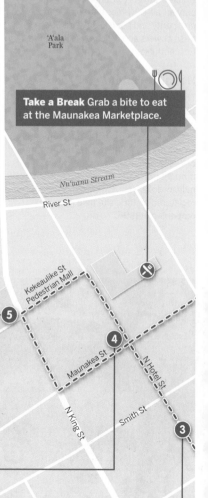

'A'ala Park

Take a Break Grab a bite to eat at the Maunakea Marketplace.

Nu'uanu Stream

River St

Kekeaulike St Pedestrian Mall

Maunakea St

N Hotel St

N King St

Smith St

5

4

3

5 On King St, continue past the red pillars coiled with dragons, then visit the buzzing 1904 **O'ahu Market**.

4 At the corner of Maunakea St, the ornate facade of the **Wo Fat Building** resembles a Chinese temple.

3 Turning right onto somewhat seedy **Hotel St**, historically Honolulu's red-light district, now filled with trendy businesses.

7 By the river, the **statue of Dr Sun Yat-sen**, 'the Father of Modern China', stands guard.

FINISH **7**

N Beretania St

Maunakea St

6

CHINATOWN

6 Heading *mauka* (towards the mountains) on Maunakea St, you'll pass **lei shops**.

Pau'ahi St

Nu'uanu Ave

2

2 On Nu'uanu Ave, the now-abandoned **Pantheon Bar** was a favorite of sailors in days past.

START **1**

Bethel St

1 Start at **Dr Sun Yat-sen Memorial Park** at the stone lions that flank the road.

Bishop St

Ⓝ 0 ————— 100 m
0 ————— 0.05 miles

Hawaiian coat of arms at 'Iolani Palace

PASHACO/SHUTTERSTOCK ©

UA MAU KE EA O KA AINA I KA PONO

'Iolani Palace

No other place evokes a more poignant sense of Hawaii's history. Built in 1882, it was modern and opulent for its time, but did little to secure Hawaii's sovereignty.

Great For...

☑ Don't Miss

The huge banyan tree on the palace grounds allegedly planted by Queen Kapi'olani.

Palace History

The palace was built under King David Kalakaua in 1882. At that time, the Hawaiian monarchy observed many of the diplomatic protocols of the Victorian world. The king traveled abroad meeting with leaders around the globe and received foreign emissaries here. Although the palace was modern and opulent for its time, it did little to assert Hawaii's sovereignty over powerful US-influenced business interests who overthrew the kingdom in 1893.

Two years after the coup, the former queen, Lili'uokalani, who had succeeded her brother David to the throne, was convicted of treason and spent nine months imprisoned in her former home. Later the palace served as the capitol of the republic, then the territory and later the state of Hawaii. In 1969 the government finally moved

Lei on statue of Queen Lili'uokalaniw

❶ Need to Know

'Iolani Palace (☎808-522-0832; www.
iolanipalace.org; 364 S King St; grounds free,
basement galleries adult/child $7/3, self-guid-
ed audio tour $15/6, guided tour $22/6;
⏱9am-pm Mon-Sat)

✕ Take a Break

Sip Kona-estate coffee and savor city
views at **Honolulu Coffee Company**.

★ Top Tip

Call ahead to confirm tour schedules
and reserve tickets during peak periods.

into the current state capitol, leaving
'Iolani Palace a shambles. After a decade
of painstaking renovations, the restored
palace reopened as a museum, although
many original royal artifacts had been lost
or stolen before work even began.

Interior Tours

Visitors must take a docent-led or
self-guided tour (no children under five
years of age) to see 'Iolani's grand interior,
including recreations of the throne room
and residential quarters upstairs. The palace
was quite modern by Victorian-era standards. Every bedroom had its own bathroom
with flush toilets and hot running water, and
electric lights replaced the gas lamps years
before the White House in Washington, DC,
installed electricity. You can independently browse the historical exhibits in the

basement, including royal regalia, historical
photographs and reconstructions of the
kitchen and chamberlain's office.

Palace Grounds

The palace grounds are open during
daylight hours and are free of charge. The
former barracks of the Royal Household
Guards, a building that looks oddly like the
uppermost layer of a medieval fort, now
houses the ticket booth.

'Iolani Palace Bandstand

Formerly known as the Coronation Pavilion,
the 'Iolani Palace Bandstand was erected in
front of 'Iolani Palace in 1883 as a pavilion
for the coronation of King Kalakaua. As
there was no other ranking person to perform the duty, Kalakaua placed the crown
on his own head. The pavilion was later
moved to its present site and used as a
bandstand. These days, the Royal Hawaiian
Band plays free concerts at 'Iolani Palace at
noon on Fridays.

USS Arizona Memorial (p49)

Pearl Harbor

Pearl Harbor has a resonance for all Americans. The site of the December 7, 1941 attack that brought the US into WWII is accessible, evocative and moving.

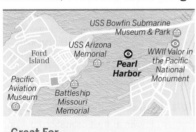

USS Bowfin Submarine Museum & Park

USS Arizona Memorial

Ford Island

Pearl Harbor

WWII Valor in the Pacific National Monument

Pacific Aviation Museum

Battleship Missouri Memorial

Great For...

❶ Need to Know

WWII Valor in the Pacific National Monument (☎808-422-3399; www.nps. gov/valr; 1 Arizona Memorial Pl; ⊗visitor center 7am-5pm) **FREE**

☑ **Don't Miss**

A shore-side walk passes signs illustrating how the attack unfolded in the now-peaceful harbor.

A Surprise Attack

December 7, 1941 – 'a date which will live in infamy,' President Franklin D Roosevelt later said – began at 7:55am with a wave of more than 350 Japanese planes swooping over the Ko'olau Range headed toward the un-suspecting US Pacific Fleet in Pearl Harbor. The battleship USS *Arizona* took a direct hit and sank in less than nine minutes, with most of its men killed in the explosion which destroyed the ship. The average age of the 1177 enlisted men who died in the attack on the ship was 19 years. It wasn't until 15 minutes after the bombing started that American anti-aircraft guns began to shoot back at the Japanese warplanes. Twenty other US military ships were sunk or seriously damaged and 347 airplanes were destroyed during the two-hour attack.

Ultimately, the greatest cost of the Pearl Harbor attack was human. Except for three ships sunk that day – the *Arizona*, the USS *Oklahoma* and the USS *Utah* – all the rest of the navy ships damaged were repaired and fought in WWII. While the destruction and damage of the US battleships was massive, events soon proved that such vessels were already obsolete. The war in the Pacific was fought by aircraft carriers, none of which were in Pearl Harbor during the attack.

WWII Valor in the Pacific National Monument

One of the USA's most significant WWII sites, this National Park Service monument narrates the history of the Pearl Harbor attack and commemorates fallen service members. The monument is entirely wheelchair accessible. The main entrance also leads to Pearl Harbor's other parks and museums.

The monument grounds are much more than just a boat dock for the USS Arizona Memorial. Be sure to stop at the two superb museums, where multimedia and interactive displays bring to life the Road to War and the Attack and Aftermath through historic photos, films, illustrated graphics and taped oral histories.

The bookstore sells many books and movies about the Pearl Harbor attack and WWII's Pacific theater, as well as

Interior of USS *Missouri*

BENNY MARTY/SHUTTERSTOCK ©

informative illustrated maps of the battle. If you're lucky, one of the few remaining, 95-plus-year-old Pearl Harbor veterans who volunteer might be out front signing autographs and answering questions.

Various ticket packages are available for the three attractions that have admission fees. The best deal is a seven-day pass that includes admission to all. Tickets are sold online at www.pearlharborhistoricsites.org, at the main monument ticket counter, and at each attraction.

USS Arizona Memorial

One of the USA's most significant WWII sites, this somber **monument** (☑808-422-3399; www.nps.gov/valr; 1 Arizona Memorial Pl; free, boat-tour reservation fee $1.50; ☺7am-5pm, boat tours 7:30am-3pm) FREE commemorates the Pearl Harbor attack and its fallen service members with an offshore shrine reachable by boat.

The USS Arizona Memorial was built over the midsection of the sunken USS *Arizona*, with deliberate geometry to represent initial defeat, ultimate victory and eternal serenity. In the furthest of three chambers inside the shrine, the names of crewmen killed in the attack are engraved onto a marble wall. In the central section are cutaways that allow visitors to see the skeletal remains of the ship, which even now oozes about a quart of oil each day into the ocean. In its rush to recover from the attack and prepare for war, the US Navy exercised its option to leave the servicemen inside the sunken ship; they remain entombed in its hull, buried at sea.

Boat Tours to USS Arizona Memorial

Boat tours to the shrine depart every 15 minutes from 7:30am until 3pm (weather permitting). For the 75-minute tour program, which includes a 23-minute documentary film on the attack, make reservations online (fee per ticket $1.50) at www.recreation.gov up to 60 days before your visit. You can also try to secure tickets on the website the day before your visit beginning at 7am Hawaii time – but these are very limited. Best to reserve in advance.

Battleship Missouri Memorial

The last battleship built by the US (it was launched in 1944), the **USS Missouri** (☑877-644-4896; www.ussmissouri.com; 63 Cowpens St, Ford Island; admission incl tour adult/child from $27/13; ☺8am-4pm, to 5pm Jun-Aug) provides a unique historical 'bookend' to the US campaign in the Pacific during WWII. Nicknamed the 'Mighty Mo', this decommissioned battleship saw action during the decisive late WWII battles of Iwo Jima and Okinawa.

USS Bowfin Submarine Museum & Park

Adjacent to the visitor center, this **park** (☑808-423-1341; www.bowfin.org; 11 Arizona Memorial Dr; museum adult/child $6/3, incl self-guided submarine tour $12/5; ☺7am-5pm, last entry 4:30pm) harbors the moored WWII-era submarine USS *Bowfin* and a museum that traces the development of submarines from their origins to the nuclear age, including wartime patrol footage. The highlight is exploring this historic submarine.

Pacific Aviation Museum

This **military aircraft museum** (☑808-441-1000; www.pacificaviationmuseum.org; 319 Lexington Blvd, Ford Island; adult/child $25/12, incl guided tour $35/12; ☺8am-5pm, last entry 4pm) covers WWII through the US conflicts in Korea and Vietnam. The first aircraft hangar has been outfitted with exhibits on the Pearl Harbor attack, the Doolittle Raid on mainland Japan in 1942 and the pivotal Battle of Midway, when the tides of WWII in the Pacific turned in favor of the Allies.

✕ **Take a Break**

Settle in at **Restaurant 604** (☑808-888-7616; www.restaurant604.com; 57 Arizona Memorial Dr; mains $12-25; ☺10:30am-10pm) on the waterfront.

Star projector, planetarium

Bishop Museum

The Bishop Museum showcases a remarkable array of cultural and natural history exhibits. It is often ranked as the finest Polynesian anthropological museum in the world.

Great For...

☑ Don't Miss

The two-story exhibits inside Pacific Hall covering Polynesian, Micronesian and Melanesian culture.

Like Hawaii's version of the Smithsonian Institution in Washington, DC, the Bishop Museum showcases a remarkable array of cultural and natural history exhibits. It is often ranked as the finest Polynesian anthropological museum in the world. Founded in 1889 in honor of Princess Bernice Pauahi Bishop, a descendant of the Kamehameha dynasty, the museum originally housed only Hawaiian and royal artifacts. These days it honors all of Polynesia.

Hawaiian Hall

The main gallery, the Hawaiian Hall, resides inside a dignified three-story Victorian building. The three floors are designed to take visitors on a journey through the different realms of Hawai'i. On the 1st floor is Kai Akea, which represents the Hawaiian gods, legends, beliefs, and the world

Ancient Hawaiian statue

PRINT COLLECTOR / CONTRIBUTOR/GETTY IMAGES ©

Kamehameha Park

Lunalilo Fwy

Kalihi St

Bishop Museum 🏛

Bernice St

Kapalama Ave

ℹ Need to Know

📞808-847-3511; www.bishopmuseum.org; 1525 Bernice St; adult/child $23/15; ⊙9am-5pm; P♿)♪

✕ Take a Break

Chow down on kalua pig and *lomilomi* salmon (minced, salted salmon, diced tomato and green onion) at **Helena's Hawaiian Food** (p67).

★ Top Tip
The gift shop sells books on the Pacific not easily found elsewhere.

of pre-contact Hawai'i. One floor up, Wao Kanaka focuses on the importance of the land and nature in daily life. The top floor, Wao Lani, is inhabited by the gods.

Pacific Hall

The fascinating two-story exhibits inside the adjacent Pacific Hall cover the myriad cultures of Polynesia, Micronesia and Melanesia. It shows how the peoples of Oceania are diverse, yet deeply connected, and is filled with cultural treasures such as canoes, woven mats and contemporary artwork.

Planetarium

The Bishop Museum is also home to O'ahu's only planetarium, which has an ever-changing range of shows, including

traditional Polynesian methods of wayfaring (navigation). Check the museum website for upcoming shows.

Other Exhibit Areas

The eye-popping, state-of-the-art multi-sensory **Science Adventure Center** is based on better understanding Hawaii's environment. You can explore areas of science in which Hawaii has gained international recognition, including volcanology, oceanography, and biodiversity.

The **Na Ulu Kaiwi'ula Native Hawaiian Garden** features species important to Hawaiian culture ranging from endemic plants to others like breadfruit that were brought to Hawaii by Polynesians centuries ago.

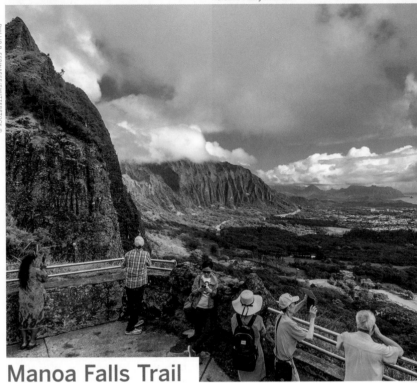

Nu'uanu Valley Lookout

PHILLIP B ESPINASSE/SHUTTERSTOCK ©

Manoa Falls Trail

The city's most rewarding short hike leads to a lacy cascade inside Honolulu's green belt.

Great For...

☑ Don't Miss

Unique and colorful plants growing near the falls.

The Hike

Honolulu's most rewarding short hike, this 1.6-mile round-trip trail runs above a rocky streambed before ending at a pretty little cascade. Tall tree trunks line the often muddy and slippery path. Wild orchids and red ginger grow near the falls, which drop about 100ft into a small, shallow pool. It's illegal to venture beyond the established viewing area.

Getting There

On public transport, take bus 5 Manoa Valley from Ala Moana Center or the university area to the end of the line; from there, it's a half-mile walk uphill to the trailhead. By car, drive almost to the end of Manoa Rd, where a privately operated parking lot charges $5 per vehicle. Free on-street parking may be available just downhill from the bus stop.

Makiki Valley Trails

ROSANNA U/GETTY IMAGES ©

❶ Need to Know

For more info on the island's trail system, see http://hawaiitrails.ehawaii.gov.

✕ Take a Break

Enjoy a buffet lunch after your hike at **Treetops Restaurant** (☑808-988-6839; http://manoatreetops.wixsite.com; 3737 Manoa Rd, Manoa Valley; buffet $15.95; ⏱9am-4pm Mon-Sat).

★ Top Tip

Need more mileage? There are several trails near Manoa Falls in the Honolulu Watershed Forest Reserve.

Watch Your Step

Falling rocks and the risk of leptospirosis (a waterborne bacterial infection) make entering the water dangerous.

Nu'uanu Valley Lookout

Just before Manoa Falls, the marked 'Aihualama Trail heads up to the left and scrambles over boulders. The trail quickly enters a bamboo forest with some massive old banyan trees, then contours around the ridge, offering broad views of Manoa Valley.

Another mile of gradual switchbacks brings hikers to an intersection with the Pauoa Flats Trail, which ascends to the right for more than half a mile over muddy tree roots to the spectacular Nu'uanu Valley Lookout. High atop the Ko'olau Range, with O'ahu's steep *pali* (cliffs) visible all around, it's possible to peer through a gap over to the Windward Coast. The total round-trip distance to the lookout from the Manoa Falls trailhead is approximately 5.5 miles. You can also get to the lookout on tracks from the Makiki Valley and Tantalus Dr.

Makiki Valley Trails

A favorite workout for city dwellers, the 2.5-mile Makiki Valley Loop links three Tantalus-area trails. These trails are usually muddy, so wear shoes with traction and pick up a walking stick. The loop cuts through a lush tropical forest, mainly composed of non-native species introduced to reforest an area denuded by Hawaii's 19th-century *'iliahi* (sandalwood) trade.

◎ SIGHTS

Honolulu's compact downtown is just a lei's throw from the harborfront. Nearby, the buzzing streets of Chinatown are packed with food markets, antique shops, art galleries and hip bars. Between downtown and Waikiki, Ala Moana has Hawaii's biggest mall and the city's best beach. The University of Hawaii campus is a gateway to the Manoa Valley. A few outlying sights, including the Bishop Museum, are worth putting into your schedule.

◎ Downtown

This area was center stage for the political intrigue and social upheavals that changed the fabric of Hawaii during the 19th century. Major players ruled here, revolted here, worshipped here and still rest, however restlessly, in the graveyards.

Hawai'i State Art Museum Museum
(☎808-586-0300; http://sfca.hawaii.gov/; 2nd fl, No 1 Capitol District Bldg, 250 S Hotel St; ☺10am-4pm Tue-Sat, also 6-9pm 1st Fri each month)
✦FREE With its vibrant, thought-provoking collections, this public art museum brings together traditional and contemporary art from Hawaii's multiethnic communities. The museum inhabits a grand 1928 Spanish Mission Revival–style building, formerly a YMCA and today a nationally registered historic site. The museum is also home to a lovely gift shop and an excellent cafe, Artizen by MW (p68).

Upstairs, revolving exhibits of paintings, sculptures, fiber art, photography and mixed media are displayed around themes, such as the island's Polynesian heritage, modern social issues or the natural beauty of land and sea. Hawaii's complex confluence of Asian, Pacific Rim and European cultures is evident throughout, shaping an aesthetic that captures the soul of the islands and the hearts of the people.

On the first Friday of each month, galleries are open 6pm to 9pm with live entertainment and a family-friendly atmosphere. Drop by at noon on the last Tuesday of the month for free 'Art Lunch' lectures, or between 11am and 3pm on the second Saturday for hands-on Hawaiian arts and crafts, often designed with kids in mind.

Ala Moana Beach Park (p59)

JEFF WHYTE/SHUTTERSTOCK

Ali'iolani Hale

State Capitol
Notable Building

(☏808-586-0178; 415 S Beretania St; ⏱7:45am-4:30pm Mon-Fri) FREE Built in the architecturally interesting 1960s, Hawaii's state capitol is a poster child of conceptual postmodernism: two cone-shaped legislative chambers have sloping walls to represent volcanoes; the supporting columns shaped like coconut palms symbolize the eight main islands; and a large encircling pool represents the Pacific Ocean surrounding Hawaii. Visitors are free to walk through the open-air rotunda and peer through viewing windows into the legislative chambers. Pick up a self-guided tour brochure on the 4th floor from Room 415.

Queen Lili'uokalani Statue
Statue

Pointedly positioned between the state capitol building and 'Iolani Palace is a life-size bronze statue of Queen Lili'uokalani, Hawaii's last reigning monarch. She holds a copy of the Hawaiian constitution she wrote in 1893 in an attempt to strengthen Hawaiian rule; 'Aloha 'Oe,' a popular song she composed; and 'Kumulipo,' the traditional Hawaiian chant of creation.

Father Damien Statue
Statue

In front of the capitol is a highly stylized statue of Father Damien, the Belgian priest who lived and worked with victims of Hansen's disease who were exiled to the island of Moloka'i during the late 19th century. He later died of the disease himself. In 2009, the Catholic Church canonized Father Damien as Hawaii's first saint after the allegedly miraculous recovery from cancer in 1988 of a Honolulu schoolteacher who had prayed over Damien's original grave site on Moloka'i.

Ali'iolani Hale
Historic Building

(☏808-539-4999; www.jhchawaii.net; 417 S King St; ⏱8am-4:30pm Mon-Fri) FREE The first major government building ordered by the Hawaiian monarchy in 1874, the 'House of Heavenly Kings' was designed by Australian architect Thomas Rowe to be a royal palace, although it was never used as such. Today, it houses the Supreme Court of

Downtown Honolulu & Chinatown

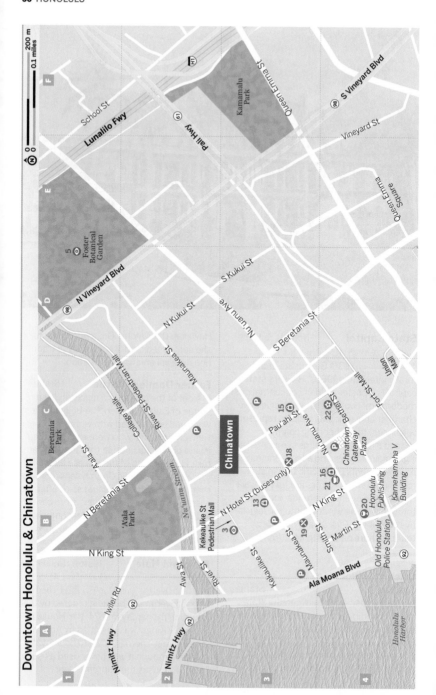

0 0
200 m
0.1 miles
N

F
School St
Lunalilo Fwy
Kamamalu Park
Queen Emma St
S Vineyard Blvd 98
Vineyard St
Pali Hwy 19
H1

E
Queen Emma Square

D
Foster Botanical Garden 5
N Vineyard Blvd 98
S Kukui St
N Kukui St
Nu'uanu Ave
Maunakea St
S Beretania St

C
Beretania Park
'A'ala St
College Walk
River St Pedestrian Mall
Nu'uanu Stream
Chinatown
P
P
Pau'ahi St 15
Nu'uanu Ave
22
Chinatown Bethel St
Gateway Plaza
Fort St Mall
Union Mall

B
N Beretania St
'A'ala Park
Kekaulike St Pedestrian Mall
N King St
3
N Hotel St (buses only) 13
X 18
P
Kekaulike St
Maunakea St
16 21
X 19
Smith St
Martin St
N King St
20
Old Honolulu Police Station
Honolulu Publishing
Kamehameha V Building
92

A
Nimitz Hwy
Iwilei Rd
92
Awa St
River St
Nimitz Hwy 92
Ala Moana Blvd
Honolulu Harbor

1
2
3
4

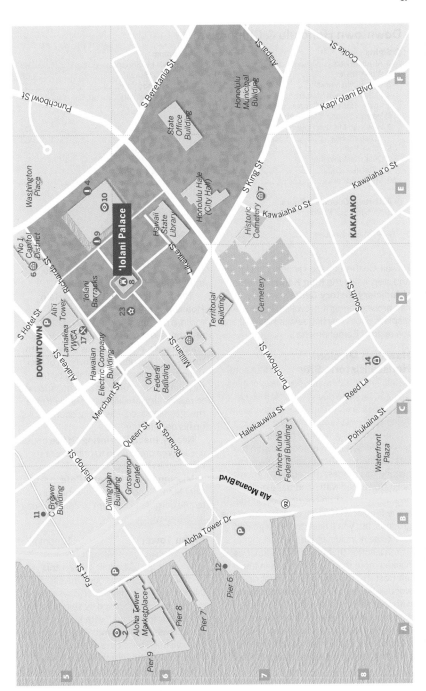

Downtown Honolulu & Chinatown

◎ **Sights**
1	Ali'iolani Hale	D6
2	Aloha Tower	A6
3	Chinatown Markets	B3
4	Father Damien Statue	E5
5	Foster Botanical Garden	D1
6	Hawai'i State Art Museum	D5
7	Hawaiian Mission Houses Historic Site	E7
8	'Iolani Palace	D6
9	Queen Lili'uokalani Statue	E5
10	State Capitol	E5

⊕ **Activities, Courses & Tours**
11	Architectural Walking Tour	B5
12	Atlantis Adventures	B7

⊞ **Shopping**
13	Cindy's Lei Shoppe	B3
14	Kamaka Hawaii	C8
15	Madre Chocolate	C3
16	Tin Can Mailman	B4

⊗ **Eating**
17	Cafe Julia	D5
18	Lucky Belly	C3
19	Pig & the Lady	B3

⊝ **Drinking & Nightlife**
20	Murphy's Bar and Grill	B4
21	Tea at 1024	B4

⊕ **Entertainment**
22	Hawaii Theater	C4
23	Royal Hawaiian Band	D6

Hawaii. Go through the security checkpoint and step inside the **King Kamehameha V Judiciary History Center**, where you can browse thought-provoking historical displays about martial law during WWII and the reign of Kamehameha I.

Hawaiian Mission Houses Historic Site
Museum

(☏808-447-3910; www.missionhouses.org; 553 S King St; 1hr guided tour adult/child 6-18yr & college student with ID $10/6; ⊗10am-4pm Tue-Sat, guided tours usually 11am, noon, 1pm, 2pm & 3pm) Occupying the original headquarters of the Sandwich Islands mission that forever changed the course of Hawaiian history, this modest museum is authentically furnished with handmade quilts on the beds and iron cooking pots in the stone fireplaces. It's free to walk around the grounds, but you'll need to take a guided tour to peek inside any of the buildings.

You'll notice that the first missionaries packed more than their bags when they left Boston – they brought a prefabricated wooden house, called the **Frame House**, with them around the Horn. Designed to withstand New England winter winds, the small windows instead blocked out Honolulu's cooling tradewinds, which kept the two-story house hellaciously hot and stuffy.

Erected in 1821, it's the oldest wooden structure in Hawaii.

The 1831 coral-block **Chamberlain House** was the early mission's storeroom, a necessity because Honolulu had few shops in those days. Upstairs are hoop barrels, wooden crates packed with dishes, and the desk and quill pen of Levi Chamberlain. He was appointed by the mission to buy, store and dole out supplies to missionary families, who survived on a meager allowance – as the account books on his desk testify.

Nearby, the 1841 **Printing Office** houses a lead-type press used to print the first bible in the Hawaiian language.

Mission Social Hall and Cafe, run by Chef Mark 'Gooch' Noguchi, serves up foodie delights from 11am to 2pm Tuesday to Saturday.

Aloha Tower
Landmark

(www.alohatower.com; 1 Aloha Tower Dr; ⊗9am-5pm; P) FREE Built in 1926, this 10-story landmark was once the city's tallest building. In the golden days when all tourists to Hawaii arrived by ship, this pre-WWII waterfront icon – with its four-sided clock tower inscribed with 'Aloha' – greeted every visitor. These days, Hawaii Pacific University has bought the Aloha Tower Marketplace and is revitalizing it for retail, dining and student housing. Take the elevator to the top-floor tower observation deck for 360-degree views of Honolulu and the waterfront.

Ala Moana & Around

Ala Moana means 'Path to the Sea' and its namesake road, Ala Moana Blvd (Hwy 92), connects the coast between Waikiki and Honolulu. Although most people think of Ala Moana only for its shopping mall, **A**la Moana Beach Park, which happens to be O'ahu's biggest beach park, makes a relaxing alternative to crowded Waikiki.

Ala Moana Beach Park   Beach

(1201 Ala Moana Blvd; P ♿) Opposite the Ala Moana Center shopping mall, this city park boasts a broad, golden-sand beach nearly a mile long buffered from passing traffic by shade trees. Ala Moana is hugely popular, yet big enough that it never feels too crowded. This is where Honolulu residents come to go running after work, play beach volleyball and enjoy weekend picnics. The park has full facilities, including tennis courts, ball fields, picnic tables, drinking water, restrooms, outdoor showers and lifeguard towers.

The peninsula jutting from the southeast side of the park is **Magic Island**. Yearround, you can take an idyllic sunset walk around the peninsula's perimeter, within an anchor's toss of sailboats pulling in and out of neighboring Ala Wai Yacht Harbor.

Honolulu Museum of Art   Museum

(☏808-532-8700; www.honolulumuseum.org; 900 S Beretania St; adult/child $10/free, 1st Wed & 3rd Sun each month free; ⏱10am-4:30pm Tue-Sat, 1-5pm Sun; P ♿) This exceptional fine-arts museum may be the biggest surprise of your trip to O'ahu. The museum, dating to 1927, has a classical facade that's invitingly open and airy, with galleries branching off a series of garden and water-fountain courtyards. Plan on spending a couple of hours at the museum, possibly combining a visit with lunch at the Honolulu Museum of Art Cafe (p69). Admission tickets are also valid for same-day visits to Spalding House (p62).

Mr Obama's Neighborhood

During the 2008 race to elect the 44th president of the United States, Republican vice-presidential candidate Sarah Palin kept asking the country, 'Who is Barack Obama?' It was Obama's wife, Michelle, who had an answer ready: 'You can't really understand Barack until you understand Hawaii.'

Obama, who grew up in Honolulu's Makiki Heights neighborhood, has written that 'Hawaii's spirit of tolerance... became an integral part of my world view, and a basis for the values I hold most dear.' The local media and many *kama'aina* (those who were born and grew up in Hawaii) agree that Hawaii's multiethnic social fabric helped shape the leader who created a rainbow coalition during the 2008 election.

Obama has also said Hawaii is a place for him to rest and recharge. 'When I'm heading out to a hard day of meetings and negotiations, I let my mind wander back to Sandy Beach, or Manoa Falls...It helps me, somehow, knowing that such wonderful places exist and I'll always be able to return to them.'

Manoa Falls Trail
BARRY WINIKER/GETTY IMAGES ©

Stunningly beautiful exhibits reflect the various cultures that make up contemporary Hawaii, and include one of the country's finest Asian art collections, featuring everything from Japanese woodblock prints by Hiroshige and Ming dynasty—era Chinese calligraphy and painted scrolls to temple carvings and

Ala Moana & University Area

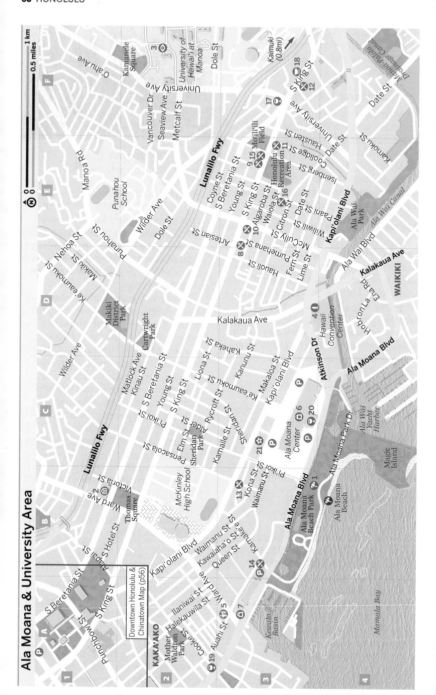

Downtown Honolulu & Chinatown Map (p56)

KAKA'AKO

WAIKIKI

Kalakaua Ave

Kapi'olani Blvd

Ala Moana Blvd

0 N   0.5 miles   1 km

Ala Moana & University Area

◎ Sights
1 Ala Moana Beach Park...............................B3
2 Honolulu Museum of Art............................B1
3 University of Hawai'i at Manoa..................F2
4 Water Giver Statue.....................................D3

⊕ Activities, Courses & Tours
Native Books/Nā Mea Hawaii............(see 7)
5 Surf HNL Girls Who Surf.............................A3

⊚ Shopping
6 Ala Moana Center......................................C3
Honolulu Museum of Art Shop..........(see 2)
7 Native Books/Nā Mea Hawaii...................A3

⊗ Eating
8 Alan Wong's..E3
9 Aloha Vietnamese Food............................E3

10 Chef Mavro..E3
Honolulu Museum of Art Cafe...........(see 2)
11 Kahai Street Kitchen..................................E3
12 Kokua Market Natural Foods.....................F3
13 Nanzan Girogiro B3
14 Nobu Honolulu...B3
15 Sweet Home Café E3
16 Waiola Shave Ice E3

⊜ Drinking & Nightlife
17 Beer Lab HI F3
18 Glazers Coffee...F3
19 Honolulu Beerworks A2
20 Mai Tai Bar C3

⊛ Entertainment
Doris Duke Theatre............................(see 2)
21 Republik..C3

statues from Cambodia and India. Another highlight is the striking contemporary wing with Hawaiian works on its upper level, and modern art by such luminaries as Henri Matisse and Georgia O'Keeffe below. Or be bewitched by the Pacific and Polynesian artifacts, such as ceremonial masks, war clubs and bodily adornments.

Check the museum website for upcoming special events, including gallery tours and art lectures; film screenings and music concerts at the Doris Duke Theatre (p71); ARTafterDARK parties with food, drinks and live entertainment on the last Friday of some months; and family-friendly arts and cultural programs on the third Sunday of every month.

Entry to the Honolulu Museum of Art Shop (p66), the cafe (p69) and the Robert Allerton Art Library is free.

Parking at the Museum of Arts Center is at Linekona lot, diagonally opposite the museum at 1111 Victoria St (enter off Beretania or Young Sts), and costs $5. From Waikiki, take bus 2 or 13 or B City Express!.

Water Giver Statue Statue
(Hawaii Convention Center, 1801 Kalakaua Ave) Fronting the Honolulu Convention Center, this magnificent statue symbolically acknowledges the Hawaiian people for their generosity and expressions of goodwill to newcomers. Sister-statue is the Storyteller Statue in Waikiki.

◎ University Area

In the foothills of Manoa Valley, the neighborhood surrounding the University of Hawai'i (UH) Manoa campus feels youthful, with a collection of cafes, eclectic restaurants and one-of-a-kind shops. There's plenty of action around the University Ave and S King St intersection.

University of Hawai'i at Manoa University
(UH Manoa; ☎808-956-8111; http://manoa.hawaii.edu; 2500 Campus Rd; ℗) About 2 miles northeast of Waikiki, the main campus of the statewide university system was born too late to be weighed down by the tweedy academic architecture of the mainland. Today, its breezy, tree-shaded campus is crowded with students from islands throughout Polynesia and Micronesia. The university has strong programs in astronomy, oceanography and marine biology, as well as Hawaiian, Pacific and Asian studies.

From Waikiki or downtown Honolulu, take bus 4 or 13; from Ala Moana, catch bus 6 or 18.

Tantalus–Round Top Scenic Drive

Offering skyline views to drivers and cyclists alike, the Tantalus–Round Top Scenic Drive climbs almost to the top of Mt Tantalus (2013ft), aka Pu'u 'Ohi'a. Bamboo, ginger, elephant-eared taro and eucalyptus trees make up the roadside profusion of tropical plants, as vines climb to the tops of telephone poles and twist their way across the wires. Starting above downtown Honolulu and the H-1 Fwy, this 10-mile circuit is a two-way loop called Tantalus Dr on its western side, and Round Top Dr to the east. Many hiking trails branch off the loop, which passes by Pu'u 'Ualaka'a State Wayside with its magnificent views.

Native red ginger flower
PILIALOHA/SHUTTERSTOCK ©

⊙ Upper Manoa Valley, Tantalu & Makiki

Welcome to Honolulu's green belt. Roads into the verdant upper Manoa Valley wind north of the UH Manoa campus, passing exclusive residential homes and entering forest reserve land in the hills above downtown's high-rises. It can be pouring with rain up here while beachgoers are basking in the sunshine at Waikiki. Further west lies Makiki Heights, the neighborhood where Barack Obama spent much of his boyhood.

Lyon Arboretum   Gardens
(📞808-988-0456; https://manoa.hawaii.edu/lyonarboretum/; 3860 Manoa Rd; donation $5, guided tour $10; ⊙8am-4pm Mon-Fri, 9am-3pm Sat, tours usually 10am Mon-Sat; P🚻)

🌿 Beautiful walking trails wind through this highly regarded 200-acre arboretum managed by the University of Hawai'i. It was originally founded in 1918 by a group of sugar planters growing native and exotic flora species to restore Honolulu's watershed and test their economic benefit. This is not your typical overly manicured tropical flower garden, but a mature and largely wooded arboretum, where related species cluster in a seminatural state. For a guided tour, call at least 24 hours in advance.

Key plants in the Hawaiian ethnobotanical garden are *'ulu* (breadfruit), *kalo* (taro) and *ko* (sugarcane) brought by early Polynesian settlers; *kukui,* once harvested to produce lantern oil; and *ti,* which was used for medicinal purposes during ancient times and for making moonshine after Westerners arrived. It's a short walk to **Inspiration Point**, or keep walking uphill for about 1 mile along a jeep road, then a narrow, tree root–ridden path to visit seasonal **'Aihualama Falls**, a lacy cliff-side cascade.

Pu'u 'Ualaka'a State Wayside   Viewpoint
(www.hawaiistateparks.org; ⊙7am-7:45pm Apr-1st Mon in Sep, to 6:45pm 1st Tue in Sep-Mar; P)
At this hillside park, sweeping views extend from Diamond Head on the left, across Waikiki and downtown Honolulu, to the Wai'anae Range on the right. The sprawling UH Manoa campus is easily recognized by its sports stadium. The airport is visible on the coast and Pearl Harbor beyond that. It's less than 2.5 miles up Round Top Dr from Makiki St to the park entrance, from where it's another half-mile drive to the lookout (bear left at the fork).

Spalding House   Museum
(📞808-237-5225; www.honoluluacademy.org; 2411 Makiki Heights Dr; adult/child $10/free, 1st Wed of the month free; ⊙10am-4pm Tue-Sat, noon-4pm Sun; P) Embraced by tropical sculpture gardens, this art museum occupies an estate house constructed in 1925 for O'ahu-born Anna Rice Cooke, a missionary descendant and wealthy arts patron.

Inside the main galleries are changing exhibits of paintings, sculpture and other contemporary artwork from the 1940s through to today by international, national and island artists. There is a small cafe and gift shop on-site. Tickets are also valid for same-day admission to the Honolulu Museum of Art (p59).

From Waikiki, take bus 2, 13 or B CityExpress! toward downtown Honolulu and get off at the corner of Beretania and Alapa'i Sts; walk one block *makai* (seaward) along Alapa'i St and transfer to bus 15 bound for Pacific Heights, which stops outside Spalding House.

⊙ ACTIVITIES

Honolulu is an active city and there's always something going on. Both the beaches and the mountains are close at hand, meaning outdoor activities are available for all. Think surfing, bodyboarding, stand-up paddleboarding and swimming in the sea to hiking around the inland mountains. Free lit tennis courts dot the city and an abundance of golf courses are nearby. It's an outdoor activities paradise.

Atlantis Adventures   Whale-Watching (☑800-381-0237; http://atlantisadventures. com/waikiki/whale-watch-cruise/; Pier 6, Aloha Tower Dr; 2½hr tour adult/child 7-12yr from $87/50) From mid-December through mid-April, Atlantis runs whale-watching cruises with an onboard naturalist on a high-tech boat designed to minimize rolling. Tours are run daily at 11:30am. Reservations are essential; book online for discounts, or look for coupons in free tourist magazines. There is a 'whale watch guarantee' and transportation is available from select Waikiki hotels.

**Blue Hawaiian
Helicopters**   Scenic Flights (☑808-831-8800; www.bluehawaiian.com; 99 Kaulele Pl; 45min flight per person $240) This may well be the most exciting thing you do on O'ahu. The 45-minute Blue Skies of O'ahu flight takes in Honolulu, Waikiki, Diamond Head, Hanauma Bay and the whole of the Windward Coast, then the North

Waikiki trolley, Kalakaua Ave

Shore, central O'ahu and Pearl Harbor. Everything you need to know, including video clips, is on the website. Book well ahead.

Makiki Valley & Manoa Cliffs Trails

Hiking

(https://hawaiitrails.org) A favorite workout for city dwellers, the 2.5-mile Makiki Valley Loop links three Tantalus area trails. These trails are usually muddy, so wear shoes with traction and pick up a walking stick. The loop cuts through a lush tropical forest, mainly composed of nonnative species introduced to reforest an area denuded by Hawaii's 19th-century *'iliahi* (sandalwood) trade.

The **Maunalaha Trail** crosses a small stream, passes taro patches and climbs up the eastern ridge of Makiki Valley, passing Norfolk pine, banyans, bamboo and some clear views. Look out below for the tumbled-down remains of ancient Hawaiian stone walls and a historic coffee plantation. After 0.7 miles, you'll reach a four-way junction. Continue uphill on the 1.1-mile **Makiki Valley Trail**, which traverses small gulches and crosses gentle streams bordered by

patches of ginger and guava trees, while offering glimpses of the city below. The 0.7-mile **Kanealole Trail** begins as you cross Kanealole Stream, then follows the stream back down through a field of Job's tears – the bead-like pseudocarps ('false fruit') of the female flowers of this tall grass are sometimes used for lei – to return to the forest baseyard.

Alternatively, a more strenuous 6.2-mile hike beginning from the same trailhead eventually leads to sweeping views of the valley and the ocean beyond. This **Manoa Cliffs Circuit**, aka the 'Big Loop,' starts on the Maunalaha Trail, then takes the **Moleka Trail** to the **Manoa Cliff**, **Kalawahine** and **Nahuina Trails**. At the Kalawahine Trail intersection, you can detour right onto the **Pauoa Flats Trail** to reach the **Nu'uanu Valley Lookout** (https://hawaiitrails.org). From the lookout, backtrack to the Kalawahine Trail, then connect via the Nahuina Trail with the Kanealole Trail, which rolls downhill back to the forest baseyard.

The starting point for both hiking loops is Makiki Forest Recreation Area, less than 0.5 miles up Makiki Heights Dr from Makiki St.

From left: Surfers' van, Ala Moana Beach; Banh mi, Pig & the Lady (p68)

THEODORE TRIMMER/SHUTTERSTOCK ©

MATT MUNRO/LONELY PLANET ©

Park in the 'carpark for hikers' as indicated, then follow the signs and walk along the hillside nature path toward the main trailheads near the **Hawai'i Nature Center** (☎808-955-0100; http://hawaiinaturecenter. org/; 2131 Makiki Heights Dr; program fees from $10; 👶), which organizes family-friendly hikes and outdoor education programs.

Native Books/Nā Mea Hawaii
Arts, Culture

(☎808-596-8885; www.nameahawaii.com; Ward Warehouse, 1050 Ala Moana Blvd) 🎫 FREE Highly recommended community-oriented bookstore, art gallery and gift shop hosts free classes, workshops and demonstrations in hula dancing, Hawaiian language, traditional feather lei making and *lauhala* weaving, ukulele playing and more. Check the website for schedules and if pre-registration is required. There's at least one cultural class on each day.

Surf HNL Girls Who Surf
Surfing, SUP

(☎808-772-4583; http://surfhnl.com/; 210 Ward Ave #329; 2hr lesson from $99, SUP sets rental per hr/day $20/50; ☺8am-6pm) Award-winning surf and stand up paddling (SUP) lessons are on offer in Ala Moana Beach Park and Ko Olina. Free hotel transportation to/from Waikiki for Ala Moana. For surfboard, bodyboard and SUP rentals, delivery to Ala Moana Beach costs $15 and $40 to Ko Olina.

Wa'ahila Ridge Trail
Hiking

(https://hawaiitrails.org) Popular even with novice hikers, this boulder-strewn trail offers a cool retreat amid Norfolk pines and endemic plants, with ridgetop views of Honolulu and Waikiki. Rolling up and down a series of small saddles and knobs before reaching a grassy clearing, the 4.8-mile round-trip trail covers a variety of terrain in a short time, making an enjoyable afternoon's walk.

Look for the Na Ala Hele trailhead sign beyond the picnic tables inside Wa'ahila Ridge State Recreation Area, at the back of the St Louis Heights subdivision, east of Manoa Valley.

If you are traveling by car, turn left off Wai'alae Ave onto St Louis Dr at the stoplight. Heading uphill, veer left onto Bertram St, turn left onto Peter St, then turn left again onto Ruth Pl, which runs west into the park. From Waikiki, bus 14 St Louis Heights stops at the intersection of Peter and Ruth Sts, which is about a half-mile walk from the trailhead.

☺ TOURS

Just west of Ala Moana Regional Park, fishing boats, sunset sails, dinner cruises and party boats leave daily from Kewalo Basin. More expensive guided tours may include transportation to/from Waikiki and advertise various specials in the free tourist magazines available at the airport and around town. Many, such as helicopter flights and food tours, are cheaper if booked directly online.

Architectural Walking Tour
Walking

(☎808-628-7243; www.aiahonolulu.org; 828 Fort Street Mall; tours $15; ☺usually 9-11:30am Sat) Led by professional architects, these historical-minded walking tours will literally change your perspective on downtown Honolulu's capitol district. The state's business center and financial district also harbors some of Hawaii's most significant and cherished architectural treasures. Reservations required – check the calendar and register online.

Hawaii Food Tours
Tours

(☎808-926-3663; www.hawaiifoodtours. com; tours from $139) These guys offer two extremely popular tours. The five-hour 'Hole-in-the-Wall' tour hits all sorts of spots around Honolulu such as Chinatown, island plate-lunch stops, beloved bakeries, crackseed candy shops and more. The seven- to eight-hour 'North Shore Food Tour' heads to the other side of the island. Tours include food, fun, transportation and taxes. Reservations are essential.

🅐 SHOPPING

Although not a brand-name mecca like Waikiki, Honolulu has unique shops and multiple malls offering plenty of local flavor, from traditional flower lei stands and ukulele factories to Hawaiiana souvenir shops, and from contemporary island-style clothing boutiques to vintage and antiques stores. The Ala Moana Center alone has over 340 stores and restaurants in the world's largest open-air shopping center.

Cindy's Lei Shoppe   Arts & Crafts
(📞808-536-6538; www.cindysleishoppe.com; 1034 Maunakea St, Chinatown; ⊙usually 6am-6pm Mon-Sat, to 5pm Sun) At this inviting little shop, a Chinatown landmark, you can watch aunties craft flower lei made of orchids, plumeria, twining maile, lantern *'ilima* (flowering ground-cover) and ginger for all occasions. Several other lei shops clustered nearby will also pack lei for you to carry back home. If worried about parking, you can order online and arrange curbside pick-up.

Honolulu Museum of Art Shop   Arts & Crafts
(📞808-532-8701; http://shop.honolulumuseum.org/; 900 S Beretania St; ⊙10am-4:30pm Tue-Sat, 1-5pm Sun) The shop at the Honolulu Museum of Art provides an opportunity to purchase pieces of Hawaiian art and craft and to benefit the local community, as all proceeds directly support the museum's programs. On offer are publications, stationery, prints and posters, and works by Hawaiian artisans and designers that won't be found outside the islands.

Kamaka Hawaii   Music
(📞808-531-3165; www.kamakahawaii.com; 550 South St, Kaka'ako; ⊙8am-4pm Mon-Fri) 🖋 Kamaka specializes in gorgeous hand-crafted ukuleles made on O'ahu since 1916 (they've just topped 100 years!), with prices starting at around $1000. Call ahead for free 30-minute factory tours, usually starting at 10:30am Tuesday through Friday. There are no retail sales on-site, but they can tell you where to purchase both new and secondhand Kamaka ukuleles nearby.

Madre Chocolate   Food
(📞808-377-6440; http://madrechocolate.com; 8 N Pau'ahi St, Chinatown; ⊙11am-6pm Mon-Sat) The Honolulu outpost of this Kailua chocolate company is serving up a storm in Chinatown, claiming to make the best bean-to-bar chocolate in the state. A must for chocolate lovers, but it doesn't come cheap! Extremely innovative, these guys offer the chance to make your own chocolate bar, or try wine or whiskey and chocolate pairings. Check the website for details.

Native Books/Nā Mea Hawaii   Books, Gifts
(📞808-596-8885; www.nameahawaii.com; Ward Warehouse, 1050 Ala Moana Blvd, Kaka'ako; ⊙10am-9pm Mon-Sat, to 6pm Sun) So much more than just a bookstore stocking Hawaiiana tomes, CDs and DVDs, this cultural gathering spot also sells beautiful silk-screened fabrics, koa-wood bowls, Hawaiian quilts, fish-hook jewelry and hula supplies. Call or check online for special events, including author readings, live local music and cultural classes. There is at least one class going on each day; check the calendar online.

Tin Can Mailman   Antiques, Books
(📞808-524-3009; http://tincanmailman.net; 1026 Nu'uanu Ave, Chinatown; ⊙11am-5pm Mon-Fri, to 4pm Sat) If you're a big fan of vintage tiki wares and 20th-century Hawaiiana books, you'll fall in love with this little Chinatown antiques shop. Thoughtfully collected treasures include jewelry and ukuleles, silk aloha shirts, tropical-wood furnishings, vinyl records, rare prints and tourist brochures from the post-WWII tourism boom. No photos allowed. Hawaiiana aficionados will be stuck in here for a while.

⊗ EATING

If O'ahu weren't so far away from the US mainland, you'd hear a lot more buzz about this multiethnic chowhound capital. Restaurants dot the city, ranging from high-class dining to cheap eateries on nearly every corner. During **Restaurant Week Hawaii** (www.restaurantweekhawaii. com), in mid-November, dozens of locally owned restaurants offer serious discounts for dining out, with a portion of proceeds to support the Culinary Institute of the Pacific at Diamond Head.

Alan Wong's Hawaii Regional **$$$**
(☎808-949-2526; www.alanwongs.com; 1857 S King St, Ala Moana & Around; mains from $35; ☺5-10pm) ✔ One of O'ahu's big-gun chefs, Alan Wong offers his creative interpretations of Hawaii Regional cuisine with a menu inspired by the state's diverse ethnic cultures. Emphasis is on fresh seafood and local produce. Order Wong's time-tested signature dishes such as ginger-crusted *onaga* (red snapper), steamed shellfish bowl, and twice-cooked *kalbi* (short ribs). Make reservations weeks in advance.

Cafe Julia Cafe **$$**
(☎808-533-3334; www.cafejuliahawaii.net; 1040 Richards St, Downtown; mains from $10; ☺11am-2pm Mon-Fri) In the charming old YWCA Laniakea building opposite 'Iolani Palace, Cafe Julia is a gem. Named after Julia Morgan, one of America's first female architects, who designed the building, the service and cuisine is superb in an open-air setting. Perfect for *poke* tacos or garlic ahi for lunch.

Cafe Kaila Cafe **$**
(☎808-732-3330; www.cafe-kaila-hawaii.com; 2919 Kapi'olani Blvd, Market City Shopping Center, Kaimuki; mains from $8; ☺7am-8pm Wed-Fri, 7am-3:30pm Sat & Sun, 7am-3pm Mon & Tue) This place at the top of Kapi'olani Blvd has racked up Best Breakfast gold medals in local culinary awards. And Kaila is so successful that she has opened two more shops...in Japan! Expect to queue to get in for the legendary lineup of incredibly

well-presented breakfast specials. Good news is that Cafe Kaila is now open for dinner Wednesday to Friday.

Ethel's Grill Fusion **$**
(☎808-847-6467; www.facebook.com/pages/ Ethels-Grill/117864404905639; 232 Kalihi St, Greater Honolulu; mains from $8; ☺5:30am-2pm Mon-Sat) One of the greatest hole-in-the-wall restaurants in Honolulu, head to Ethel's for the tastiest food and the homely atmosphere. This bustling, cash-only place has 24 seats and six parking spots and both are usually full when Ethel's is open. Incredibly inexpensive for tongue-tingling options such as garlic 'ahi, *mochiko* chicken, pig's feet soup, deep-fried turkey tails and oxtail soup.

Helena's Hawaiian Food Hawaiian **$**
(☎808-845-8044; http://helenashawaiianfood. com; 1240 N School St, Greater Honolulu; dishes from $3; ☺10am-7:30pm Tue-Fri) ✔ Walking through the door is like stepping into another era at this legendary institution. Even though longtime owner Helena Chock has passed away, her relatives still command the family kitchen, which opened in 1946. Most people order à la carte; cash only. A few blocks southeast of the Bishop Museum, Helena's received a James Beard Award for 'America's Classics'.

Kokua Market Natural Foods Supermarket **$**
(☎808-941-1922; www.kokua.coop; 2643 S King St, University area; ☺8am-9pm; 🅿) ✔ Hawaii's only natural-food co-op is extremely good value and has an organic hot-and-cold meal and salad bar, plus a vegetarian- and vegan-friendly deli for takeout on S King St near UH. Kombucha is on tap in different flavors for $3 per cup. Free parking and picnic tables to eat your goodies, off Kahuna Lane behind the store.

Lucky Belly Asian, Fusion **$**
(☎808-531-1888; www.luckybelly.com; 50 N Hotel St, Chinatown; mains from $10; ☺11am-2pm & 5pm-midnight Mon-Sat) Sleek bistro tables are packed elbow-to-elbow at this arts-district noodle bar that crafts hot and spicy Asian fusion bites, knockout artisanal cocktails

and amazingly fresh, almost architectural salads that the whole table can share. A 'Belly Bowl' of *ramen* soup topped with buttery pork belly, smoked bacon and pork sausage is carnivore heaven.

Pig & the Lady   Asian, Fusion $$
(☑808-585-8255; http://thepigandthelady. com; 83 N King St, Chinatown; mains from $10; ☺10:30am-2pm Mon-Sat, 5:30-10pm Tue-Sat) An award-winning Vietnamese fusion restaurant that you'll need to reserve in the evening, the Pig & the Lady is one of the hottest spots to dine on the island. Imaginative lunch sandwiches come with shrimp chips or pho broth; delicious dinner options include Laotian fried chicken. It doesn't stop there though; there's takeout and you'll spot these guys at farmers' markets.

Sweet Home Café   Taiwanese $
(☑808-947-3707; 2334 S King St, University area; shared dishes $2-15; ☺4-11pm) Expect lines of locals waiting outside this place's door. On wooden family-style tables sit steaming-hot pots; choose your broth, then peruse the refrigerators and figure out what to cook in it. Countless choices of all kinds of vegetables, tofu, lamb, chicken or tender beef tongue. Besides the great food and good fun, there is complimentary shave ice for dessert.

Tamura's Poke   Seafood $
(☑808-735-7100; www.tamurasfinewine.com/ pokepage.html; 3496 Wai'alae Ave, Kaimuki; ☺11am-8:45pm Mon-Fri, 9:30am-8:45pm Sat, 9:30am-7:45pm Sun; P) Arguably the best *poke* on the island is up on Wai'alae Ave in undistinguished-looking Tamura's Fine Wines & Liquors. Head inside, turn right, wander down to *poke* corner and feast your eyes. The 'spicy ahi' and the smoked marlin are to die for. Ask for tasters before you buy and take away.

Waiola Shave Ice   Desserts $
(☑808-949-2269; www.waiolashaveice.com; 2135 Waiola St, University area; snacks $2-6; ☺9:30am-6:30pm) The flagship store from the 1940s for this growing business that

also has super-popular outlets just off Kapahulu Ave and in Kaka'ako. For a lesson in old-school shave ice, Waiola's is superfine with add-ons that set it apart: try the azuki beans, *mochi* (Japanese sticky-rice cakes), *iliko'i* (passion fruit) syrup or condensed milk.

12th Avenue
Grill   Modern American $$$
(☑808-732-9469; http://12thavegrill.com; 1120 12th Ave, Kaimuki; mains from $27; ☺5:30-10pm Sun-Thu, to 11pm Fri & Sat) Hidden in a side road off Waialae Ave, this Kaimuki grill has been picking up a number of best-restaurant awards. Combining the efforts of an impressive team and using as much local produce as possible, 12th Avenue Grill has the locals drooling. The grilled kimchi marinated Hawaii ranchers skirt steak ($32) is more than just a mouthful to say!

Artizen by MW   Hawaiian $
(☑808-524-0499; www.artizenbymw.com; 250 S Hotel St, Downtown; bentō from $8; ☺7:30am-2:30pm Mon-Fri) This impressive cafe at the Hawaii State Museum of Art is the perfect spot for breakfast or lunch, or just for a coffee while perusing the museum's stunning collections. There are ready-made grab-and-go bento, or sit and try the kimchi Portuguese bean soup ($6), spicy Korean pork bowl ($10), or the hot turkey sandwich with gravy ($13).

Chef Mavro   Fusion $$$
(☑808-944-4714; www.chefmavro.com; 1969 S King St, Ala Moana & Around; multicourse tasting menus from $105; ☺6-9pm Wed-Sun) At Honolulu's most avant-garde restaurant, maverick chef George Mavrothalassitis creates conceptual dishes, all paired with Old and New World wines. This is award-winning fine dining and a fusion of Hawaiian and chef Mavro's home region of Provence in France. Choose between the four- or the six-course menu and don't forget your wallet. Reservations essential.

Mission Social Hall & Cafe   Cafe $
(☑808-447-3913; www.missionhouses. org/visitor-information/cafe; 553 S King St,

Downtown; 3 items for $11; ⊙11am-2pm Tue-Sat) At the historic Hawaiian Mission Houses, this counter-serve cafe, run by well-known local chef Mark Noguchi, serves lunch five days per week. This is staple stuff with an island twist in a lovely setting. The menu rotates, but dishes include a *kajiki* (marlin) sandwich, and a *liliko'i*-guava-calamansi tart for dessert. There's a patio and lawn for family-friendly events.

Honolulu Museum
of Art Cafe   Modern American $$
(☎808-532-8734; http://honolulumuseum.org/; Honolulu Museum of Art, 900 S Beretania St, Ala Moana & Around; mains from $15; ⊙11:30am-1:30pm Tue-Sat) Market-fresh salads and sandwiches made with O'ahu-grown ingredients, a decent selection of wines by the glass and tropically infused desserts make this an indulgent way to support the arts. Romantic tables face the courtyard and fountain with spectacular sculptures by Jun Kaneko. Reservations recommended; last seating at 1.30pm. There is no museum admission charge to lunch at the cafe.

Aloha Vietnamese
Food   Vietnamese $
(☎808-941-1170; 2320 S King St, University area; mains under $12; ⊙2pm-midnight Tue-Sun, 4-11pm Mon) This is no -rills family-run Vietnamese at its best. A locals favorite, don't be fazed by lines out the door or the lack of decor. The menu is extensive, the service is friendly and the food is superb. Try the brisket and sirloin pho. Plenty of parking out front and open until late.

Andy's Sandwiches
& Smoothies   Sandwiches $
(☎808-988-6161; www.andyssandwiches.com; 2904 E Manoa Rd, Manoa Valley; items from $4; ⊙7am-5pm Mon-Thu, to 4pm Fri, to 2.30pm Sun) Family run, Andy's is a hidden gem up the Manoa valley (next to Starbucks across the road from Manoa Marketplace) that doesn't see too many tourists. Popular with UH students, it can be a squeeze to

get in, but it's definitely worth the effort. The sandwiches, smoothies, açai bowls and salads are superb, especially the bird's-nest salad.

Kahai Street Kitchen   Hawaiian $
(☎808-845-0320; www.kahaistreet-kitchen. com; 946 Coolidge St, University area; plate lunches from $9; ⊙10:30am-7:30pm Tue-Sat) This hole-in-the-wall place is ragingly popular with locals (you'll notice lines of people at the order counters at the two-story white corner building). There are four sizeable tables out front on Coolidge St, or you can head inside for more seating through the door on King St. We're talking gourmet plate lunches, salads and sandwiches.

Nanzan Girogiro   Japanese $$$
(☎808-521-0141; www.guiloguilo.com; 560 Pensacola St, Ala Moana & Around; chef's tasting menu from $50; ⊙6pm-midnight Thu-Mon) Traditional *kaiseki ryōri* (seasonal small-course) cuisine infused with Hawaii-grown fruits and vegetables, fresh seafood and, frankly, magic. Akin to eating small pieces of art in an art gallery, bar seats ring the open kitchen. Ceramic turtles hide savory custard in their shells and pottery bowls harbor tea-soaked rice topped with delicately poached fish. Reservations essential.

Nobu Honolulu   Asian $$$
(☎808-237-6999; www.noburestaurants.com; Waiea Tower, 1118 Ala Moana Blvd, Kaka'ako; shared dishes from $7, mains from $25; ⊙restaurant 5-10pm Sun-Thu, to 10:30pm Fri & Sat, lounge 5pm-close daily) Nobu Matsuhisa's legendary Japanese-fusion restaurant and sushi bar has made the move from Waikiki to the new Waiea Tower in Ward Village. Good news is that Nobu's signature dishes such as black miso cod and yellowtail jalapeno have made the move too. With clean, fresh decor and Nobu's excellent service, the new location is proving a hit in Honolulu.

🍸 DRINKING & NIGHTLIFE

Every self-respecting bar in Honolulu has a *pupu* menu to complement the liquid sustenance, and some bars are as famous for their appetizers as their good-times atmosphere. A key term to know is *pau hana* (literally 'stop work'), Hawaiian pidgin for 'happy hour.' Chinatown's edgy nightlife scene revolves around N Hotel St, which was the city's notorious red-light district. New gastropubs are opening up all over the city.

Beer Lab HI   Brewery

(☏808-888-0913; www.beerlabhi.com; 1010 University Ave, University area; ⊙4-10pm Tue-Thu, 4pm-midnight Fri, 3pm-midnight Sat) Love the story! Three nuclear engineers working at Pearl Harbor make beer for a hobby; decide to open a bar; can't be bothered with cooking, so go for a BYOF (Bring Your Own Food) bar! LaLa Land food truck parks across the street providing eats. Sounds a bit 'mad-scientist', but Beer Lab Hawaii is definitely a hit, with some unusual brews.

Glazers Coffee   Cafe

(☏808-391-6548; www.glazerscoffee.com; 2700 S King St, University area; ⊙7am-10pm Mon-Thu, 7am-9pm Fri, 8am-10pm Sat & Sun; 🛜) They're serious about brewing strong espresso drinks and batch-roasted coffee at this UH students' hangout, where you can kick back on comfy living-room sofas next to jazzy artwork and plentiful electrical outlets. There's fast wi-fi and strong air-conditioning; it's easy to see why the sofas are often full at this hidden gem of a coffee house.

Honolulu Beerworks   Microbrewery

(☏808-589-2337; www.honolulubeerworks.com; 328 Cooke St, Kaka'ako; ⊙11am-10pm Mon-Thu, 11am-midnight Fri & Sat) This warehouse microbrewery is fast building up a following with 10 of its brews on tap. It's hard to go past the Point Panic Pale Ale, well-rounded with a kick, just like the famous bodyboarding break. The menu of 'beer food' may be limited, but it certainly hits the spot as you work your way through the beers on offer.

La Mariana Sailing Club   Bar

(☏808-848-2800; www.lamarianasailingclub.com; 50 Sand Island Access Rd, Greater Honolulu; ⊙11am-9pm) Time warp! Who says all the great tiki bars have gone to the dogs? Irreverent and kitschy, this 1950s joint by the lagoon is filled with yachties and long-suffering locals. Classic mai tais are as killer as the other tropical potions, complete with tiki-head swizzle sticks and tiny umbrellas. Grab a waterfront table and dream of sailing to Tahiti.

Morning Glass Coffee   Coffee

(☏808-673-0065; www.morningglasscoffee.com; 2955 E Manoa Rd, Manoa Valley; coffee from $3.75; ⊙7am-4pm Mon-Fri, 7:30am-4pm Sat) Just beyond Manoa Marketplace, up the Manoa Valley, Morning Glass has a glowing reputation for serving top coffee, plus terrific breakfasts and lunches in an open-air setting. There's on-site parking, and though the building is small, the reputation is growing huge. Try the macaroni and cheese pancakes for breakfast ($10).

Murphy's Bar and Grill   Irish Pub

(☏808-531-0422; http://murphyshawaii.com/; 2 Merchant St, Chinatown; ⊙11am-2am Mon-Fri, 4pm-2am Sat & Sun) This old-fashioned Irish pub has been a haven for mariners, businessmen and locals since 1891 and is in a lovely old brick building on Merchant St. While you'll find the Guinness and Kilkenny that you expected to find on tap, you may be surprised by the discerning lunch and dinner menus. Try the shepherd's pie ($17.50).

Tea at 1024   Teahouse

(☏808-521-9596; www.teaat1024.net; 1024 Nu'uanu Ave, Chinatown; ⊙11am-2pm Tue-Fri, to 3pm Sat & Sun) Tea at 1024 takes you back in time to another era. Cutesy sandwiches, scones and cakes accompany your choice of tea as you relax and watch the Chinatown crowd rush by the window. They even have bonnets for you to don to add to the ambience. Set menus run from $22.95 per person and reservations are recommended.

⭐ ENTERTAINMENT

For what's going on after dark this week, from live music and DJ gigs to theater, movies and cultural events, check the *Honolulu Star-Advertiser's TGIF* (www.staradvertiser.com/tgif) section, which comes out every Friday, and the free alternative tabloid *Honolulu Weekly* (http://honoluluweekly.com), published every Wednesday. Other websites worth checking out are *Honolulu Now* (www.hnlnow.com) and that of the popular monthly mag *Honolulu Magazine* (www.honolulumagazine.com).

Doris Duke Theatre   Cinema

(☎808-532-8768; www.honolulumuseum.org; Honolulu Museum of Art, 900 S Beretania St; tickets $10) The Doris Duke Theatre shows a mind-bending array of experimental, alternative, retro-classic and art-house films, especially ground-breaking documentaries, inside the Honolulu Museum of Art. The theater also hosts lectures, performances and concerts. The museum has had a film program from the 1930s, showing classic films in Central Courtyard; screenings moved to what is now the Doris Duke Theatre in 1977.

Hawaii Theater   Performing Arts

(☎808-528-0506; www.hawaiitheatre.com; 1130 Bethel St, Chinatown) ✆ Beautifully restored, this grande dame of O'ahu's theater scene is a major venue for dance, music and theater. Performances include top Hawaii musicians, contemporary plays, international touring acts and film festivals. The theater also hosts the annual Ka Himeni Ana competition of singers in the traditional *nahenahe* style. Listed on both the State and National Registers of Historic Places.

Republik   Live Music

(☎808-941-7469; http://jointherepublik.com; 1349 Kapi'olani Blvd, Ala Moana & Around; ⊙lounge 6pm-2am Tue-Sat, concert schedules vary) Honolulu's most intimate concert hall for touring and local acts – indie rockers, punk and metal bands, even ukulele players – has a graffiti-bomb vibe and backlit black walls that trippily light up. Check out the calendar online and buy tickets for shows in advance, both to make sure you get in and to save a few bucks.

Royal Hawaiian Band   Live Music

(☎808-922-5331; www.rhb-music.com) Founded in 1836 by King Kamehameha III, the Royal Hawaiian Band is the only band in the US with a royal legacy, and is the only full-time municipal band in the country. The band plays all over O'ahu (check the calendar online) and plays a free concert each Friday at noon at 'Iolani Palace (p45).

ℹ GETTING THERE & AWAY

Once you're on O'ahu, getting to Honolulu is easy using either your own rental wheels or TheBus public transportation system.

ℹ GETTING AROUND

Just northwest of Waikiki, the Ala Moana Center mall is the central transfer point for TheBus, O'ahu's public-transportation system. Several direct bus routes run between Waikiki and Honolulu's other neighborhoods.

Major car-rental companies are found at Honolulu International Airport and in Waikiki.

Traffic jams up during rush hours, roughly from 7am to 9am and 3pm to 6pm weekdays. Expect heavy traffic in both directions on the H-1 Fwy during this time, as well as on the Pali and Likelike Hwys headed into Honolulu in the morning and away from the city in the late afternoon. Some major roads are 'coned' during rush hours to add lanes to the directions that are busy.

WAIKIKI

In this Chapter

Kuhio Beach Park 76
Surfing.. 78
Sights 80
Beaches 86
Activities 88
Tours 89
Shopping 89
Eating 91
Drinking & Nightlife......................... 96
Entertainment 98
Getting There & Away 100
Where to Stay 101

Waikiki at a Glance...

Once a Hawaiian royal retreat, Waikiki today revels in its role as a retreat for the masses. This famous strand of sand moves to a rhythm of Hawaiian music at beachfront high-rises. In this pulsing jungle of modern hotels and malls, you can still hear whispers of Hawaii's past, from the chanting of hula troupes at Kuhio Beach to the legacy of Olympic gold medalist Duke Kahanamoku.

Distractions? Surfing lessons. Sunbathing. Hopping aboard a catamaran and sailing toward Diamond Head. At night, sip a mai tai and enjoy the lilting harmonies of slack key guitar.

Waikiki in One Day

Start with a stroll to **Kuhio Beach Park** (p76) and genuflect at the **Duke Kahanamoku statue** (p78). Snorkel off **Kapi'olani Beach Park** (p87). Head inland for classic Hawaiian fare at **Rainbow Drive-In** (p93). Then, zip across the water aboard the **Na Hoku II Catamaran** (p89). Back on land, enjoy authentic hula and music at the **Kuhio Beach Torchlighting & Hula Show** (p77).

Waikiki in Two Days

On the second day cross the grassy expanses of **Kapi'olani Regional Park** (p85), then follow the sand to **Kahaloa & Ulukou Beaches** (p87) for a surfing lesson where the sport began. Indulge in the buffet at **Orchids** (p92), then relax at uncrowded **Fort DeRussy Beach** (p99). Enjoy sunset melodies at **House Without a Key** (p98) and dinner at **Hy's Steakhouse** (p96).

Waikiki Map (p82)

Arriving in Waikiki

Honolulu International Airport About 9 miles northwest of Waikiki.

Express Shuttle Operates 24-hour door-to-door shuttle buses from the airport to Waikiki's hotels.

You can reach Waikiki via **TheBus** routes 19 or 20. Buses run every 20 minutes from 6am to 11pm daily.

The most atmospheric drive to Waikiki is **Nimitz Highway (Hwy 92)**.

Sleeping

Waikiki's main beachfront strip, along Kalakaua Ave, is lined with hotels and sprawling resorts. Further from the sand, look for inviting small hotels on Waikiki's backstreets. Many are quite affordable year-round. Hundreds of condos and apartments are on offer on Airbnb and HomeAway. For more on where to stay, see p101.

DAVID MADISON/GETTY IMAGES ©

Kuhio Beach Park

If you're the kind of person who wants it all, this beach offers everything from protected swimming to outrigger-canoe rides, and even a free sunset-hula and Hawaiian-music show.

Great For...

☑ Don't Miss

Prince Kuhio statue honors the Prince of the People.

Kapahulu Groin

The beach is marked on its opposite end by Kapahulu Groin, a walled storm drain with a walkway on top that juts out into the ocean. A low stone breakwater, called the Wall, runs out from Kapahulu Groin, parallel to the beach. It was built to control sand erosion and, in the process, two nearly enclosed swimming pools were formed.

The pool closest to Kapahulu Groin is best for swimming. However, because circulation is limited, the water gets murky. Kapahulu Groin is one of Waikiki's hottest bodyboarding spots. If the surf's right, you can find a few dozen bodyboarders riding the waves. These experienced local kids ride straight for the groin's cement wall and then veer away at the last mo-

❶ Need to Know

The Waikiki Beach Center has restrooms, outdoor showers, a snack bar and beach-gear-rental stand.

✕ Take a Break

Order sushi and watch the sunset from **Sansei Seafood Restaurant & Sushi Bar** (p95).

★ Top Tip
Never leave your valuables unattended on the beach.

ment, thrilling the tourists watching them from the little pier above.

Kuhio Beach Torchlighting & Hula Show

It all begins at the Duke Kahanamoku statue with the sounding of a conch shell and the lighting of torches after sunset. At the nearby hula mound, lay out your beach towel and enjoy a truly authentic Hawaiian music and dance show. This is no bit of tourist fluff either, as top talent regularly performs, including much-lauded hula experts from the University of Hawai'i.

Kuhio Beach Surfboard Lockers

Where most cities have bike racks and others have huge parking garages, Waikiki has a public facility that embodies the very spirit of the beach: a huge locker area for surfboards right near the sand. Located next to the police substation, this iconic storage area for local surfers is the perfect offbeat photo op. Hundreds of boards are stored here by locals in between their time out on the water.

Outrigger Canoes

Some surf outfits offer outrigger-canoe rides ($110 for four people) that take off from the beach and ride the tossin' waves home – kids especially love those thrills.

Waikiki Beach

MATT MUNRO/LONELY PLANET ©

Surfing

Waikiki has good surfing year-round, with the largest waves rolling in during winter. Gentler summer surf breaks are best for beginners.

Great For...

☑ **Don't Miss**

The statue of Duke Kahanamoku in Kuhio Beach Park (off Kalakaua Ave).

Duke Kahanamoku

The Duke was a true Hawaiian hero, winning numerous Olympic swimming medals, breaking the world record for the 100yd freestyle in his first competitive event, and becoming known as 'the father of modern surfing.' He even had stints as sheriff of Honolulu and as a Hollywood actor. Duke also pioneered the Waikiki 'beachboys', teaching visitors how to surf. His statue on Kalakaua Ave is always draped in colorful lei.

Getting Started: Diamond Head Surfboards

One of the best Waikiki-area shops for board rentals of all kinds. It has a huge range on offer. As well as renting out surfboards, stand up paddleboards and bodyboards by the hour, day or week, it has excellent personalized surfing lessons

Duke Kahanamoku sculpture (p86) by artist Jan Gordon Fisher

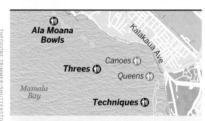

❶ Need to Know

If you need nonemergency help, stop by the **Waikiki Police Substation** (☎808-723-8566; www.honolulupd.org; 2425 Kalakaua Ave; ⏱24hr) next to Kuhio Beach Park.

✕ Take a Break

Enjoy happy hour every day from 3pm to 5pm at festive **Lulu's Waikiki** (p97).

★ Top Tip

Stands offering surfing lessons and surfboard rentals line the sand at Kuhio Beach Park near Kapahulu Groin.

based out of its well-stocked shop. Its Hawaii Republic T-shirts are popular.

Surf Spots for Beginners

Canoes is one of the most famous spots and often busy with surfing classes. It's an easygoing mix of left and right breaks with a crowd from around the world enjoying long, consistent rides. Once Canoes is mastered, try Queens, which is an all round great wave. It's a longboard dream and is usually crowded, especially when any of the many surf contests are on.

Threes

Very reliable at low tide, Threes has a big following with locals, who appreciate its picture-perfect form in almost all conditions (when highest, it forms small barrels). It's a half-mile out, so be ready for a long paddle.

Ala Moana Bowls

Literally known for its 'bowls', this break has barrels you can stand up in when conditions are right. It's near the entrance to Ala Wai Harbor and is a fast hollow left. There's usually a serious crew of locals here.

Techniques

The name of this break dates to the 1930s when surfers developed hollow boards in order to execute the maneuvers needed to surf these breaks. Previously, the cumbersome heavy redwood boards couldn't be used here.

Get your Gear

Surfing lessons and surfboard, stand up paddling (SUP) and bodyboard rentals can be arranged at the concession stands along the sand at Kuhio Beach Park, near the bodyboarding hot spot of Kapahulu Groin.

◉ SIGHTS

Yes, the beach is the main sight, but Waikiki also has historic hotels, evocative public art, amazing artifacts of Hawaiian history and even a zoo and an aquarium.

Wizard Stones of
Kapaemahu   Statue
(off Kalakaua Ave, Kuhio Beach Park) Near the police substation at Waikiki Beach Center, four ordinary-looking boulders are actually the legendary Wizard Stones of Kapaemahu, said to contain the mana (spiritual essence) of four wizards who came to O'ahu from Tahiti around AD 400. According to ancient legend, the wizards helped the island residents by relieving their aches and pains, and their fame became widespread. As tribute when the wizards left, the islanders placed the four boulders where the wizards had lived.

The stones weigh 7 tons; how the ancients moved them the 2 miles from a quarry east of Diamond Head is a mystery.

Royal Hawaiian
Hotel   Historic Building
(☎808-923-7311; www.royal-hawaiian.com; 2259 Kalakaua Ave; ⊙tours 1pm Tue & Thu) **FREE** With its Moorish-style turrets and archways, this gorgeously restored 1927 art-deco landmark, dubbed the 'Pink Palace,' is a throwback to the era when Rudolph Valentino was *the* romantic idol and travel to Hawaii was by Matson Navigation luxury liner. Its guest list reads like a who's who of A-list celebrities, from royalty to Rockefellers, along with luminaries such as Charlie Chaplin and Babe Ruth. Today, historic tours explore the architecture and lore of this grande dame.

Don't miss the remarkable painting of Hawaii completed by Ernest Clegg for the hotel's opening. Painted directly on the plaster, it has been a permanent feature outside the elevators in the original building since the hotel opened.

King David
Kalakaua Statue   Statue
(off Kalakaua Ave) Born in 1836, King Kalakaua ruled Hawaii from 1874 until his death

Body boarder, Waikiki

Beach promenade

in 1891. With his wife, Queen Kapi'olani, Kalakaua traveled the world extensively. This statue, designed by Native Hawaiian sculptor Sean Browne, greets visitors coming into Waikiki and was donated by the Japanese-American Community of Hawaii to mark 100 years of Japanese immigration in 1985. Kalakaua was instrumental in the signing of the Japan-Hawaii Labor Convention that brought 200,000 Japanese immigrants to Hawaii between 1885 and 1924.

Waikiki Aquarium   Aquarium

(☑808-923-9741; www.waikikiaquarium.org; 2777 Kalakaua Ave; adult/child $12/5; ⊗9am-5pm, last entry 4:30pm; ⊞) ⏹ Located on Waikiki's shoreline, this university-run aquarium recreates diverse tropical Pacific reef habitats. You'll see rare fish species from the Northwestern Hawaiian Islands, as well as hypnotic moon jellies and flashlight fish that host bioluminescent bacteria. Especially hypnotizing are the Palauan chambered nautiluses with their unique spiral shells – in fact, this is the world's first aquarium to breed these endangered creatures in captivity, a ground-breaking

Waikiki is perfect for any tropical distraction; or simply doing nothing at all

achievement. It's a pleasant 15-minute walk southeast of the main Waikiki beach strip.

An outdoor pool is home to rare and endangered Hawaiian monk seals. A new garden with native Hawaiian plants features a self-guided tour. Check the website or call ahead to make reservations for special family-friendly events and fun educational programs for kids, such as Aquarium After Dark adventures.

Moana Surfrider
Hotel   Historic Building

(☑808-922-3111; www.moana-surfrider.com; 2365 Kalakaua Ave; ⊗tours 11am Mon, Wed & Fri) **FREE** Christened the Moana Hotel when it opened in 1901, this beaux-arts plantation-style inn was once the haunt of Hollywood movie stars, aristocrats and business tycoons. The historic hotel embraces a seaside courtyard with large banyan trees and a wraparound veranda,

Waikiki

Waikiki Ocean Club (0.1mi)

Hawaii Surfboard Rentals (0.2mi)

808 Smart Cars Rentals

Ena Rd

25

Cruzin Hawaii

Keoniana St

Pau St

Kuamo'o St

Namahana St

Ala Moana Blvd

10

Olohana St

Kalaimoku St

Ala Wai Blvd

Launiu St

University Ave

Kamoku St

1

Ala Wai Park

Kai'olu St

Kalakaua Ave

Kuhio Ave

54

Aloha Dr

Hilton Lagoon

Rainbow Dr

87 86

Kalia Rd

Maluhia Rd

17

68

Manukai St

Paoa Pl

Chase Hawaii Rentals

Fort DeRussy Military Reservation

Saratoga Rd

62 74

72

78

7

81

59

Beach Walk

64

Lewers St

Royal Hawaiian Ave

69

Seaside Ave

71

Nohonani St

55

49

63

Kalia Rd

Helumoa Rd

3 4 83

Duke's La

76

Gray's Beach

58 50

31 21

35

26

40

37

Ka'iulani Ave

82

16 80

70

77

39

12

27

41

6

29

28

65

Kuhio Beach Park

20

Mamala Bay

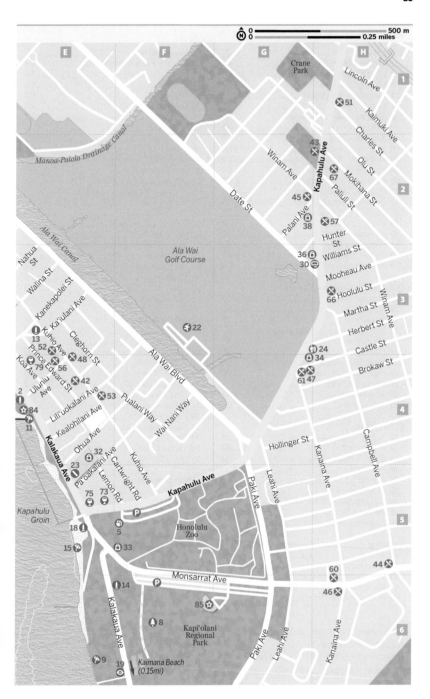

Waikiki

◎ Sights
1 Ala Wai Canal D1
2 Duke Kahanamoku Statue.....................E4
3 Fort DeRussy Beach.........................B3
4 Hawaii Army Museum..........................B3
5 Honolulu Zoo...............................F5
6 Kahaloa & Ulukou Beaches...................D4
7 Kahanamoku Beach...........................A2
8 Kapi'olani Regional Park F6
9 Kapi'olani Beach Park.......................E6
10 King David Kalakaua Statue C2
11 Kuhio Beach Park...........................E4
12 Moana Surfrider Hotel D4
13 Princess Kaiulani Statue...................E3
14 Queen Kapi'olani Statue F6
15 Queen's Surf Beach.........................E5
16 Royal Hawaiian Hotel C3
17 Storyteller Statue C2
18 Surfer on a Wave Statue....................E5
19 Waikiki Aquarium...........................F6
20 Wizard Stones of Kapaemahu.................D4

⊕ Activities, Courses & Tours
21 Abhasa Spa C3
22 Ala Wai Golf Course........................F3
23 AquaZone...................................E5
24 Diamond Head Surfboards....................H3
25 Hiking Hawaii B1
26 Holokai Catamaran..........................B3
27 Maita'i Catamaran..........................C3
28 Na Hoku II Catamaran.......................D4
29 Na Ho'ola Spa D4
30 Snorkel Bob's..............................H3
31 Spa Khakara................................C3

◎ Shopping
32 Angels by the Sea..........................E4
33 Art on the Zoo Fence.......................F5
34 Bailey's Antiques & Aloha Shirts...........G4
35 Fighting Eel...............................D3
36 Island Paddler.............................G3
37 Malie Organics.............................C3
38 Na Lima Mili Hulu No'eau...................G2
39 Rebecca Beach..............................D3
40 Ukulele PuaPua.............................C3

⊗ Eating
41 Azure C4
42 Blue Ocean.................................E4
43 Da Hawaiian Poke Company H2
44 Diamond Head Market & Grill................H5
45 Haili's Hawaiian Foods G2
46 Hawaii Sushi...............................H6
47 Hawaii's Favorite Kitchens.................G4
48 Hy's Steakhouse E4
49 Kaiwa......................................C3
50 La Mer C3
51 Leonard's..................................H1
52 Lovin' Oven................................E3
53 MAC 24/7...................................E4
54 Mahina & Sun's D2
55 Marukame Udon..............................D3
56 Musubi Cafe Iyasume........................E4
57 Ono Seafood................................H2
58 Orchids....................................C3
59 Pau Hana Market............................C3
60 Pioneer Saloon.............................H6
61 Rainbow Drive-In...........................G4
62 Ramen Nakamura.............................C2
63 Roy's Waikiki..............................C3
Sansei Seafood Restaurant &
   Sushi Bar........................ (see 23)
64 Tonkatsu Ginza Bairin C3
65 Veranda....................................D4
66 Wada.......................................H3
67 Waiola Shave Ice...........................H2

◎ Drinking & Nightlife
68 Bacchus Waikiki............................D2
Beach Bar .... (see 65)
69 Cuckoo Coconuts............................D3
70 Duke's Waikiki.............................D4
71 Fusion Waikiki.............................D3
72 Gorilla in the Cafe........................C3
73 Hula's Bar & Lei Stand.....................E5
74 In Between.................................C2
75 Lulu's Waikiki.............................E5
76 Maui Brewing Co............................D3
77 RumFire....................................C3
78 Tapa's Restaurant & Lanai Bar..............D2
79 Wang Chung's E4

⊕ Entertainment
80 'Aha 'Aina.................................D3
Beach Bar .... (see 65)
81 Hilton Hawaiian Village Fireworks A2
82 House Without a Key........................C3
83 Kani Ka Pila Grille........................B3
84 Kuhio Beach Torchlighting & Hula
   Show E4
85 Royal Hawaiian Band F6
86 Tapa Bar A2
87 Waikiki Starlight Luau.....................A2

where island musicians and hula dancers perform in the evenings.

Upstairs from the lobby, you'll find displays of memorabilia from the early days: everything from scripts of the famed Hawaii Calls radio show broadcast live from the courtyard here between 1935 and 1975 to woolen bathing suits, historical period photographs and a short video of Waikiki back in the days when the Moana was the only hotel on the oceanfront horizon.

Princess Kaiulani Statue   Statue

(off Kuhio Ave) Princess Kaiulani was heir to the throne when the Kingdom of Hawaii was overthrown in 1893. This statue of the princess feeding her beloved peacocks sits in Waikiki's Kaiulani Triangle Park and was unveiled in 1999 on the 124th anniversary of her birth. Known for her beauty, intelligence and determination, the princess visited President Cleveland in Washington after the overthrow, but could not prevent the annexation of Hawaii by the US. She died at the tender age of 23.

Kapiʻolani Regional Park   Park

(☎808-768-4623; off Kalakaua & Paki Aves) In its early days, horse racing and band concerts were the biggest attractions at Waikiki's favorite green space. Although the racetrack is long gone, this park named after Queen Kapiʻolani is still a beloved outdoor venue for live music and local community gatherings, from farmers markets and arts-and-crafts fairs to festivals and rugby matches. The tree-shaded Kapiʻolani Bandstand is ideal for catching a concert by the time-honored Royal Hawaiian Band, which performs classics here on many Sunday afternoons.

Queen Kapiʻolani Statue   Statue

(off Kalakaua Ave, Kapiʻolani Regional Park) This bronze statue depicts Queen Kapiʻolani, the wife of King David Kalakaua – his statue at the other end of Waikiki greets visitors to Waikiki. The queen was a beloved philanthropist, known as the queen who loved children. Among other accomplishments, she founded a maternity home in 1890 for disadvantaged Hawaiians and today you'll hear her name often – the park, a hospital, a major boulevard and a community college are named for her.

Hawaii Army Museum   Museum

(☎808-955-9552; www.hiarmymuseumsoc. org; 2161 Kalia Rd; donations welcome, audiotour $5; ⏰9am-5pm Tue-Sat, last entry 4:15pm; P)

🔭 Diamond Head

The extinct crater of Diamond Head is now a state monument, with picnic tables and a spectacular hiking trail up to the 761ft-high summit. The trail was built in 1908 to service military observation stations located along the crater rim.

Inside the crater rim, the park has information and historical displays, restrooms, drinking fountains and a picnic area. From Waikiki, catch bus 23 or 24; from the closest bus stop, it's about a 20-minute walk to the trailhead. By car, take Monsarrat Ave to Diamond Head Rd and turn right immediately after passing Kapiʻolani Community College (KCC). Enter the park through Kahala Tunnel.

From the **Diamond Head Lookout**, there are fine views over Kuilei Cliffs Beach Park and up the coast toward Kahala. On the east side of the parking area, look for the Amelia Earhart Marker, which recalls the aviator's 1935 flight from Hawaii to California. It's an enjoyable 1.4-mile walk beyond Kaimana Beach in Waikiki.

VUK8691/GETTY IMAGES ©

FREE At Fort DeRussy, this museum exhibits an almost mind-numbing array of military paraphernalia as it relates to Hawaii's history, starting with shark-tooth clubs that Kamehameha the Great used to win control of the island more than two centuries ago. Old photographs and stories help bring an understanding of the influence of the US military presence in Hawaii.

Extensive exhibits include displays on the 442nd, the Japanese American regiment that became the most decorated regiment in WWII, and on Kaua'i-born Eric Shinseki, a retired four-star army general who spoke out against the US invasion of Iraq and who served as Secretary of Veterans Affairs. The building was once the fortified Shore Battery Randolph, which housed large defense guns.

Surfer on a Wave Statue   Statue
(off Kalakaua Ave) Opposite the entrance to Honolulu Zoo and right on the beach, the *Surfer on a Wave* statue celebrates surfing as a major part of the culture of Waikiki. Cast in bronze by Robert Pashby, it was unveiled in 2003.

Storyteller Statue   Statue
(off Kalakaua Ave) This bronze statue just off Kalakaua Ave represents 'The Story-tellers', the keepers of Hawaiian culture. For centuries, women have been at the top of Hawaiian oral traditions, and the storytellers preserve the identity of their people and land by reciting poems, songs, chants and genealogies. The Storyteller's companion-statue is the Water Giver statue at the Hawaiian Convention Center.

🏖 BEACHES

Queen's Surf Beach   Beach
(Wall's; off Kalakaua Ave, Kapi'olani Beach Park; 👤) Just south of Kuhio Beach, the name-sake beach for the famous surf break is a great place for families as the waves are rarely large when they reach shore but they are still large enough for bodyboarding, which means older kids can frolic for hours. At the south end of the beach, the area in front of the beach pavilion is popular with the local gay community.

Kahanamoku Beach   Beach
(Paoa Pl; 👤) Fronting the Hilton Hawaiian Village, Kahanamoku Beach is Waikiki's westernmost beach. It takes its name from Duke Kahanamoku (1890–1968), the legendary Waikiki surfer whose family once owned the land where the resort now stands. Hawaii's champion surfer

and Olympic gold medal winner learned to swim right here. The beach offers calm swimming conditions and a gently sloping, if rocky, bottom. Public access is at the end of Paoa Pl, off Kalia Rd, and Holomoana St (where there's easy parking).

Behind the beach, **Duke Kahanamoku Lagoon** offers very family-friendly placid waters and sand.

Kaimana Beach   Beach
(Sans Souci Beach) At the Diamond Head edge of Waikiki, Kaimana is a prime sandy stretch of oceanfront that's far from the frenzied tourist scene. It's commonly called Sans Souci Beach for the name of the hotel that once stood on the site of today's New Otani Kaimana Beach Hotel. Local residents often come here for their daily swims. A shallow reef close to shore makes for calm, protected waters and provides good snorkeling.

Kahaloa & Ulukou Beaches   Beach
The beach between the Royal Hawaiian and Moana Surfrider hotels is Waikiki's busiest section of sand and surf, making it great for people-watching. Most of the beach has a shallow bottom with a gradual slope. The only drawback for swimmers is its popularity with beginner surfers, and the occasional catamaran landing hazard. Queens and Canoes, Waikiki's best-known surf breaks, are just offshore. Paddle further offshore over a lagoon to Populars (aka 'Pops'), a favorite of long-boarders.

Kapiʻolani Beach Park   Beach
(off Kalakaua Ave, Kapiʻolani Regional Park)
Where did all the tourists go? From Kapahulu Groin south to the Natatorium, this peaceful stretch of beach, backed by a green space of banyan trees and grassy lawns, offers a relaxing niche with none of the frenzy found on the beaches fronting the Waikiki hotel strip. Facilities include restrooms and outdoor showers. Kapiʻolani Beach is a popular weekend picnicking spot for local families, who unload the kids to splash in the ocean while adults fire up the BBQ.

The widest northern end of Kapiʻolani Beach is nicknamed Queen's Surf Beach (p86). On a few summer nights, classic movies are shown for free on a huge outdoor screen (www.sunsetonthebeach.net).

the 'Surfer on a Wave' statue celebrates surfing as a major part of the culture of Waikiki

From left: Beachgoers in Waikiki; The Royal Hawaiian Hotel (p80); *Surfer on a Wave* (2003), by artist Robert Pashby

OSUGI/SHUTTERSTOCK ©

VICTOR WONG/SHUTTERSTOCK ©

ACTIVITIES

Waikiki is good for swimming, bodyboarding, surfing, sailing and other watersports most of the year, and there are lifeguards, restrooms and outdoor showers scattered along the beachfront. Between May and September, summer swells make the water a little rough for swimming, but great for surfing.

Inland, you can run, play tennis and enjoy a round of golf.

 WATERSPORTS

Hawaii Surfboard Rentals
Surfing, SUP

(☑808-689-8989; www.hawaiisurfboardrentals.com; 1901 Kapi'olani Blvd; surfboard rental minimum 2 days from $45; ⊘9:30am-2pm) Has a huge variety of boards to rent. Free surfboard, SUP, bodyboard and car-rack delivery and pick-up across Waikiki; weekly rates are an especially good deal.

 SNORKELING & SCUBA DIVING

Waikiki's crowded central beaches are not particularly good for snorkeling, so pick your spot carefully. Two top choices are Kaimana Beach (p87) and Queen's Surf Beach (p86), where you'll find some live coral and a decent variety of tropical fish. But to really see the gorgeous stuff – coral gardens, manta rays and more exotic tropical fish – head out on a boat. You can easily rent snorkel sets and scuba-diving equipment, or book ahead for boat trips and PADI open-water certification courses.

Snorkel Bob's
Snorkeling

(☑808-735-7944; www.snorkelbob.com; 700 Kapahulu Ave; snorkel set rental per week from $9; ⊘8am-5pm) A top spot to get your gear. Rates vary depending on the quality of the snorkeling gear and accessories packages, but excellent weekly discounts are available and online reservations taken. You can even rent gear on O'ahu, then return it to a Snorkel Bob's location on another island.

O'ahu Diving
Diving

(☑808-721-4210; www.oahudiving.com; 2-dive trips for beginners $130) Specializes in first-time experiences for beginner divers without certification, as well as deep-water boat dives offshore and PADI refresher classes if you're already certified and have some experience under your diving belt. Trips depart from various locations near Waikiki.

AquaZone
Diving, Snorkeling

(☑808-923-3483; www.aquazonescuba.com; 2552 Kalakaua Ave, Waikiki Beach Marriott Resort; beginner divers 1 tank $120; ⊘8am-5pm) Dive shop and tour outfitter in the front of the Waikiki Beach Marriott. Sign up for a beginner's scuba-diving pool lesson (no PADI certification required) and boat dive, a sea-turtle snorkeling tour or a morning deep-water boat dive, including out to WWII shipwrecks. Rental snorkel and diving gear available.

 HIKING

Hiking Hawaii
Hiking

(☑855-808-4453; http://hikinghawaii808.com; 1956 Ala Moana Blvd; per person from $45) These guys offer a number of hiking options daily all over O'ahu, from a Makap'u Lighthouse walk to a hike to Manoa Falls to a full-day trip to the North Shore. Check out the options online. Waikiki hotel pick-ups, transportation and guide are included. Custom hikes arranged for $50 per hour.

 GOLF

Ala Wai Golf Course
Golf

(☑reservations 808-733-7387; www.honolulu.gov/des/golf/alawai.html; 404 Kapahulu Ave; green fees $19-55; ⊘6am-5:30pm) With views of Diamond Head and the Ko'olau Range, this flat 18-hole, par-70 layout scores a Guinness World Record for being the world's busiest golf course. Local golfers are allowed to book earlier in the week and grab most of the starting times, leaving few for visitors (who may call to reserve up to three days in advance).

If you get there early in the day and put yourself on the waiting list – and as long as your entire party waits at the course –

you'll probably get to play. Driving range and club rentals available.

RUNNING

If you're into running, you're in good company: statistics estimate that Honolulu has more joggers per capita than any other city on the planet. Two of the best places in Waikiki to break out your running shoes in the early morning or late afternoon are along the **Ala Wai Canal** and around Kapi'olani Regional Park (p85).

SPAS
Abhasa Spa Spa
(☎808-922-8200; www.abhasa.com; 2259 Kalakaua Ave, Royal Hawaiian Hotel; 50min massage from $150; ☺9am-9pm) Locally inspired experiences include traditional Hawaiian-style *lomilomi* ('loving hands') and *pohaku* (hot stone) massage, sea-salt scrubs, and *kukui* (candlenut), coconut and coffee-oil body treatments. A sister spa to **Spa Khakara** (☎808-685-7600; www.khakara.com; 2255 Kalakaua Ave, Sheraton Waikiki; 50min massage from $135; ☺9am-9pm).

Na Ho'ola Spa Spa
(☎808-237-6330; www.nahoolaspawaikiki. com; 2424 Kalakaua Ave, Hyatt Regency Waikiki; 50min massage from $160; ☺8:30am-9pm) At this bi-level spa, *limu* (seaweed) wraps detoxify, *kele-kele* (mud) wraps soothe sore muscles and *ti*-leaf wraps heal sun-ravaged skin, while macadamia-nut oil and fresh pineapple scrubs exfoliate. Ocean views are blissful.

TENNIS

If you've brought your own rackets, the Diamond Head Tennis Center, at the Diamond Head end of Kapi'olani Regional Park, has 10 courts. For night play, go to the Kapi'olani Regional Park Tennis Courts, opposite the aquarium; all four courts are lit. All of these public courts are free and first-come, first-served.

TOURS

Several catamaran cruises leave right from Waikiki Beach – just walk down to the sand, step into the surf and hop aboard. There is the option of a 90-minute, all-you-can-drink 'booze cruise'. Reservations are recommended for sunset sails, which sell out fast.

Na Hoku II Catamaran Cruise
(☎808-554-5990; www.nahokuiiandmanukai. com; near Outrigger Waikiki Beach Resort; 90min catamaran trips $40-45) With its unmistakable yellow-and-red striped sails, this catamaran is a local icon. These hard-drinkin' tours (drinks included in ticket price) set sail four times daily, shoving off from in front of Duke's Waikiki (p98) bar. The sunset sail usually sells out, so book early.

Maita'i Catamaran Cruise
(☎808-922-5665; www.leahi.com; on shore, off Kalakaua Ave; adult/child from $34/17; ⛵) Departing from shore between the **Halekulani** (199 Kalia Rd) and **Sheraton Waikiki** (2255 Kalakaua Ave) hotels, this white catamaran with green sails offers a big variety of boat trips. Reserve ahead for a 90-minute daytime or sunset boozecruise (children allowed, yes they serve mai tais) or a moonlight sail to take in the Hilton Hawaiian Village's Friday fireworks show. Family-friendly reef-snorkeling tours include an onboard picnic lunch.

SHOPPING

Amid the chains in Waikiki's upscale malls and resorts, you can find excellent local boutiques with island designs and creations.

For mundane needs, you won't be able to miss the ubiquitous **ABC Stores**, conveniently cheap places to pick up essentials such as beach mats, sunblock, snacks, cold beer, macadamia-nut candy and sundries, not to mention 'I got lei'd in Hawaii' T-shirts and motorized, grass-skirted hula girls for the dashboard of your car.

Bailey's Antiques
& Aloha Shirts   Clothing, Antiques

(☏808-734-7628; http://alohashirts.com; 517 Kapahulu Ave; ☺10am-6pm) Bailey's has, without a doubt, the finest aloha-shirt collection on O'ahu, possibly the world! Racks are crammed with thousands of collector-worthy vintage aloha shirts in every conceivable color and style, from 1920s kimono-silk classics to 1970s polyester specials to modern offerings. Prices dizzyingly vary from 10 bucks to several thousand dollars.

Fighting Eel   Clothing

(☏808-738-9295; www.fightingeel.com; 2233 Kalakaua Ave, Royal Hawaiian Center, B-116; ☺10am-10pm) Hawaiian-made fashion is the hallmark of this impressive four-store group from local designers Rona Bennett and Lan Chung. Also look for swimsuits, children's clothing, jewelry and accessories.

Malie Organics   Cosmetics

(☏808-922-2216; www.malie.com; 2259 Kalakaua Ave, Royal Hawaiian Resort, A2; ☺9am-9pm) Beauty oils, creams, perfumes and more are sold in this shop that looks as good as it smells. Everything is locally made from organic and natural ingredients, mostly derived from native Hawaiian plants and flowers.

Angels by the Sea   Clothing

(☏808-922-9747; http://angelsbytheseahawaii. com; 2552 Kalakaua Ave, 1st fl, Waikiki Beach Marriott Resort; ☺8am-10pm) Hard to find inside a mega chain hotel, this airy boutique owned by a Vietnamese fashion designer (who was once crowned Ms Waikiki) is a gem for handmade beaded jewelry and hobo bags, effortlessly beautiful resort-style dresses, tunic tops and aloha shirts in tropical prints of silk and linen. Has a second location inside the Sheraton Waikiki (p89).

Island Paddler   Clothing

(☏808-737-4854; www.islandpaddlerhawaii. com; 716 Kapahulu Ave; ☺10am-6pm) Besides having a great selection of paddles and paddling gear, these guys have T-shirts, aloha shirts, beachwear and everything you might need for a day at the beach – along with a friendly and relaxed atmosphere.

Art on the Zoo Fence   Arts & Crafts

(www.artonthezoofence.com; Monsarrat Ave, opposite Kapi'olani Regional Park; ☺9am-4pm Sat & Sun) Dozens of artists hang their works along the fence on the south side of the **Honolulu Zoo** (☏808-971-7171; www. honoluluzoo.org; cnr Kapahulu & Kalakaua Aves; adult/child $14/6; ☺9am-4:30pm; P) every weekend, weather permitting. Browse the contemporary watercolor, acrylic and oil paintings and colorful island photography as you chat with the artists themselves.

Na Lima Mili Hulu
No'eau   Arts & Crafts

(☏808-732-0865; www.featherlegacy.com; 762 Kapahulu Ave; ☺usually 9am-4pm Mon-Sat) The late Aunty Mary Louise Kaleonahenahe Kekuewa's daughter and granddaughter keep alive the ancient craft of feather lei-making at this small storefront, whose name means 'the skilled hands that touch the feathers.' It can take days to produce a single feather lei, prized by collectors. Call ahead to check opening hours or make an appointment for a personalized lesson.

Rebecca Beach   Clothing

(☏808-931-7722; www.rebeccabeach.com; 2259 Kalakaua Ave, Royal Hawaiian Resort, #7; ☺9am-9pm) Swimwear, casual looks and more dressy duds for a night out are sold at this high-end boutique.

Ukulele PuaPua   Gifts & Souvenirs

(☏808-923-9977; www.hawaiianukuleleonline. com; 2255 Kalakaua Ave #13, Sheraton Waikiki; ☺8am-10:30pm) Avoid those flimsy souvenir ukuleles and head here to find the real thing. These guys are passionate and offer free group beginner lessons every day. On Wednesdays at 3pm, the staff plays.

EATING

Waikiki has a lot of restaurants aimed at the vacationing masses, but among the over-priced underwhelmers, you can find some real gems, including a few where a nice view doesn't equal dull food.

Waikiki Beach Area

You can have a good meal and a view along Waikiki Beach. Just inland, there are many more decent options. Along Kalakaua Ave, chains overflow with hungry tourists – most of whom can probably find the same chains in their hometowns.

Pau Hana Market   Food Truck $

(☎808-591-1981; http://pauhanawaikiki.com; 234 Beach Walk; most mains under $15; ⊙11am-10pm) An entire cluster of food trucks can be found here on any given day. Choices change by the week, but there's usually a couple specializing in Asian, veggie, sandwiches, seafood and more. The chefs inside the vans are creative, the prices low and the picnic tables accommodating. There's always a beer and wine vendor.

Mahina & Sun's   American $$

(☎808-924-5810; http://surfjack.com/eat-shop/; 412 Lewers St, Surfjack Hotel & Swim Club; mains $12-32; ⊙6:30am-10pm Sun-Thu, to midnight Fri & Sat) ✒ Overlooking the stylish pool at the Surfjack Hotel, this open-air bistro has a well-imagined casual and comfortable menu of classics, such as burgers, salads, pizza and seafood (which is carefully sourced to be sustainable). Most ingredients are organic. Enjoy drinks until late from the creative bar. Up early? Try the banana bread or the avocado toast at breakfast.

Tonkatsu Ginza Bairin Japanese $$

(☎808-926-8082; www.pj-partners.com/bairin/; 255 Beach Walk; mains $18-24; ⊙11am-9:30pm Sun-Thu, to midnight Fri & Sat) Why go to Tokyo for perfect pork *tonkatsu* when you can enjoy the lightly breaded bits of deep-fried pork goodness right here in Waikiki? Since 1927 the family behind this restaurant has

Waikiki's Mystery Observer

Nobody knows his or her name, but on Instagram, **@misterver** has a huge following thanks to a steady stream of brilliant candid photos shot on Waikiki's streets and beaches. Don't look for glossy tourist moments; instead you'll see longtime residents at home in a neighborhood more known for its ever-changing flood of visitors. You'll see dogs, decrepit buildings, unguarded moments and idiosyncratic looks captured anonymously and on the fly.

been serving *tonkatsu* at a Ginza restaurant. At this far-flung expansion, nothing has been lost. Besides the namesake, there is great sushi, rice bowls and more.

Azure   Seafood $$$

(☎808-921-4600; www.azurewaikiki.com; 2259 Kalakaua Ave, Royal Hawaiian Resort; mains from $38, 5-course tasting menu $85; ⊙5:30-9pm) ✒ Azure is the signature restaurant at the Royal Hawaiian Resort. Seafood fresh from the market, such as Kona abalone, red snapper and *ono* (white-fleshed mackerel), are all exquisitely prepared island-style. Daily specials are usually just that. The wine, beer and cocktail list will delight. You can dine right near the sand under a 'Royal Hawaiian' pink-and-white awning.

Roy's Waikiki   Hawaii Regional $$$

(☎808-923-7697; www.royshawaii.com; 226 Lewers St; mains $24-53; ⊙9am-9:30pm Mon-Thu, to 10pm Fri-Sun) This contemporary incarnation of Roy Yamaguchi's island-born chain is perfect for a flirty date or just celebrating the good life. The ground-breaking chef's signature *misoyaki* butterfish, blackened ahi and macadamia-nut-crusted mahimahi (white-fleshed fish also called 'dolphin') are always on the menu. The famous hot chocolate soufflé for dessert is a must. The bar makes great cocktails and there's seating outside under tiki torches.

From left: Shave ice; Eating Portugese style donuts at Leonard's (p94); Ahi (tuna) *poke* bowls

Kaiwa   Japanese $$$

(☎808-924-1555; http://kai-wa.com; 226 Lewers St, 2nd fl, Waikiki Beach Walk; mains $15-36; ⏱11:30am-2pm & 5-10pm) While prowling the sanitized climes of the Waikiki Beach Walk, you can pause at a generic chain staple, or you can stop off for excellent Japanese fare here. Tables on the terrace overlook the milling hordes below, while inside the dining room exudes a stylish, high-concept style in dark wood and tall banquettes.

La Mer   French $$$

(☎808-923-2311; www.halekulani.com; 2199 Kalia Rd, Halekulani; 3-/4-course prix-fixe dinner menu $110/145; ⏱6-10pm; Ⓟ) At the luxury Halekulani resort, La Mer is rated by traditionalists as Waikiki's top fine-dining destination. A neoclassical French menu puts the emphasis on Provençal cuisine with the addition of fresh Hawaii-grown ingredients, such as lobster gelée with sea urchin or big-eye tuna tartare. Wines are perfectly paired; diners are required to have jackets. The beach views are superb. Valet-parking is free for diners.

Orchids   Buffet $$$

(☎808-923-2311; www.halekulani.com; 2199 Kalia Rd, Halekulani; Sun brunch buffet $68, mains other times $12-60; ⏱7:30am-10pm Mon-Sat, 9:30am-2:30pm Sun) O'ahu's most elegant Sunday brunch spread covers all the bases, with a made-to-order omelet station; a buffet of *poke*, sashimi, sushi and salads; and a decadent dessert bar with coconut pie and homemade Kona coffee ice cream.

But don't come just for the food – it's the smashing ocean view, tropical flowers and cheesy harp and flute music that set the honeymoon mood. Make reservations in advance. Resort attire required. On other days, the restaurant serves a full menu through the day. At night there's a dress code.

Veranda   Cafe $$$

(☎808-921-4600; www.moana-surfrider.com; 2365 Kalakaua Ave, Moana Surfrider; afternoon tea from $34; ⏱6-11am, noon-3pm & 5:30-9:30pm; Ⓟ) For colonial atmosphere that harks back to early-20th-century tourist traditions, traditional afternoon tea comes

complete with finger sandwiches, scones with pillowy Devonshire cream and tropically flavored pastries. Portions are small, but the oceanfront setting and house-blended teas are memorable. Make reservations and come prepared to shoo away pesky hungry birds. It's also a fine place for a waterfront breakfast.

🞨 Kapahulu Avenue

On the outskirts of Waikiki, Kapahulu Ave is always worth a detour for its growing number of creative bistros and cafes. Look for standout neighborhood eateries, drive-ins and bakeries, cooking up anything from Hawaiian soul food to Japanese country fare.

Rainbow Drive-In   Hawaiian $

(☎808-737-0177; www.rainbowdrivein.com; 3308 Kanaina Ave; meals $4-9; ☺7am-9pm; 🞀)
If you only hit one classic Hawaiian plate lunch joint, make it this one. Wrapped in rainbow-colored neon, this famous drive-in is a throwback to another era. Construction workers, surfers and gangly teens order all their down-home favorites such as burgers, mixed-plate lunches, *loco moco* and Portu-

guese sweet-bread French toast from the takeout counter. Many love the hamburger steak.

The owners' family donates part of the profits to local schools and charities. Started by an island-born US army cook after WWII, its customers have included a teenage Barack Obama (he still drops by on his Hawaiian visits today).

Waiola Shave Ice   Desserts $

(☎808-949-2269; www.waiolashaveice.com; 3113 Mokihana St; shave ice $2-5; ☺11am-5:30pm; 🅿🞀) This clapboard corner shop has been making the same superfine shave ice since 1940, and we'd argue that it's got the formula exactly right. Get yours doused with 20-plus flavors of syrup and topped by azuki beans, *liliko'i* cream, condensed milk, Hershey's chocolate syrup or spicy-sweet *li hing mui* (crack seed).

It's one building in on Mokihana St and a tad hard to spot from Kapahulu Ave.

Haili's Hawaiian Foods   Hawaiian $

(☎808-735-8019; http://hailishawaiianfood. com; 760 Palani Ave; meals $11-16; ☺10am-7pm Tue-Sat, to 2pm Sun; 🞀) ✔ Haili's has been cooking up homegrown Hawaiian fare since 1950. Locals cheerfully shoehorn themselves into kid-friendly booths and tables, then dig into heaping plates of *kalua* pig (cooked in an underground pit), *lomilomi* salmon (minced, salted salmon, diced tomato and green onion) and *laulau* (meat wrapped in *ti* leaves and steamed) served with poi (mashed taro) or rice. Even the sides like mac salad are tops.

For a little variety, try the grilled ahi plate lunches, bowls of tripe stew, *poke* bowls or fat tortilla wraps.

Hawaii's Favorite Kitchens   Hawaiian $

(☎808-744-0465; http://hawaiisfavoritekitchens.com; 3111 Castle St; mains $4-12; ⊙10am-7pm) Why drive all over Oʻahu looking for favorite local foods when you can get many of them right here? Fittingly owned by the iconic Rainbow Drive-In (p93) next door, this brightly lit storefront has dishes from **Mike's Huli Chicken** (☎808-277-6720; https://sites.google.com/site/mikeshulihulichicken; 47-525 Kamahameha Hwy, Kahaluʻu; meals $7-12; ⊙10:30am-7pm), **Poke Stop** (☎808-676-8100; http://poke-stop.com; 94-050 Farrington Hwy, Waipahu Town Center; mains $8-14; ⊙10am-8pm Mon-Sat, to 5pm Sun), Shimazu Shave Ice and more.

Ono Seafood   Seafood $

(☎808-732-4806; 747 Kapahulu Ave; mains $7-12; ⊙9am-6pm Mon & Wed-Sat, 10am-3pm Sun) Arrive early at this addictive, made-to-order *poke* shop, before it runs out of fresh fish marinated in *shōyu* (soy sauce), house-smoked *tako* (octopus), spicy ahi rice bowls or boiled peanuts spiked with star anise. Very limited free parking. The *shōyu* ahi is beloved by regulars. There's a couple of humble tables right outside by the door.

Leonard's   Bakery $

(☎808-737-5591; www.leonardshawaii.com; 933 Kapahulu Ave; snacks from $1; ⊙5:30am-10pm Sun-Thu, to 11pm Fri & Sat; 🚻) It's almost impossible to drive by the Leonard's eye-catching vintage 1950s neon sign without seeing a crowd of tourists. This bakery is famous for its *malasadas* (sweet deep-fried dough rolled in sugar) Portuguese-style – like a doughnut without

Sashimi

the hole. Order variations with *haupia* (coconut cream) or *liliko'i* filling for more flavor. Be sure to get yours straight from the fryer nice and hot.

Other baked goods like the bland sausage croissants aren't worth the hype. If there's a line, there are displays of logo-emblazoned T-shirts to divert you.

Sansei Seafood Restaurant & Sushi Bar   Japanese $$
(☏808-931-6286; www.sanseihawaii.com; 2552 Kalakaua Ave, 3rd fl, Waikiki Beach Marriott Resort; shared plates $5-20, mains $16-35; ⊙5:30-10pm Sun-Thu, to 1am Fri & Sat) From the mind of one of Hawaii's top chefs, DK Kodama, this Pacific Rim menu rolls out everything from creatively stylish sushi and sashimi to Dungeness crab ramen with black-truffle broth – all to rave reviews. Tables on the torch-lit veranda equal prime sunset views.

Da Hawaiian Poke Company   Hawaiian $$
(☏808-425-4954; www.dahawaiianpokecompany.com; 870 Kapahulu Ave; mains $9-20; ⊙10am-9pm Mon-Sat, to 6pm Sun) Ignore the location in a Safeway strip mall parking lot (enjoy the plentiful parking) and concentrate on the premium *poke* on offer. Choose from sustainably caught seafood, then pick your flavor (wasabi and miso garlic are especially good) and then select your toppings. It's very fresh and smartly prepared. The setting is casual, which won't divert you from your *poke*.

Wada   Japanese $$
(☏808-737-0125; www.restaurantwada.com; 611 Kapahulu Ave; mains $11-30; ⊙4-11pm) Superb Japanese fare is creatively presented at this deceptively simple dining room on the Kapahulu Ave strip. Without the Waikiki glitz, the focus is on the food. The mostly local crowd come here to celebrate with authentic cuisine. Changing tasting menus can be paired with wine and sake.

✪ Kuhio Avenue Area
Along Kuhio Ave, and the many nearby streets and alleys, are small places to eat with an array of meal types. Many are filled with locals.

Marukame Udon   Japanese $
(☏808-931-6000; www.toridollusa.com; 2310 Kuhio Ave; mains $2-8; ⊙7am-10pm; 🚹) Everybody loves this Japanese noodle shop, which is so popular there is often a line stretching down the sidewalk. Watch those thick udon noodles get rolled, cut and boiled fresh right in front of you, then stack mini plates of giant tempura and *musubi* (rice balls) stuffed with salmon or a sour plum on your cafeteria tray.

Wash it all down with iced barley or green tea; there's no booze.

Blue Ocean   Seafood $
(☏808-542-5587; 2449 Kuhio Ave; mains $9-17; ⊙10:30am-10pm) Shrimp in all forms are the stars at this vibrant blue food truck. The spicy garlic shrimp po' boy is a spicy delight, with succulent little crustaceans spilling out all over. Other treats include some excellent salmon dishes. There are a few rudimentary seats here, otherwise enjoy your feast as takeout. Staff are charmers.

Musubi Cafe Iyasume   Japanese $
(☏808-921-0168; www.tonsuke.com/eomusubiya.html; 2427 Kuhio Ave, Pacific Monarch Hotel; mains $5-9; ⊙6:30am-8pm) This hole-in-the-wall keeps busy making fresh *onigiri* (rice balls) stuffed with seaweed, salmon roe and sour plums. Other specialties include salmon-roe rice bowls, Japanese curry and island-style *mochiko* fried chicken. In a hurry? Grab a bentō box to go. The namesake *musubi* is a definitive version with grilled Spam atop a block of white rice wrapped in *nori* (seaweed sheet).

Lovin' Oven   Pizza $$
(☏808-866-6489; www.lovinoven-hawaii.com; 2425 Kuhio Ave, Aqua Bamboo; pizzas $25-30; ⊙4-10pm Wed-Mon) Amid flickering tiki torches around a hotel pool, this simple cafe turns out some of Waikiki's best pizza. Choose from a full range of pizzas or build your own. Enjoy crispy thin-crust and a bounty of excellent toppings. Seating is

poolside, drinking is BYOB (there's a neighboring ABC Store). Or do takeout or, even better, delivery! Note the motto here: 'I hate pizza, said no one.'

MAC 24/7   American $$
(☏808-921-5564; http://mac247waikiki.com; 2500 Kuhio Ave, Hilton Waikiki Beach; mains $9-25; ☺24hr) It's 3am and you're famished, skip the temptation for a cold $25 burger from room service (*if* you have room service) and drop by Waikiki's best all-night diner. The dining room has a bold style palette (the better to perk you up for the menu) and by day has a lovely garden view. Food (and prices) are a cut above.

Pancakes are a real specialty here and, if you're up for it, try the famous MAC pancake challenge: eat three huge 14in pancakes in under 90 minutes and you get your picture on the wall of fame – less than 100 people have managed this in almost 10 years!

Hy's Steakhouse   Steak $$$
(☏808-922-5555; http://hyswaikiki.com; 2440 Kuhio Ave; mains $30-80; ☺6-10pm) Hy's is so old-school that you expect to find inkwells on the tables. This traditional steakhouse has a timeless old leather and wood interior. But ultimately, it's not whether you expect to see Frank and Dean at a back table, rather it's the steak at Hy's that is superb.

From a glassed-in booth off the dining room, their meat master cooks up an array of succulent cuts of beef. There's plenty of sides and salads you can order – and they're all fine – but really save room (and save some money) for the steaks. The garlic one is highly recommended.

😊 Monsarrat Avenue
Wander past the zoo and Waikiki School to reach some fine local cafes and restaurants on Monsarrat Ave.

Pioneer Saloon   Fusion $
(☏808-732-4001; www.pioneer-saloon.net; 3046 Monsarrat Ave; mains $9-14; ☺11am-8pm) It's simple stuff, but the locals can't get enough of Pioneer Saloon's Japanese fusion plate lunches, with everything from grilled ahi to fried

baby octopus to *yakisoba* (fried noodles). The chicken with garlic sauce and the chili-fried chicken are tops. Look for the potted plants outside; loads of whimsical nonsense decor inside. Don't miss the shave ice.

Diamond Head Market & Grill   Hawaiian $
(☏808-732-0077; www.diamondheadmarket.com; 3158 Monsarrat Ave; meals $9-18; ☺6:30am-9pm; 🚗) Step inside this neighborhood market for a gourmet deli packaging up the likes of roast pork loin and citrus jicama salad, perfect for a beach picnic. Outside at the takeout window, surfers and families order *char siu* (Chinese barbecued pork) plate lunches, portobello mushroom burgers and, at breakfast, tropical-fruit pancakes. Do takeout or eat at the picnic tables. Don't miss the blueberry scones.

Hawaii Sushi   Sushi $
(☏808-734-6370; 3045 Monsarrat Ave, Suite 1; mains $6-10; ☺10am-8pm) A winner for Hawaiian-style fresh sushi with rolls and bowls such as the Spicy Ahi Bowl, you can't get fresher fish anywhere else in Waikiki. The specials are excellent and change daily. There's parking outside and a few seats inside.

🍸 DRINKING & NIGHTLIFE

If you're looking for a frosty cold beer or a fruity cocktail to help you recover from a day at the beach, don't worry, there are endless options in Waikiki. Sip a sunset mai tai and be hypnotized by the playing of slack key guitars, then mingle with locals who come here to party too.

Beach Bar   Bar
(☏808-922-3111; www.moana-surfrider.com; 2365 Kalakaua Ave, Moana Surfrider; ☺10:30am-11:30pm) Waikiki's best beach bar is right on an especially lovely stretch of beach. The atmosphere comes from the historic Moana Surfrider hotel and its vast banyan tree. The people-watching of passersby, sunbathers and surfers is captivating day and night. On an island of mediocre mai tais, the version

Waikiki Beach at sunset

here is one of O'ahu's best. Although it's always busy, turnover is quick so you won't wait long for a table. There's live entertainment (p99) much of the day.

Cuckoo Coconuts   Lounge
(808-926-1620; www.cuckoococonutswaiki-ki.com; 333 Royal Hawaiian Ave; 11am-midnight) Mismatched wobbly tables under a canopy of canvas and ragged umbrellas plus a menagerie of aging potted tropical plants give this bar a carefree, unpretentious vibe. Every night there's a great lineup of musicians with a familiar list of croon-worthy classics and time-tested patter. Settle back, have some sort of deep-fried treat, enjoy a cheap drink and get carried away.

Gorilla in the Cafe   Cafe
(808-922-2055; www.facebook.com/gorillaha-waii; 2155 Kalakaua Ave; 6:30am-10pm Mon-Fri, from 7am Sat & Sun) Owned by Korean TV star Bae Yong Joon, this artisan coffee bar brews Waikiki's biggest selection of 100% Hawaii-grown beans from independent farms all around the islands. Handmade

pourovers are worth the extra wait, or just grab a fast, hot espresso or creamy frozen coffee concoction blended with banana.

Hula's Bar & Lei Stand   Gay
(808-923-0669; www.hulas.com; 134 Kapahulu Ave, 2nd fl, Waikiki Grand Hotel; 10am-2am;) This friendly, open-air bar is Waikiki's legendary gay venue and a great place to make new friends, boogie and have a few drinks. Hunker down at the pool table, or gaze at the spectacular vista of Diamond Head. The breezy balcony-bar also has views of Queen's Surf Beach, a prime destination for a sun-worshipping LGBTQ crowd.

Lulu's Waikiki   Cocktail Bar
(808-926-5222; www.luluswaikiki.com; 2586 Kalakaua Ave, Park Shore Waikiki; 7am-2am) Brush off your sandy feet at Kuhio Beach, then step across Kalakaua Ave to this surf-themed bar and grill with 2nd-story lanai (balcony) views of the Pacific Ocean and Diamond Head. Lap up sunset happy hours (3pm to 5pm daily), then chill out to acoustic acts and local bands later most

Gay & Lesbian Waikiki

Waikiki's LGBTQ community is tightly knit, but full of aloha for visitors. Start at friendly, open-air **Hula's Bar & Lei Stand** (p97), which has ocean views of Diamond Head. Stop for drinks and to play pool and boogie. More svelte and classy **Bacchus Waikiki** (☑808-926-4167; www.bacchus-waikiki.com; 408 Lewers St, 2nd fl; ⊗noon-2am) is an intimate wine bar and cocktail lounge with happy-hour specials, shirtless bartenders and Sunday afternoon parties on the terrace. For singalongs, hit **Wang Chung's** (☑808-921-9176; http://wangchungs.com; 2424 Koa Ave, Stay Waikiki; ⊗5pm-2am; � 🖥), a living-room-sized karaoke bar.

Tiki-themed **Tapa's Restaurant & Lanai Bar** (☑808-921-2288; www.tapaswaikiki.com; 407 Seaside Ave, 2nd fl; ⊗2pm-2am Mon-Fri, from 9am Sat & Sun; 🖥) is a bigger chill-out spot with cheery bartenders, pool tables, a jukebox and karaoke nights. Around the corner, **Fusion Waikiki** (☑808-924-2422; www.fusionwaikiki.co; 2260 Kuhio Ave; drag-show cover $10; ⊗midnight-4am Sun-Thu, from 9pm Fri & Sat) is a divey nightclub with weekend drag shows. Hidden up an alley, laid-back **In Between** (☑808-926-7060; www.inbetweenwaikiki.com; 2155 Lau'ula St; ⊗noon-2am) attracts an older crowd for 'the happiest of happy hours.'

evenings. DJs crank up the beats after 10pm on Saturday.

Maui Brewing Co   Brewery

(☑808-843-2739; http://mauibrewingco.com; 2300 Kalakaua Ave, 2nd fl, Holiday Inn Resort Waikiki Beachcomber; ⊗11am-11pm) Hawaii's largest bar opened in 2017 and features over two dozen of the great microbrews from Maui Brewing. Under lights made from kegs, you can lounge back in the vast and airy space, enjoying classic beers like Bikini Blonde lager, Big Swell IPA and Pineapple

Mana wheat. The large outdoor terrace has views of the resort-filled skyline.

Duke's Waikiki   Bar

(☑808-922-2268; www.dukeswaikiki.com; 2335 Kalakaua Ave, Outrigger Waikiki Beach Resort; ⊗7am-midnight) It's a raucous scene, especially when weekend concerts spill onto the beach. Taking its name from Duke Kahanamoku, the surfing theme prevails throughout this carousing landmark where selfies and holiday camaraderie are encouraged. Upstairs, the tiki torch-lit veranda at the Hula Grill has a more soothing live Hawaiian soundtrack from 7pm to 9pm almost nightly. Skip the food.

RumFire   Bar

(www.rumfirewaikiki.com; 2255 Kalakaua Ave, Sheraton Waikiki; ⊗11:30am-midnight Sun-Thu, to 1:30am Fri & Sat) The collection of vintage rum is mighty tempting at this lively and huge hotel bar, with fire pits looking out onto the beach and live contemporary Hawaiian (or jazz) music. Or wander over to the resort's cabana-like Edge of Waikiki Bar for knockout views, designer cocktails and more live Hawaiian and pop-rock music poolside.

⊛ ENTERTAINMENT

For first-rate live Hawaiian music and hula dancing, you are in the right place. On any given night in Waikiki you can see top talent for free or the price of a drink. Consult the *Honolulu Weekly* (www.honoluluweekly.com), published every Wednesday, for events listings.

⊛ Hawaiian Music & Hula

House Without a Key   Live Music

(☑808-923-2311; www.halekulani.com; 2199 Kalia Rd, Halekulani; ⊗7am-9pm) Named after a 1925 Charlie Chan novel set in Honolulu, this genteel open-air hotel lounge sprawled beneath a century-old kiawe tree simply has no doors to lock. A sophisticated crowd gathers here for sunset cocktails, excellent Hawaiian music and solo hula dancing by former Miss Hawaii pageant winners.

Panoramic ocean views are as intoxicating as the tropical cocktails.

Hilton Hawaiian Village Fireworks   Fireworks

(Kahanamoku Beach; ☺7:45pm Fri) FREE Every Friday night, the Hilton Hawaiian Village stages a booming 10-minute fireworks show. Although it's done in conjunction with a special luau (Hawaiian feast) by one of the pools, the actual show is over the water in front of the beach and can be seen from across Waikiki. For the best views, join the locals and tourists on **Fort DeRussy Beach** (off Kalia Rd).

Beach Bar   Live Music

(☎808-922-3111; www.moana-surfrider.com; 2365 Kalakaua Ave, Moana Surfrider; ☺10:30am-11:30pm) Inside this historic beachfront hotel bar, soak up the sounds of classical and contemporary Hawaiian musicians playing underneath the old banyan tree where the *Hawaii Calls* radio program was broadcast nationwide during the mid-20th century. Live-music schedules vary, but hula soloists dance from 6pm to 8pm most nights. Expect mellow tunes at lunch and through the evening.

Kani Ka Pila Grille   Live Music

(☎808-924-4990; www.outriggerreef.com; 2169 Kalia Rd, Outrigger Reef Waikiki Beach Resort; ☺11am-10pm. live music 6-9pm) Once happy hour ends, the Outrigger's lobby bar sets the scene for some of the most laid-back live-music shows of any of Waikiki's beachfront hotels, with traditional and contemporary Hawaiian musicians playing familiar tunes amid a patter of jokes.

Royal Hawaiian Band   Live Music

(☎808-922-5331; www.rhb-music.com; Kapi'olani Regional Park) The tree-shaded Kapi'olani Bandstand is the perfect venue for this time-honored troupe that performs classics from the Hawaiian monarchy era on most Sunday afternoons, special events or festivals. It's a quintessential island scene that caps off with the audience joining hands and singing Queen Lili'uokalani's 'Aloha 'Oe' in Hawaiian. Check their website

for details on the performances across Waikiki and O'ahu.

Tapa Bar   Live Music

(☎808-949-4321; www.hiltonhawaiianvillage.com; ground fl, Tapa Tower, 2005 Kalia Rd, Hilton Hawaiian Village; ☺10am-11pm, live music 7:30-8pm) FREE It's worth navigating through the gargantuan Hilton resort complex to this Polynesian-themed open-air bar just to see some of the best traditional and contemporary Hawaiian groups performing on O'ahu today. Friday and Saturday nights see longtime favorite Olomana, an acoustic trio. There is also live entertainment many nights in the hotel's Tropics cafe.

⭐ Luau & Dinner Shows

'Aha 'Aina   Luau

(☎808-921-4600; http://royal-hawaiianluau.com; Royal Hawaiian Resort, 2259 Kalakaua Ave; adult/child 5-12yr from $188/106; ☺5-8pm Mon) This oceanfront dinner show is like a three-act musical play narrating the history of Hawaiian *mele* (songs) and hula. The buffet features good renditions of traditional Hawaiian and Polynesian fare and unlimited drinks. There are cultural demonstrations, such as making cloth from bark. The literal highlight is the fire dancing. Seating is at long tables, request to be near the stage when you book.

Waikiki Starlight Luau   Luau

(☎808-947-2607; www.hiltonhawaiianvillage.com/luau; 2005 Kalia Rd, Hilton Hawaiian Village; adult/child 4-11yr from $109/65; ☺5:30-8pm Sun-Thu, weather permitting; 👶) Enthusiastic pan-Polynesian show, with buffet meal, outdoor seating at a rooftop venue, Samoan fire dancing and *hapa haole* (literally, 'half foreign') hula.

GETTING THERE & AWAY

Waikiki is a district of the city of Honolulu, so much of the transport information applies to both.

Honolulu International Airport (p313) is about 9 miles northwest of Waikiki.

BUS

You can reach Waikiki via **TheBus** (☏808-848-5555; www.thebus.org; adult $2.50, 4-day visitor pass $35; ☺infoline 5:30am-10pm) routes 19 or 20. Buses run every 20 minutes from 6am to 11pm daily. Luggage is restricted to what you can hold on your lap or stow under the seat (maximum size 22in by 14in by 9in). Both routes run along Kuhio Ave.

AIRPORT SHUTTLE

Express Shuttle (☏808-539-9400; www.airportwaikikishuttle.com; fare airport to Waikiki one-way/round-trip $16/32), run by Roberts Hawaii, operates 24-hour door-to-door shuttle buses from Honolulu International Airport to Waikiki's hotels, departing every 20 to 60 minutes. Transportation time depends on how many stops the shuttle makes before dropping you off. Surcharges apply for bicycles, surfboards, golf clubs and extra baggage. Reservations are helpful, but not always required for airport pick-ups. For return trips, reserve at least 48 hours in advance.

CAR

From the airport, the easiest and most atmospheric driving route to Waikiki is via the Nimitz Hwy (Hwy 92), which becomes Ala Moana Blvd. Alternatively, take the H-1 (Lunalilo) Fwy eastbound, then follow signs to Waikiki. The drive between the airport and Waikiki takes about 30 minutes without traffic; allow at least 45 minutes during weekday rush hours.

TAXI

Taxis from the airport to Waikiki cost $35 to $45.

GETTING AROUND

CAR & MOTORCYCLE

Major car-rental companies have branches in Waikiki.

808 Smart Cars Rentals (☏808-735-5000; www.hawaiismartcarrentals.com; 444 Niu St; rental per day from $85; ☺9am-5pm) 🌿 Offers pricey rentals of Smart cars with convertible roofs that get almost 40mpg on island highways; being smaller, they're also easier to park.

Chase Hawaii Rentals (☏808-942-4273; www.chasehawaiirentals.com; 355 Royal Hawaiian Ave; 10/24hr rental from $90/110; ☺8am-6pm) Rents Harley-Davidson, Kawasaki and Honda motorcycles and Vespa scooters (over 21 years with valid motorcycle license and credit card only).

Cruzin Hawaii (☏877-945-9595, 808-945-9595; http://cruzinhawaii.com; 1980 Kalakaua Ave; rental per 8/24hr from $100/120) Rents mostly Harley-Davidson motorcycles (over 21s with valid motorcycle license and credit card only); also mopeds and bikes.

Where to Stay

Waikiki's main beachfront strip, along Kalakaua Ave, is lined with hotels and sprawling resorts. Some of them are true beauties with either a historic or boutique atmosphere. Most are aimed at the masses, however.

Neighborhood	Atmosphere
Waikiki Beach	Big resorts line Waikiki Beach and parallel Kalakaua Ave. Some are historic, others are luxurious (or both) and some simply pack visitors in by the thousands. Obviously, being on the beach beats having to cross the road to get there.
Kuhio Avenue	The area of Waikiki east of Kalakaua Ave is getting more and more large hotels. But in the streets that radiate off Kuhio Ave you can still find lots of older and smaller hotels, many loaded with rugged charm. Here you'll get to rub elbows with the many characters and ageless beach bums who still call Waikiki home.
Kaimana Beach	South past Kapi'olani Regional Park is an outcrop of 1960s high-rise hotels and condos that enjoy great views but are removed from Waikiki's hustle.

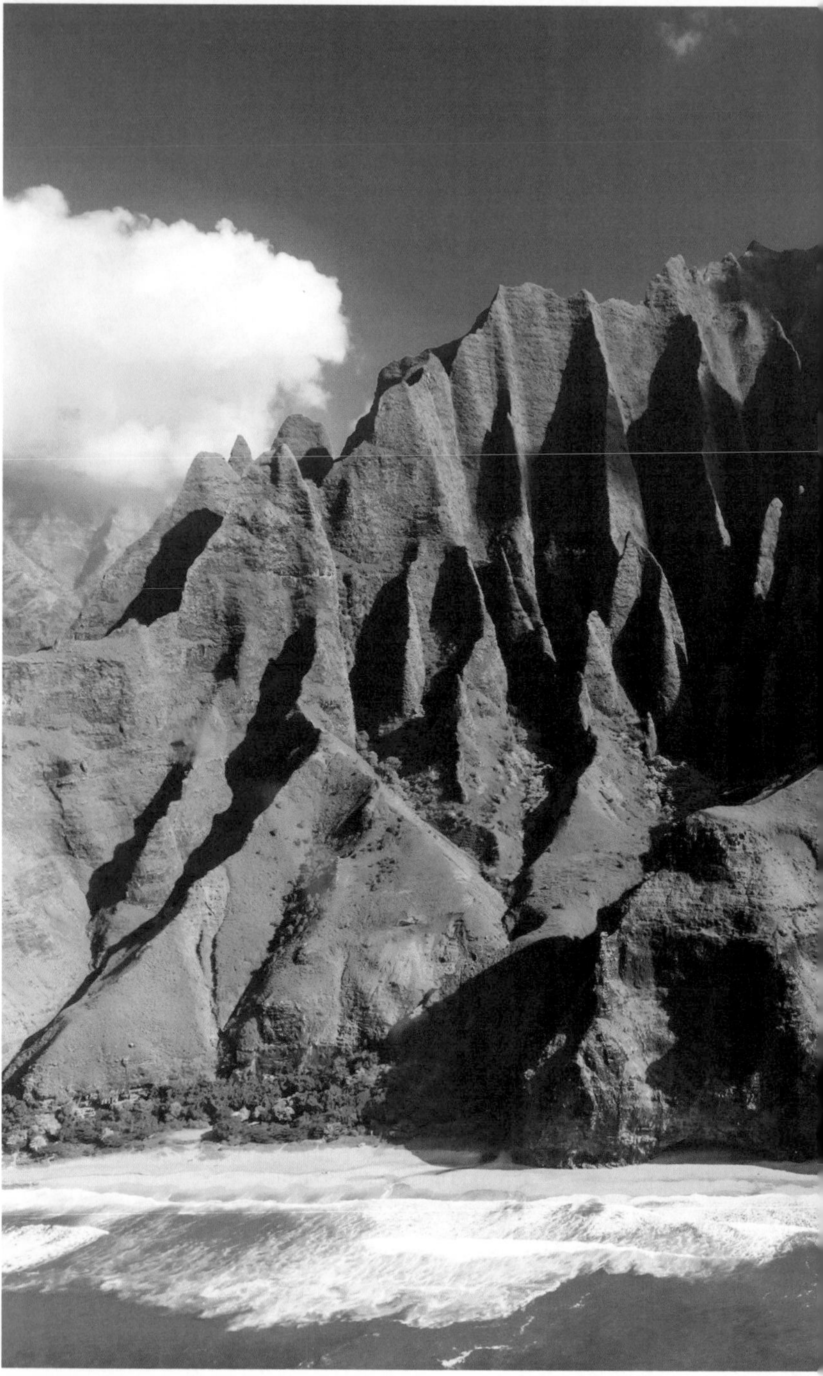

NA PALI COAST WILDERNESS STATE PARK

In this Chapter

Boat Tours of the Na Pali Coast 106
Kalalau Trail 110
Ha'ena State Park 114
Ha'ena 118
Getting There & Away 119

Na Pali Coast Wilderness State Park at a Glance...

Roadless, pristine and hauntingly beautiful, this 16-mile-long stretch of stark cliffs, white-sand beaches, turquoise coves and gushing waterfalls links the island's northern and western shores. It's arguably Kaua'i's most magnificent natural sight. While fit trekkers tackle the exposed, undulating, slippery trail from Ha'ena to Kalalau Valley, it's also possible to experience the coastline by kayak, raft or catamaran. Kalalau, Honopu, Awa'awapuhi, Nu'alolo and Miloli'i are the five major valleys along the coast, each seemingly more stunning than the last.

Na Pali Coast in One Day

Tackle the Hanakapi'ai Beach to Hanakapi'ai Falls leg of the **Kalalau Trail** (p110). The day hike offers panoramic views of the Na Pali Coast, and ends at the scenic Hanakapi'ai Falls. Cool off after your hard work with a swim at **Ke'e Beach** (p114). If you time it right, you'll be there in time for the spectacular sunset.

Na Pali Coast in Two Days

Head out on a **boat tour** (p106)to see the coast from the other side – choose from kayaking, rafting or a catamaran. Depending on your tour time, stop in Ha'ena to visit the **Limahuli Garden** (p118) or, if you surf, ride the waves at **Makua (Tunnels) Beach** (p118).

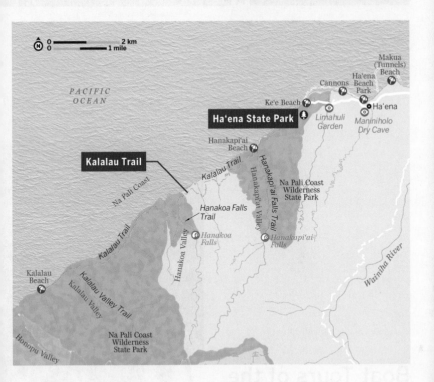

Arriving at the Na Pali Coast

The parking lot nearest the Kalalau trailhead at Ke'e Beach is quite large, but fills quickly. By midmorning and during the jam-packed summer months, it may be full. Overnight hikers should consider parking at Ha'ena Beach Park (free, but not patrolled) or possibly at private **YMCA Camp Naue** (☎808-826-6419; campnaue@yahoo.com; Kuhio Hwy; tent sites $15 per night). You can also hop the **North Shore Shuttle** (p119) to Ke'e Beach from Hanalei.

Sleeping

Within the park, camping is allowed at Hanakoa Valley (one-night maximum) and Kalalau Valley. Permits for Kalalau book out up to a year in advance.

Ha'ena Beach Park is a popular and beautiful camping spot (closed on Monday nights), and a base for exploring the North Shore, including the Na Pali Coast. Advance county camping permits are required. There is an abundance of vacation rentals in Ha'ena.

Na Pali coastline from offshore

Boat Tours of the Na Pali Coast

Glimpsing the Na Pali Coast by sea is an unforgettable experience. Depending on your craft, you can paddle, snorkel, venture into sea caves or just kick back with a tropical drink, luxuriating in one of the world's great views.

Great For...

ℹ Need to Know

Check several days of weather forecasting and ocean conditions before heading out, as high surf or foul weather may cause cancellations.

☑ **Don't Miss**

Views of the lush and corrugated cliffs towering over the coast.

Kayaking

Kayaks are for those who want a workout with their Na Pali Coast tour. They're of the sit-on-top variety, with seat backs and pedal rudders. You don't need to be a triathlete or kayaking expert to use one, but you should be in top physical condition; kayak tours can last 12 hours and you'll be paddling 17 miles.

While undoubtedly epic, kayaking the Na Pali Coast is strenuous and dangerous, and therefore not for everyone. Going with a guide helps mitigate the risks; going without one requires experience in ocean (not river) kayaking. It also means you shouldn't go alone. Always start on the North Shore, end on the Westside (due to currents) and never go in winter (potentially deadly swells). Check several days of weather forecasting and ocean conditions before heading out.

Outfitters & Rentals

Between April and October, most outfitters offer a long day trip that spans the entire Na Pali Coast. You can also rent kayaks for self-guided treks, but should only go that route if you are very experienced.

For a guided tour, try the following options:

Na Pali Kayak (p129) The Na Pali Coast trip is the only tour these folks lead, and their guides have over a decade of experience. Guided overnight camping trips start at $400 per person; a one-day trip costs from $225.

Kayak Kaua'i (p129) The original Na Pali kayaking outfitter's Summer Sea Kayaking Tour ($240) paddles the entire stretch from Ke'e to Polihale in one long day.

Catamarans

Catamarans are the cushiest way to see the Na Pali Coast, offering smoother rides, ample shade, restrooms and crowd-pleasing amenities, like onboard water slides and unlimited food and beverages. Some are equipped with sails (and actually use them), while others are entirely motorized. If you've only sailed monohulls before, this is a far more stable and roomy experience.

Rafts

Rafts are the thrill-seeker's choice, bouncing along the water, entering caves (in mellower weather) and making beach landings, but most lack any shade, restrooms or comfy seating, so they're not for everyone (bad backs beware). The best rafts are RIBs, with hard bottoms that allow smoother rides (sit at the back for less jostling but potentially more sea spray). The largest may include a canopy and even a toilet.

Booking

Book Na Pali Coast boat or kayak tours as early in your trip as possible (ideally before you arrive), as high surf or foul weather may cause cancellations.

✖ Take a Break

Recharge with fresh fish and sushi at **Hanalei Dolphin Restaurant & Sushi Lounge** (p130) in Hanalei.

★ Top Tip

If you are prone to seasickness – a very real issue – inquire about sea conditions, take medication ahead of time and opt for the catamaran. Morning trips generally see the calmest seas.

Kalalau Trail

Winding along the cliffs offers some of the most pristine, extreme views of the coast's deep, riveting pleats. This trail is the best way to connect directly with the elements.

Great For...

Don't Miss

Coast and jungle views on a 4-mile round-trip hike from Ke'e Beach to Hanakapi'ai Beach.

Trail Overview

Winding along *nā pali* (literally, 'the cliffs') offers glimpses of Kaua'i's most pristine valleys. It's also the best way to connect directly with the elements, though keep in mind that the trek – if you opt to complete the full 22-mile round-trip – is a steep, rough hike with some dangerous, eroded sections.

The hike's three segments are Ke'e Beach to Hanakapi'ai Beach, Hanakapi'ai Beach to Hanakapi'ai Falls and Hanakapi'ai Beach to Kalalau Valley. There are hunters who can do the entire trail in and out in one day, but most people will either opt for a day hike to Hanakapi'ai Beach or Hanakapi'ai Falls, or will bring camping gear for an overnight backpack all the way to Kalalau Valley.

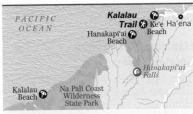

❶ Need to Know

For overnight camping at Kalalau, get an advance permit form **Hawaii State Parks** (http://hawaiistateparks.org/camping).

✕ Take a Break

Reward yourself with a rib-eye steak at **Mediterranean Gourmet** (p119).

★ Top Tip

Parking lot break-ins at Ke'e Beach are rampant; consider leaving your car empty and unlocked to prevent window-smashing.

Take safety concerns seriously. In winter, trails can become rivers, streams can become impassable and the beaches will disappear in high surf. Give thought before heading out on a rainy day and always use extreme caution when swimming at the beaches, especially Hanakapi'ai Beach, where numerous people have drowned over the years.

Ke'e Beach to Hanakapi'ai Beach

It shouldn't take more than an hour to complete this 2-mile trek (4 miles if done as a round-trip day hike) beginning at **Ke'e Beach** in Ha'ena State Park. It's a perfect mini–Na Pali experience that passes through small hanging valleys and over trickling streams. When it rises on the ridge, it offers panoramic views down the entire coast. You'll end at scenic-but-dangerous white-sand **Hanakapi'ai Beach**, at the bottom of Hanakapi'ai Valley.

Hanakapi'ai Beach to Hanakapi'ai Falls

A spur trail branches off the Kalalau Trail to the falls, an 8-mile day hike from Ke'e. The trail parallels Hanakapi'ai Stream up the valley for 2 miles, passing the remains of age-old taro fields and wild guava groves before the canyon narrows, framed by mossy rock walls. The ascending trail repeatedly crosses the stream. Watch your footing on the rocky upper part of the trail, where some of the rocks are covered with slick algae. When it rains, flash floods are likely in this narrow valley.

The steady incline leads to the spectacular **Hanakapi'ai Falls**, which tumbles 300ft into a wide pool gentle enough for swimming. Directly under the falls, falling rocks are common. Start early from Ke'e to beat the hordes. Otherwise, you'll have (a lot of) company.

Hanakapi'ai Beach to Kalalau Valley

Going past Hanakapi'ai Beach means you've got 9 miles left and that you've committed to the whole 22-mile round-trip hike. **Hanakoa Valley** is almost halfway and is a rest stop or campground for hikers – depending on how you choose to break up the trail. If you plan on seeing Hanakapi'ai Falls, this makes a good stopping point for your first night. It's also the turnoff for the 0.6-mile round-trip trail to Hanakoa Falls: a worthy stopover, but there's no swimming allowed.

Past Hanakoa the trail gets noticeably drier and more exposed and the blue Pacific lapping the base of the cliff taunts that much more. Hiking poles are helpful along the entire trail, but especially here, along the rocky ledges. Near the end, the trail takes you across the front of Kalalau Valley, where you'll feel dwarfed by 1000ft lava-rock cliffs before proceeding to the campsites on **Kalalau Beach**, just west of the valley.

Kalalau Valley feels a lot like Eden – one populated with hikers and hippies. If you're a good swimmer, consider paying your respects to the ancestors at Honopu Beach as well. Only attempt to swim during summer.

Book your campsite well in advance; a couple of days should unwind you rather well, then retrace your steps to **Ke'e Beach**. If you time it right and the weather

View over Kalalau Valley

gods conspire in your favor, the journey will end with a magical sunset.

Kalalau Trail Safety

The Kalalau Trail is *very* rugged, and hiking its entire length is not for everyone. Only fit, experienced hikers need apply. Being prepared is critical: you won't want to pack too much but you will need to stay hydrated, prepped for rain and you *must* pack out your trash. You may see hikers with machetes, walkie-talkies, climbing rope and reef shoes, but even trekkers with the least impressive gear should know not to expect a rescue. These precipices are to be taken seriously, and your safety is ultimately your own responsibility. Anyone with a police scanner can tell you 'plenty story' about the braggart from the mainland who was warned by friends, family or an onlooker, but said something along the lines of these famous last words: 'Nah, I'm from the Rockies. This is nothing.' Finally, mosquitoes here are bloodthirsty and the sun can ravage, so always wear insect repellent and sunblock.

Even if you're not planning to camp, a camping permit is legally required to day-hike beyond Hanakoa. Camping permits ($20 per person per night for nonresidents) are available from Hawaii State Parks (p107) online or in person at the Lihu'e office. There's a five-night maximum per trip, with camping allowed only at Hanakoa and Kalalau. Book permits as far in advance as possible, up to a year ahead.

Kalalau Trail Permits

Keep in mind that even if you're not planning to camp, a permit is officially required to continue on the Kalalau Trail beyond Hanakapi'ai. Free day-use hiking permits are available from the **Division of State Parks** (☑808-274-3444; www.hawaiistateparks. org; 3060 Eiwa St, Room 306, Lihu'e; ☺8am-3:30pm Mon-Fri) in Lihu'e, which also issues the required camping permits for the Hanakoa (one-night maximum) and Kalalau (five-nights maximum) Valleys.

WILDNERDPIX/SHUTTERSTOCK ©

Trail Maps

The state parks office in Lihu'e can provide a Kalalau Trail brochure with a map. Another good source sponsored by the county is **Kaua'i Explorer** (www.kauaiexplorer.com).

Danger: Hanakapi'ai Beach

Never turn your back on the ocean here, especially near the river mouth. Don't let the kids play in the shallows out of reach. Swimming at this beach is dangerous and prohibited.

Waikapala'e Wet Cave

Ha'ena State Park

Pass the botanical garden, cross a bridge over a gushing river and enter Ha'ena State Park. Sculpted from the narrow, lava-rich coastline, it burns with allure, mystique and beauty.

Pele (the Hawaiian goddess of fire) is said to have overlooked the area as a home because of the water percolating through its wet and dry caves. Today this 230-acre park remains home to the 1280ft cliff commonly known in the tourism industry as 'Bali Hai,' its name in the film *South Pacific*. Its real name is Makana ('Gift'). Apt, for sure.

Ke'e Beach is the launch point for hikes on the Kalalau Trail through the Na Pali Coast Wilderness State Park.

Ke'e Beach

Memorable North Shore sunsets happen at this spiritual spot where ancient Hawaiians came to practice hula. In summer, the beach offers a refreshing dip to hikers of the nearby Kalalau Trail. But beware that Ke'e Beach may appear calm when it is,

Great For...

Don't Miss

Taking in a superlative sunset – it's an island rite of passage.

Ke'e Beach

✕ Take a Break

There are no restaurants or snack bars in the park. Pack a picnic!

SHANE MYERS PHOTOGRAPHY/SHUTTERSTOCK ©

in fact, otherwise. Vicious currents have sucked some through a keyhole in the reef out into the open sea.

Never leave small children alone near the waterline. Facilities include outdoor showers and restrooms. Car break-ins are common in the parking lot, so don't leave any valuables behind. If you come for the sunset, and you should, bring mosquito repellent.

Kaulu Paoa Heiau

The roaring surf was a teacher to those who first practiced the spiritual art of hula, chanting and testing their skills against nature's decibel levels. Ke'e Beach is the oceanfront site of a cherished *heiau* (ancient stone temple) dedicated to Laka, the goddess of hula. It's also where the volcano goddess Pele fell in love with Lohiau.

ⓘ Need to Know

Almost everyone makes day trips here with their own wheels, but Ke'e Beach is served by the **North Shore Shuttle** (p119) every 1¼ hours. First drop-off 7:35am, last pick-up 8:05pm.

★ Top Tip

Get permits in advance. There are no restaurants or snack bars. Pack a picnic.

★ Top Tip
There is no camping in the state park, but there is camping allowed at nearby Ha'ena Beach Park and further along the coast.

CURTIS/SHUTTERSTOCK ©

Waterfall in Ha'ena State Park

Lei and other sacred offerings found on the ground should be left as is. Enter the heiau through its entryway; don't be disrespectful by crossing over the temple walls.

Wet Caves

Two wet caves lie within the boundaries of Ha'ena State Park. Formed by the constant pounding of waves many years ago, the massive cavern of **Waikapala'e Wet Cave** is as enchanting as it is spooky. It's on the opposite side and a short walk from the visitor-overflow parking area. **Waikanaloa Wet Cave** is further down on the south side of the highway.

Though some enter the water to experience the sunlight's blue reflection in Waikapala'e's deeper chamber, note the water may be contaminated with leptospira bacteria; the rocks are slippery; and there's nothing to hold onto once you're in the water. But it does make one hell of an Instagram glamour shot. Make sure you have someone watching out for you and shower immediately after.

Backyard Graveyards

Ancient burial sites lie underneath countless homes and hotels throughout Hawaii. Construction workers often dig up *iwi* (bones) and *moepu* (funeral objects), while locals swear by eerie stories of equipment malfunctioning until bones are properly reinterred and prayers given.

In 1990 Congress enacted the Native American Graves Protection and Repatriation Act (www.hawaii.gov/dlnr/hpd/hpburials.htm), which established burial councils on each island to oversee the treatment of remains and preservation of burial sites. Desecration of *iwi* is illegal, and a major affront to Native Hawaiians.

One of Kaua'i's most recent cases involved Ha'ena's Naue Point, the site of some 30 confirmed *iwi*. Starting in 2002, and lasting close to nine years, the case went through numerous phases of court hearings, public demonstrations and burial-treatment proposals and ended with the state allowing the landowner to build.

 Sacred Sharks

No doubt being attacked by a *mano* (shark) could be deadly; precautions, such as avoiding swimming in murky waters, especially after a rain, will help you avoid them. But statistically speaking, you're more likely to die from a bee sting than a shark attack and you should be more concerned about contracting leptospirosis or giardiasis in those infamous muddy waters than becoming a midday snack.

Rather than letting any hardwired phobia of large predators get you down, try considering the *mano* from another perspective while in Hawaii: as sacred. For many local families, the *mano* is their *'aumakua* (guardian spirit). *'Aumakua* are family ancestors whose *'uhane* (spirit form) lives on in the body of an animal, watching over members of their living *'ohana*. Revered for their ocean skill, *mano* were also considered the *'aumakua* of navigators. Even today, *mano 'aumakua* have been said to guide lost fishermen home, or toward areas of plentiful fish, to make for a bountiful sojourn.

What happens next? Could a landowner lose the right to build? Probably not. Most likely, the state will approve a burial-treatment proposal to remove the *iwi* and reinter them off-site (an outcome that Hawaiians find woefully inadequate).

As well, many hotels and condos were built on land with iwi now sitting in storage or still underground. And what happens to those restless spirits? Believe it or not, Po'ipu's Grand Hyatt Resort has a director of Hawaiian and community affairs who does blessings somewhere on resort grounds at least once a month to quell any 'spiritual disturbance.'

Ha'ena

Remote, resplendent and idyllic, this is where the ribbon road ends amid lava-rock pinnacles, lush wet forest and postcard-perfect beaches. In the wet season, the cliffs are positively weeping with waterfalls. It's also the site of controversy, as many of the luxury homes on the point were built atop *'iwi kupuna* (ancient Hawaiian burial grounds). No Kaua'i adventure is complete without a drive to the end of the road and at least a short hike along the roadless Na Pali Coast.

⊙ SIGHTS

Limahuli Garden   Gardens
(☏808-826-1053; http://ntbg.org/gardens/limahuli.php; 5-8291 Kuhio Hwy; self-guided adult/student/child under 18yr $20/10/free, guided tours adult/student & child over 10yr $40/20; ⊙9:30am-4pm Tue-Sat, guided tours 10am; ⋔) ✔ As beautiful as it gets for living education, this garden offers a pleasant overview of endemic botany and ancient Hawai'i's *ahupua'a* (land division) system of management. Self-guided tours take

about 1½ hours, allowing you to meditate on the scenery along a 0.75-mile loop trail; in-depth guided tours (minimum age 10 years, reservations required) last 2½ hours.

Volunteer service projects in native ecosystem restoration give ecotourists a glimpse into the entire 985-acre preserve. To get here, turn inland just before the stream that marks the boundary of Ha'ena State Park.

Makua (Tunnels) Beach   Beach
One of the North Shore's almost-too-beautiful beaches, named for the underwater caverns and lava tubes in and among the near-shore reef. In summer, this is among the best snorkel spots on the island. It's also the North Shore's most popular dive site. In winter, however, the swell picks up and the surf can be heavy.

In the shoulder season, the snorkeling can still be decent, but always use caution and check with locals or lifeguards before heading into the water. Beware especially of a regular current flowing west toward the open ocean. If you can't score a parking spot at one of the two unmarked lots down short dirt roads, park at Ha'ena State Park and walk.

Limahuli Garden

ALL A SHUTTER/SHUTTERSTOCK ©

Ha'ena Beach Park   Beach

Not ideal for swimming in winter, because of the regular pounding shore break that creates a strong undertow; this beach is nevertheless good for taking in some sun. During the summer months, the sea is almost always smooth and safe. Ask lifeguards about conditions before going in, especially between October and May.

To the left is **Cannons**, an expert local surf break. Facilities include restrooms, outdoor showers, picnic tables and a pavilion. Overnight camping is allowed. Secure permits in advance.

Maniniholo Dry Cave   Cave

Maniniholo Dry Cave is deep, broad and rather fun to explore, though the deeper you penetrate the lower the ceiling and the darker your surrounds. A constant seep of water from the cave walls keeps the dark interior dank. As you slowly step toward the rear wall, remember that you are standing below a massive monolith of Jurassic proportions.

You'll not only hear but feel the rumble of thunder and crash of the waves which reverberate all around. And if you believe in that sort of thing and are sensitive to it, you may even feel a palpable mana (spiritual essence), especially near the grouping of stones set up around what looks like a fire pit – perhaps a place of counsel or merely shelter in the days long gone. The cave is named after the head fisherman of the *menehune* (the 'little people') who, according to legend, built ponds and other structures here overnight. It sits directly across from Ha'ena Beach Park.

🅖 ACTIVITIES

Hanalei Day Spa   Spa

(📞808-826-6621; www.hanaleidayspa.com; Hanalei Colony Resort, 5-7130 Kuhio Hwy; massage 50/80min $110/165; ⏰9am-6pm Tue-Sat) If you're tired or need to revitalize, this friendly though modest spa offers some of the island's more competitively priced massages (including Hawaiian *lomilomi*) and body treatments such as an Ayurvedic body wrap.

🅐 SHOPPING

Na Pali Art Gallery   Arts & Crafts

(📞808-826-1844; www.napaligallery.com; Hanalei Colony Resort, 5-7130 Kuhio Hwy; ⏰7am-5pm; 📶) Peruse a quality array of local artists' paintings, woodwork, sculptures, ceramics, jewelry and collectibles made from Larimar – a blue volcanic glass sourced from the Dominican Republic. Not everyone loves the coffee served here, but it's the only caffeine in the immediate area.

🅧 EATING & DRINKING

There is but one restaurant and one cafe in town. The town bar is located inside the town restaurant, next door to the town coffee joint. All share the same superlative view.

Mediterranean Gourmet   Mediterranean $$$

(📞808-826-9875; www.kauaimedgourmet.com; Hanalei Colony Resort, 5-7130 Kuhio Hwy; mains $13-29; ⏰noon-8:30pm) A taste of the Mediterranean literally on the Pacific (if the windows weren't there, you'd get salty ocean mist on your face), this fish out of water offers an eclectic range of Euro-inspired dishes such as rosemary rack of lamb and pistachio-crusted ahi (yellowfin tuna). Food quality and service can be inconsistent, but the menu is unique to the island.

Lunch is served from noon to 3pm. Happy hour blooms in the bar from 3pm to 6pm and features select appetizers. Dinner seating begins at 5pm. It has live music on Saturday and Sunday evenings.

🅘 GETTING THERE & AWAY

Ha'ena is served by the Kuhio Hwy, with several one-lane bridges between here and Hanalei. If a bridge floods during a storm, you'll be cut off. **North Shore Shuttle** (📞808-826-7019; www. kauai.gov/NorthShoreShuttle; one way $4) serves the area and connects with the **Kaua'i Bus** (📞808-246-8110; www.kauai.gov/Bus; one way adult/child $2/$1) in Hanalei; still, you'll need your own wheels if you base yourself here.

HANALEI BAY

Outrigger canoe, Black Pot Beach Park (p125)

In this Chapter

Black Pot Beach Park & Around..... 124
Beaches... 128
Activities 129
Tours.. 129
Eating.. 130
Drinking & Nightlife........................... 131
Getting There & Around.................... 131

Hanalei Bay at a Glance...

There are precious few towns with the majestic natural beauty and barefoot soul of Hanalei. The bay is the thing, of course. Its half-dozen surf breaks are legendary, partly because local surf gods such as the late Andy Irons cut their teeth here. Even if you aren't here for the waves, the beach will demand your attention with its wide sweep of cream-colored sand and magnificent jade mountain views.

So too will the pint-sized town where you may take a yoga class, snack on sushi, shop for chic beach gear, vintage treasures and stunning art, or duck into a world-class dive bar.

Hanalei Bay in One Day

Start with the steep, short climb up **Okolehao Trail** (p129), grab coffee and a pastry at **Hanalei Bread Company** (p130), then rent a kayak or SUP and paddle up the Hanalei River. Decompress with a sunset beach walk at **Hanalei Beach Park** (p126) and hit the bar at **Tahiti Nui** (p131) for dinner (surprisingly good!) and drinks.

Hanalei Bay in Two Days

On day two, you'll explore your surroundings. Cruise the ribbon road north to Ha'ena and hit Makua (Tunnels) Beach, where reef-snorkeling and swimming opportunities abound in the summertime. Cap off your day with a sunset at Ke'e Beach at the end of the road then double back to Hanalei for a divine wine-splashed dinner at **BarAcuda Tapas & Wine** (p130).

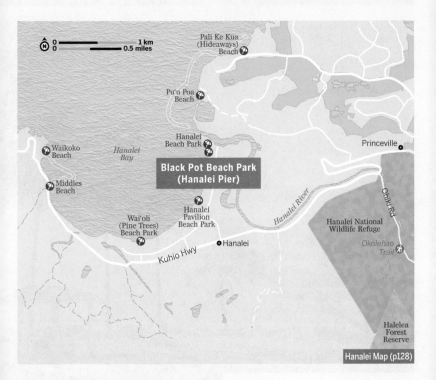

Arriving in Hanalei Bay

There are only two reliable ways to reach the region: by public transport (ie county bus, airport shuttle), or under your own steam. On Kaua'i a rental car gives you the most flexibility, with most agencies in and around the airport. Taxis are expensive and hard to wrangle.

Sleeping

Lodging in the North Shore is less about hotels and more about rental homes, B&Bs and farmstays.

Short on hotels and long on rental properties, the best option for groups and families is to rent a condo in Princeville or a beach house in Hanalei or points north. The best value will be in Kilauea and Princeville.

Black Pot Beach Park

Black Pot Beach Park & Around

Dying to surf those beautiful waves, aren't ya? If you're a beginner, you are in luck. Head to Hanalei Pier for a lesson.

Great For...

☑ Don't Miss

A tropical cocktail at a Hanalei grass shack tiki bar.

The Setting

Well-known for being filmed in *The Descendants,* Hanalei Bay is easily Kaua'i's most famous beach and for good reason. Really one long beach that's divided into several sections with different names, there's something for almost everyone here: sunbathing, swimming, snorkeling, standup paddle surfing, kayaking, bodyboarding and surfing.

The winter months can make this stretch of water an expert spot for board riders only (no swimming or snorkeling). In summer, the water is sometimes so calm it's hard to distinguish between sky and sea, except for a smattering of yachts bobbing on the horizon.

Black Pot Beach Park (Hanalei Pier)

PRINCEVILLE

Hanalei Bay

HANALEI

Weke Rd

Hanalei River

Kuhio Hwy

❶ Need to Know

Restrooms, showers and lifeguards are all available here.

✕ Take a Break

Post-surfing snack at **BarAcuda Tapas & Wine** (p130).

★ Top Tip

Park along Weke Rd if you have to, as the public lot gets crowded.

Black Pot Beach (Hanalei Pier)

This small section of gorgeous Hanalei Bay sits to the north of the bay, near the mouth of the Hanalei River. It usually offers the calmest surf among the wild North Shore swells. Also known as Hanalei Pier for its unmistakable landmark, the sand is shaded by ironwood trees and is popular mainly with novice surfers. In summer, swimming and snorkeling are decent, as are kayaking and SUP.

Use extreme caution during periods of high surf because dangerous shore breaks and rip currents are common. At the park's eastern end, where the Hanalei River empties onto the beach, is a small boat ramp where kayakers launch for trips upriver.

Surf Lessons Here

The sandy-bottomed beach slopes gently, making it safe for beginning surfers. Lessons are typically taught just west of the pier, where you'll find surf schools galore.

Camping

Lodging in the North Shore is covered by rental homes, B&Bs and farmstays. Though it requires getting an advance county permit, camping at Black Pot Beach Park (Hanalei Pier) is fun and safe. Amenities are limited to restrooms, picnic tables and cold-water outdoor showers. Camping is allowed on Fridays, Saturdays and holidays only.

Hanalei Beach Park

This pleasant beach is just north of Black Pot Beach. With its sweeping views, it makes a great place for a picnic, sunset or lazy day at the beach. Ideally located, its downside is the parking, which can be a challenge. Park along Weke Rd if you have to, as the public lot gets crowded. Facilities include restrooms and outdoor showers. Camping is allowed only with an advance county permit.

Hanalei Town

This pint-sized town will enchant you; take a yoga class, snack on sushi, shop for chic beach gear, vintage treasures and stunning art, or duck into a world-class dive bar. Sure, Hanalei has more than its share of adults with Peter Pan syndrome, and you'll see as many men in their sixties waxing their surfboards as you will groms with 'guns' (big-wave surfboards). Which begs the query: why grow up at all when you can grow old in Hanalei?

Wai'oli Hui'ia Church

A popular site for quaint church weddings, the original Wai'oli Hui'ia Church was built by Hanalei's first missionaries, William and Mary Alexander, who arrived in 1834 in a

Hawaiian girls' outrigger team in Hanalei

double-hulled canoe. Today the church, hall and mission house remain in the middle of town, set on a huge manicured lawn with a beautiful mountain backdrop.

The green American Gothic–style wooden church that passers-by can see today was donated in 1912 by three sons of Abner Wilcox, another island missionary. The doors remain open during the day, and visitors are welcome. A 19th-century Bible printed in Hawaiian is displayed on top of the old organ. The church choir sings hymns in Hawaiian at the 10am Sunday service.

Hanalei National Wildlife Refuge

Anywhere west of Kilauea will set you on a path ever more pristine the further you go. Following Kalihiwai, you'll catch your first glimpses of even more vast Eden-esque landscapes. Rolling hills abound as you pass through Princeville, where you'll spot the Hanalei Valley Lookout, across from the Princeville Center. It's arguably the best vantage point for the Hanalei National Wildlife Refuge.

One of the largest rivers in the state, the Hanalei River has nurtured its crops since the first kanaka maoli (Native Hawaiians) began cultivating taro in its fertile valley fields. Other crops have come and gone. In the mid-1800s, rice paddies were planted here to feed the Chinese sugar-plantation laborers. By the 1930s, four rice mills were operating in the Hanalei area. Today, taro again dominates, with only 5% of its original acreage.

The wildlife refuge, established in 1972, is closed to the public. However, from the lookout you might be able to spot the 49 varieties of birds using the habitat, including the valley's endangered native species: *ae'o* (Hawaiian stilt; slender with black back, white chest and long pink legs), *'alae kea* (Hawaiian coot; slate gray with white forehead), *'alae 'ula* (Hawaiian moorhen; dark gray with black head and distinctive red-and-yellow bill) and *koloa maoli* (Hawaiian duck; mottled brown with orange legs and feet).

🛈 Need to Know

You can enter the Hanalei National Wildlife Refuge only on the **Ho'opu-lapula Haraguchi Rice Mill Tour** (p129).

TRAVEL BUG/GETTY IMAGES ©

BEACHES

Hanalei Bay is a long crescent comprised of several sections with different names.

Hanalei Pavilion Beach Park   Beach

Toward the middle of Hanalei Bay, you'll find this scenic beach park that possesses a white-sand crescent made for strolling. Waters are typically not as calm as further east by the pier, but swimming and paddling are possible during the calmest summer months. Facilities include restrooms and outdoor showers. Parking is limited. Street parking is often available.

Wai'oli (Pine Trees) Beach Park   Beach

Offering respite from the sun, this park is equipped with restrooms, outdoor showers, beach volleyball courts and picnic tables. Winter months bring big swells and locals dominate the surf spot here known as **Pine Trees**. The shore break is harder here than any other spot on Hanalei Bay and swim-

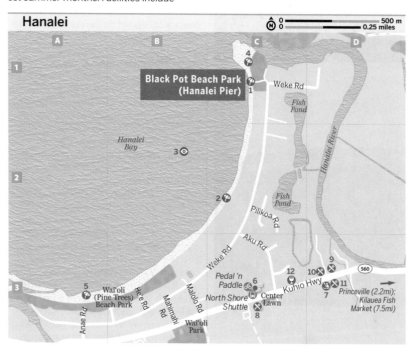

Hanalei

⊙ Sights
1 Black Pot Beach Park (Hanalei Pier).........C1
2 Hanalei Pavilion Beach Park....................C2
3 Hanalei Bay.....................................B2
4 Hanalei Beach Park C1
5 Wai'oli (Pine Trees) Beach Park A3

➕ Activities, Courses & Tours
6 Na Pali Catamaran.................................C3
7 Na Pali Kayak....................................D3

✖ Eating
8 BarAcuda Tapas & Wine C3
   Hanalei Bread Company ....(see 8)
9 Hanalei Dolphin Restaurant &
   Sushi Lounge D3
10 Hanalei Taro & Juice Co D3
11 Postcards Café.....................................D3

🍷 Drinking & Nightlife
12 Tahiti Nui C3

ming is dangerous, except during calm summer surf.

ACTIVITIES

Less crowded than the Eastside's Wailua River, Hanalei River offers roughly 6 miles of tranquil scenery, ideal for kayaking or standup paddle surfing.

Na Pali Kayak   Kayaking
(☏808-826-6900; www.napalikayak.com; 5075 Kuhio Hwy, Hanalei; tours per person $225 plus tax & state park fees) Hiking the Na Pali Coast can be a magnificent experience, but the trail ends at the midway point of the roadless coastline defined by sheer 4000ft cliffs. Join this full-day tour and you can see it all.

Kayak Kaua'i   Kayaking
(☏808-826-9844; www.kayakkauai.com; Kuhio Hwy; Na Pali tour packages from $240, Blue Lagoon Tour $85-95, kayak rental per day with delivery $45-55) This island-wide kayak outfitter with a base on the Wailua River on the Eastside offers extended paddling/camping trips along the Na Pali shore to Kalalau

or Miloi'i, and Blue Lagoon paddling and snorkeling day trips around Hanalei. It will also rent and deliver camping and paddling gear island-wide.

Okolehao Trail   Hiking
(Ohiki Rd) This steep 2.5-mile round-trip trail affords panoramic views of Hanalei's taro fields, the start of the Na Pali Coast and, on a clear day, Kilauea Lighthouse. It's rumored to be named for 'moonshine,' referring to distilled liquor made from the roots of *ti* plants. The visual spoils are worth the sweaty climb through the forest.

TOURS

Ho'opulapula Haraguchi Rice Mill & Taro Farm Tours   Tours
(☏808-651-3399; www.haraguchiricemill. org; tours incl lunch adult/child 5-12yr $87/52; ⊙tours usually 9:45am Wed, by reservation only) ✐ Learn about cultivating taro on Kaua'i at this sixth-generation family-run nonprofit farm and rice mill (the last remaining in the Hawaiian Islands). On farmer-guided tours, which take you out into the *lo'i kalo*, you'll

Taro fields near Hanalei Bay

SEAN XU/GETTY IMAGES ©

Overlook of Hanalei Bay

get a glimpse of the otherwise inaccessible Hanalei National Wildlife Refuge (p127) and learn about Hawaii's immigrant history.

Na Pali Catamaran
Boating

(☑808-826-6853, 866-255-6853; www.napalicatamaran.com; Ching Young Village, 5-5190 Kuhio Hwy; 4hr tours $180-199) This exceptional outfit has been running tours for over 35 years, offering comfy catamaran cruises along the Na Pali Coast from Hanalei Bay. Depending on ocean conditions and the time of year, you might venture into some sea caves. Remember, though, the surf can pound and there's no reprieve from the elements. Minimum age five years.

Na Pali Explorer
Boating

(☑808-338-9999; www.napaliexplorer.com; 4½hr tours $99-129; ♠) Take a coastal snorkeling trip on a rigid-hull inflatable raft, which is hard-bottomed and gives a smoother ride than all-inflatable Zodiacs. The longer 49ft raft, which carries up to 36 passengers, has a restroom and a canopy for shade. Tours run out of Hanalei Bay.

Minimum age for participants is five to eight years, depending on the boat.

🍴 EATING

BarAcuda Tapas & Wine
Mediterranean $$$

(☑808-826-7081; www.restaurantbaracuda.com; Hanalei Center, 5-5161 Kuhio Hwy; shared plates $7-26; ⊙5:30-10pm, kitchen closes at 9:30pm) ✔ This is the most chef-driven spot in Hanalei and its best kitchen. The wine list is expertly curated with a blend of new- and old-world vintners, and the tapas-style plates, featuring local beef, fish, pork and veg, are meant to be shared.

Hanalei Bread Company
Bakery $

(☑808-826-6717; www.restaurantbaracuda.com/hanalei-bread-shop; Hanalei Center, 5-5183 Kuhio Hwy; mains $9-14; ⊙7am-5pm) A new organic bakery and cafe in the old Hanalei Coffee Roasters building owned by the BarAcuda team. Expect fresh-baked crusty breads and baguettes, great coffee, breakfast pizzas with onion, bacon and a soft egg cracked on top, gluten-free crepes, roasted vegetable and goat's cheese sandwiches, and long lines that move fast.

Kilauea Fish Market   Seafood $$

(☎808-828-6244; Kilauea Plantation Center, 4270 Kilauea Rd; mains $10-18; ☺11am-8pm Mon-Sat) Serves healthy versions of over-the-counter plate lunches such as fresh *ono* (white-fleshed wahoo) or Korean BBQ chicken, *mahimahi* (white-fleshed fish also called 'dolphin') tacos and tasty *ahi* (yellow-fin tuna) wraps. It's around back of the Kilauea Plantation Center and has outdoor picnic tables. Bring your own beer or wine and be prepared to wait.

Hanalei Dolphin Restaurant & Sushi Lounge   Seafood $$$

(☎808-826-6113; www.hanaleidolphin.com; 5-5016 Kuhio Hwy; mains lunch $12-16, dinner $25-40; ☺restaurant 11:30am-9pm, market 10am-7pm) At one of Hanalei's oldest restaurants, the incisive sushi chefs will play culinary jazz with their daily fresh fish if decision-making is not your forte. Opt for the cooked-food menu if raw fish doesn't grab you. Everything is good here.

Postcards Café   Fusion $$$

(☎808-826-1191; http://postcardscafe.com; 5-5075 Kuhio Hwy; mains $24-38; ☺5:30-9pm; ♫) ✔ With innocent charm, this garden cottage with the rusted anchor out front could just as easily be found in the New England countryside. Vegan and seafood dishes often have an appealing world-fusion twist, such as the wasabi-crusted ahi or fennel-crusted lobster tail. A genteel atmosphere will induce nostalgia like a Robert Redford film. Reservations recommended for groups of four or more.

🍷 DRINKING & NIGHTLIFE

Tahiti Nui   Bar

(☎808-826-6277; http://thenui.com; 5-5134 Kuhio Hwy; ☺11am-10pm Sun-Thu, to midnight Fri & Sat) The legendary Nui (which made a cameo appearance in *The Descendants*) is a tiki dive bar with heart and history, and

---

🍴 **Homage to Kalo**

According to Hawaiian cosmology, Papa (earth mother) and Wakea (sky father) gave birth to Haloa, a stillborn brother to man. Haloa was planted in the earth and from his body came *kalo* (taro), a plant that has long sustained the Hawaiian people and been a staple for oceanic cultures around the world.

Kalo is still considered a sacred food, full of tradition and spirituality for Hawaiians. Hanalei is home to the largest taro-producing farm in the state, Hoʻopulapula Haraguchi Rice Mill & Taro Farm, where the purple, starchy potato-like plant is grown in *loʻi kalo* (wet taro fields). Rich in nutrients, *kalo* is often boiled and pounded into poi, an earthy, starchy and somewhat sweet and sticky pudding-like food.

---

a rather tasty dinner menu. It's usually crowded from mid-afternoon onward, and can get rollicking nightly with live Hawaiian music. It's especially busy on weekends, when it's the only place open past 10pm.

ℹ️ GETTING THERE & AWAY

There's one road into and out of Hanalei. During heavy rains (common in winter), the Hanalei Bridge occasionally closes due to flooding and those on either side are stuck until it reopens.

If you opted not to rent a car, the **North Shore Shuttle** (p119) links Hanalei to Keʻe with multiple stops in Waniha and Haena along the way.

ℹ️ GETTING AROUND

Pedal ʻn Paddle (☎808-826-9069; Ching Young Village, 5-5105 Kuhio Hwy; ☺9am-6pm) rents cruisers (per day/week $15/60) and hybrid road bikes ($20/80), all including helmets and locks.

MARTIN M303/SHUTTERSTOCK ©

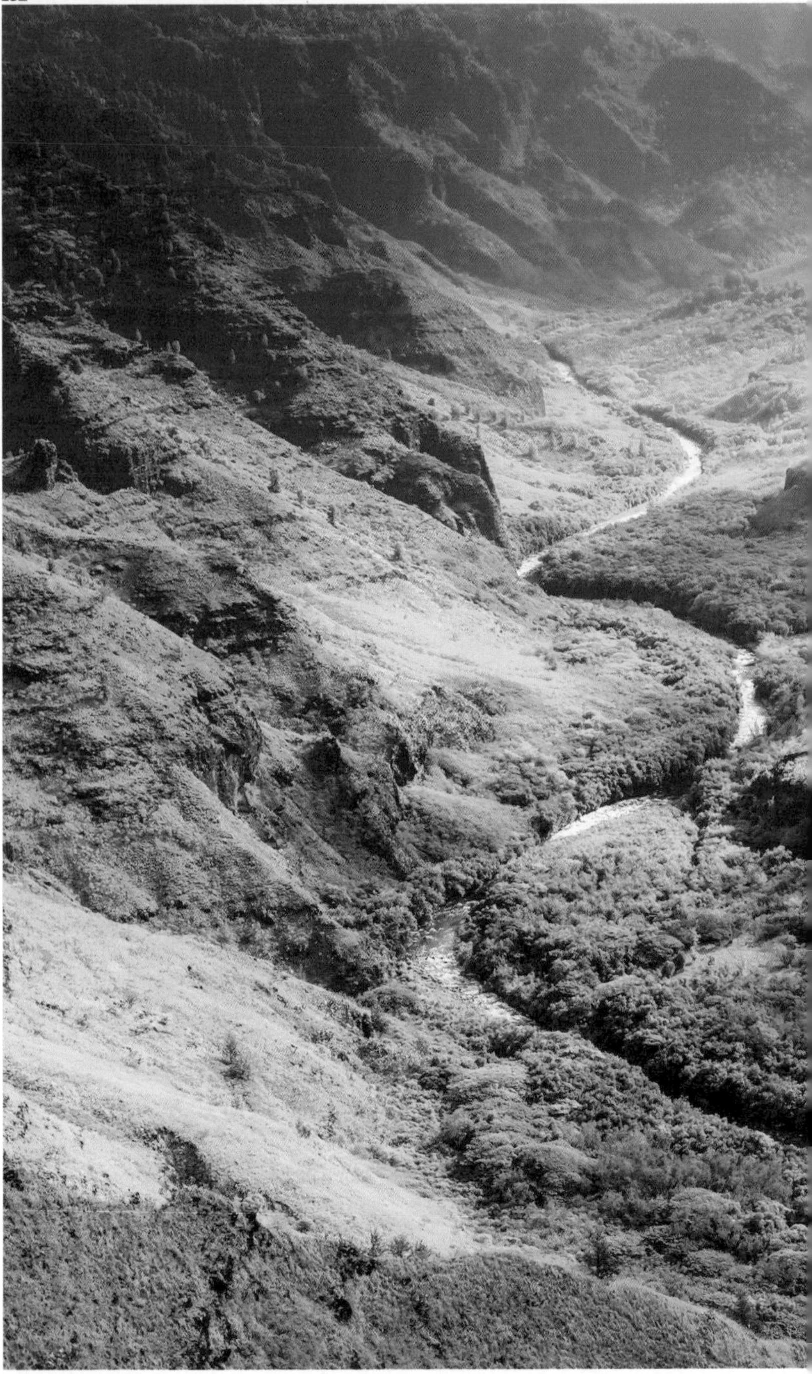

WAIMEA CANYON

In this Chapter
Hiking Waimea Canyon 136
Hiking Koke'e State Park 140
Sights 144
Activities 145
Eating 147
Entertainment 147
Getting There & Around 147

Waimea Canyon at a Glance...

This is the edge of the world. And everything from the people to the landscape is somehow more wild than on the rest of Kaua'i. You won't find many top-notch resorts or restaurants, but you will experience a genuine broad-grinned spirit that is proud, authentic and directly Hawaiian.

With noteworthy parks, lots of sunshine and access to the world-famous Na Pali Coast, this is an adventurer's dream come true. There are deep, riveting red canyons, impossibly steep jungle cliffs, forgotten surf breaks, empty beaches, chart-topping views, waterfalls and a seemingly infinite expanse of ocean.

Waimea Canyon in Two Days

Follow Rte 550 through Waimea Canyon and Koke'e State Park, stopping at the many stunning lookouts. Pause at the **Koke'e Museum** (p140) then stroll the main street in historic Hanapepe. On day two, see the great Na Pali from the sea. Then head to the **Waimea Town Center** (p144) to learn about the past.

Waimea Canyon in Four Days

On day three, hike in **Koke'e** (p140), one of nature's great works of art. Day four provides spectacular views along the **Waimea Canyon Drive** (p138). Dine at **Wranglers' Steakhouse** (p143) because you deserve a juicy steak. End with a sunset at **Kekaha Beach Park**.

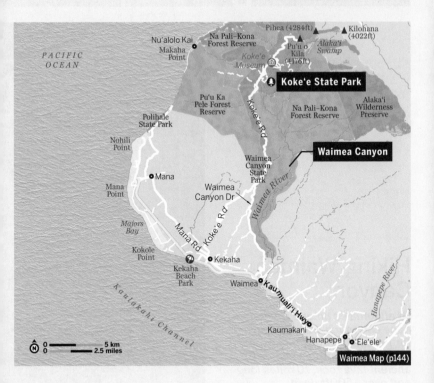

Arriving in Waimea Canyon

Waimea is easily reached by rental car. **Kaua'i Bus** (p119) also services the village.

Sleeping

There are some lovely vacation homes in Waimea Canyon and the Westside, several looking right on to the beach, as well as a handful of cute inns and one resort-like historic hotel. In Koke'e State Park, accommodations in basic cabins or your own tent.

Waterfall into Waimea Canyon

Hiking Waimea Canyon

Of all Kaua'i's unique wonders, none can touch Waimea Canyon for grandeur. Few would expect to find a gargantuan chasm of ancient lava rock, 10 miles long and over 3500ft deep.

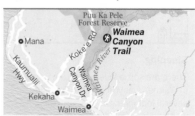

Great For...

ⓘ Need to Know

Cell phones do not work here. Hike with a companion or tell someone your expected return.

★ **Top Tip**

Do not drink fresh water found along the trails without treating it.

Geography

Known as the Grand Canyon of the Pacific, Waimea Canyon was formed when Kaua'i's original shield volcano, Wai'ale'ale, slumped along an ancient fault line. The horizontal striations along the canyon walls represent successive volcanic eruptions. The red colors indicate where water has seeped through the rocks, creating mineral rust from the iron ore inside. Flowing through the canyon is Waimea River, Kaua'i's longest, fed by tributaries that bring reddish-brown waters from Alaka'i Swamp's mountaintop.

Drives here on a clear day are phenomenal. Don't be disappointed by rain, as that's what makes the waterfalls gush. Sunny days following rain are ideal for prime views, though slick mud makes hiking challenging at these times.

Waimea Canyon Drive

This spectacular drive, the best on the island, follows the entire length of Waimea Canyon into Koke'e State Park, ascending 19 miles from the coast to Pu'u o Kila Lookout. It begins as Waimea Canyon Dr by Waimea's West Kaua'i Technology & Visitor Center, then merges into and becomes Koke'e Rd. You can stop at scenic lookouts and take short hikes during the drive. The breathtaking Waimea Canyon Lookout is about 0.3 miles north of Mile 10, at an elevation of 3400ft.

In addition to jaw-dropping canyon vistas and ocean views, you can also see several fine specimens of native trees, including koa and ohia, as well as invasive species such as kiawe. The valuable hardwood koa proliferates at the hunter's check station. Look for the trees with narrow, crescent-shaped leaves.

The canyon running in an easterly direction off Waimea Canyon is Koai'e Canyon, an area accessible to backcountry hikers.

There are no gas stations along the way, but major signposted lookouts have restrooms. Consider going to the end of the road in the morning and making your way backwards to avoid traffic.

Waimea & Koai'e Canyon Trail

The relatively flat, 11.5-mile (one way) Waimea Canyon Trail fords the Waimea River several times. Pick it up at the bottom of Waimea Canyon at the end of Kukui Trail. An entry permit is required (available at self-service trailhead registration boxes). Bring mosquito repellent.

You'll intersect the Koai'e Canyon Trail about half a mile up the canyon. This moderate 3-mile (one way) trek takes you

Hikers in Waimea Canyon State Park

down the south side of the canyon to some swimming holes (avoid them during rainy weather due to the possibility of hazardous flash floods).

Hiking Tips

For experienced hikers, several rugged trails lead deep into Waimea Canyon. Keep in mind these trails are shared with pig hunters and are busiest on weekends and holidays. Trail maps are available at the Koke'e Museum in Koke'e State Park.

Hiking poles or a sturdy walking stick will ease the steep descent into the canyon. Note the time of sunset and plan to return well before dark, as daylight will fade inside the canyon long before sunset. Beware of rain, which creates hazardous conditions in the canyon: red-dirt trails quickly become slick and river fords rise to impassable levels.

While packing light is recommended, take enough water for your entire trip, especially the uphill return journey. Do not drink freshwater found along the trails without treating it.

✕ Take a Break

Carry your food for the day. Many of the lookouts have little food stands offering up fresh fruit, snacks and drinks.

Camping

In Waimea Canyon State Park, all four backcountry campgrounds (per night $18) along the canyon's trails are on forest reserve land. Advance camping permits are required.

Hiker on the Awa'awapuhi Trail

CHASE CLAUSEN/SHUTTERSTOCK ©

Hiking Koke'e State Park

Expansive Koke'e (ko-keh-eh) State Park is a playground for ecotourism. It's home to inspirational views, as well as some of the island's most precious ecosystems.

Great For...

☑ Don't Miss

Views of the Kalalau Valley from the Kalalau Lookout at Mile Marker 18.

Botanists will revel in the variety of endemic species, while birders will have their binoculars full. Hikers enjoy some reprieve from the sun as they tackle a variety of trails for all skill levels.

The park boasts 45 miles of trails that range from swampy bogs to wet forest to red-dirt canyon rim with clifftop views that can cause vertigo even in wannabe mountain goats. Hiking here offers chances to spy endemic species of animals and plants, including Kaua'i's rare, endangered forest birds.

Koke'e Museum

At this museum (☎808-335-9975; www. kokee.org; donation $3; ⏰9am-4:30pm; 🚻) 🐾 you'll find detailed topographical maps, exhibits on flora and fauna, and local historical photographs. It also has botanical

Honeycreeper

sketches of endemic plants and taxidermic representations of some of the wildlife that calls Koke'e home. The gift shop sells a handy fold-out map of the park and its hiking trails.

Getting to the Trails

Halemanu Rd, just north of Mile 14 on Koke'e Rd, is the starting point for several scenic hikes. Whether or not the road is passable in a non-4WD vehicle depends on recent rainfall. Note that many car-rental agreements forbid any off-road driving.

Awa'awapuhi Trail

The Awa'awapuhi Trail (3.2 miles one way) is arguably the best in Koke'e, and a little easier than its nearby counterpart, the equally spectacular Nu'alolo Trail. The trail

❶ Need to Know

For trail information, stop at the Koke'e Museum and consult the Nā Ala Hele website (www.hawaiitrails.org/trails).

✕ Take a Break

Refuel with a burger and drink at **Koke'e Lodge** (☏808-335-6061; Koke'e Rd; mains $5-9; ⊙cafe 9am-2:30pm, takeout until 3pm; 👪).

offers unforgettable vistas of 2000ft cliffs rising above the Na Pali Coast.

The trail requires a good amount of endurance, but is less steep and technical, making it a better fit for families than the other iconic trail. Because it's more accessible, the Awa'awapuhi Trail sees more people, and there are some steep steps where you might find yourself hugging a tree. At the trail's end you'll arrive at a breathtaking view of the cliffs below Awa'awapuhi Lookout.

Nu'alolo Trail

The Nu'alolo Trail (3.8 miles) is one of the steeper and more technical trails in the area. Like the Awa'awapuhi Trail, it affords sky-bound views of the Na Pali Coast, but with half the traffic. The trailhead for the Nu'alolo Trail is just south of the Koke'e Museum.

There's a 1400ft drop in the first mile of this hike. The first half has good shade, while the second half can be more exposed. The trail takes about five hours round-trip. Remember, what goes up must come down, so save enough water for the hike back up.

Cliff & Canyon Trails

The 0.1-mile Cliff Trail is a relatively easy walk with rewarding canyon views. Keep going on the 1.7-mile Canyon Trail, a steep forested trail that descends before opening up to a vast red-dirt promontory with cliffs to one side and charming log steps to guide you further. Shortly thereafter it'll take some huff-and-puff climbing to get to Waipo'o Falls.

This is the best family-hiking area in the park. If it's getting too much, you could turn around at the falls. Otherwise, follow the trail across the stream to the canyon rim. The trail ends at Kumuwela Lookout, where you can rest at a picnic table before backtracking to Halemanu Rd.

For an alternate return route, make a right at the signed intersection with the Black Pipe Trail at the top of the switchback where you leave the canyon rim. This

0.5-mile alternative trail stops at the 4WD road, where you turn left (downhill) and walk back to where you started.

To get to the trailhead for the Cliff and Canyon Trails, walk down Halemanu Rd over 0.8 miles. Keeping Halemanu Stream on your left, turn right onto a footpath leading to the Cliff and Canyon Trails. At the next junction, the Cliff Trail veers right and uphill to a viewpoint. You can skip the steps on the road if you have a 4WD by accessing the trail system from the end of Kumuwela Ridge.

Pihea Trail to Alaka'i Swamp Trail

This rugged, strenuous 7.5-mile round-trip trek begins off Koke'e Rd at Pu'u o Kila Lookout. A mere mile in, Pihea Lookout appears. After a short scramble downhill, the board-

Alakai Swamp Trail

★ **Top Tip**
Rainy season lasts October to May, although you may need a waterproof layer any time of the year.

walk begins. About 1.8 miles later, you'll come to a crossing with the Alaka'i Swamp Trail. Taking a left at this crossing puts you on the trail toward Kilohana Lookout.

Continuing straight on the Pihea Trail will take you to Kawaikoi Campground instead. Most hikers begin this trip at Pu'u o Kila Lookout because it's accessible via the paved road.

Both of these trails may be muddy and not recently maintained. The stretch between Alaka'i Crossing and Kilohana Lookout includes hundreds of steps, which can be hell on your knees. Expect to take all day to finish the hike.

Koke'e Resource Conservation Program

If you are so taken with Koke'e's spectacular beauty that you want to contribute your time and energy into keeping it beautiful, get into the backcountry with this ecological restoration organization to eradicate invasive species and restore the island's native habitat.

In exchange for work, you can get transport to and from the airport, plus a unique way of learning about native flora and fauna. It's backbreaking work, but think of it as a hike with some weed-whacking in between.

> ### ★ Eo e Emalani I Alaka'i
>
> A one-day outdoor dance festival at the Koke'e Museum in early October commemorating Queen Emma's 1871 journey to Alaka'i Swamp. The festival includes a royal procession, hula dancing, live music and more.

⊙ SIGHTS

West Kaua'i Technology & Visitor Center
Museum

(☎808-338-1332; www.westkauaivisitorcenter. org; 9565 Kaumuali'i Hwy; ⊙10am-4pm Mon-Fri; ⓘ) 🖉 FREE Orient yourself historically to the Westside with modest exhibits on Hawaiian culture, Captain Cook, sugar plantations

and the US military. The gift shop sells locally made artisan crafts, including rare Ni'ihau shell lei.

This complex doubles as a visitor center and offers a free, three-hour historic Waimea walking tour at 8:30am Mondays (call to register by noon on the previous Friday).

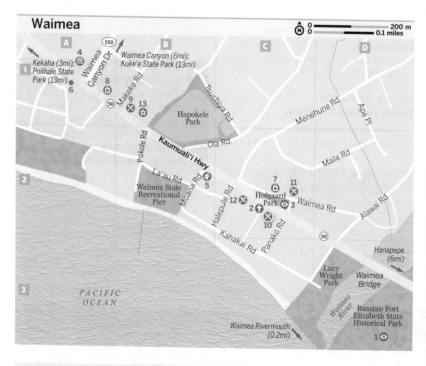

Waimea

Waimea

⊙ Sights
1 Russian Fort Elizabeth State
   Historical Park..D3
2 Waimea Hawaiian Church C2
3 Waimea Town Center...................................C2
4 West Kaua'i Technology & Visitor
   Center...A1

⊕ Activities, Courses & Tours
5 Na Pali Explorer..B2
6 Na Pali Riders..A1

ⓐ Shopping
7 Aunty Lilikoi Passion Fruit Products........C2

8 Kaua'i Granola A1

⊗ Eating
9 G's Juicebar B1
10 Ishihara Market C2
11 Jo-Jo's Anuenue Shave Ice &
    Treats..C2
12 Wrangler's Steakhouse C2
    Yumi's ....(see 13)

⊕ Entertainment
13 Waimea Theater..B1

Russian Fort Elizabeth State Historical Park   Historic Site

(http://dlnr.hawaii.gov/dsp/parks/kauai; off Kaumuali'i Hwy; ☺dawn-dusk) `FREE` A Russian fort in Hawaii? Yes, it's true. Constructed in 1817 and named after the Empress of Russia, Fort Elizabeth commanded the entrance to Waimea River. The octagonal design ranges from 350ft to 450ft across. In addition to a cannon, it once harbored a Russian Orthodox chapel. Apart from impressive walls, some 20ft high, there is little else to see nowadays. There's a pretty beach here. It's by the riverfront so it isn't great for swimming, but it makes for a pleasant afternoon stroll.

Waimea Hawaiian Church   Church

(4491 Halepule Rd; ☺services 9am Sun) This simple low-slung replica of an original missionary church hosts a Sunday Hawaiian-language mass that can be a fun and interesting way to connect with local culture. History buffs will be interested to know that the first Christian missionaries came to Waimea in 1820. The original church was built here by the Reverend George Rowell in 1865 after a theological dispute with his missionary partner.

✪ ACTIVITIES

Taking Na Pali Coast tours that start from Kekaha's Kikiaola Small Boat Harbor (instead of Port Allen near Hanapepe) means the journey isn't as rough.

Na Pali Riders   Boating

(☎808-742-6331; www.napaliriders.com; 9600 Kaumuali'i Hwy; 4hr tour adult/child 5-12yr $1559/119) Get a firsthand peek at sea caves (weather permitting) with Captain Chris Turner, who likes to think of his Zodiac raft tour as being 'National Geographic' in style (read: he likes to travel fast, blare Led Zeppelin and talk story). Warning: the no-shade, bumpy ride isn't for the faint of heart. Morning and afternoon departures available. Cash discounts.

Alaka'i Swamp

Nothing provides an out-of-the-ordinary hiking experience the way Alaka'i Swamp does. Designated a wilderness preserve in 1964, this soggy paradise has a hiking trail that is almost completely lined with wooden planks, mainly to discourage off-trail trekking. Nevertheless, you'll traverse truly fantastic terrain on this hike, including misty bogs with knee-high trees and tiny, carnivorous plants. On a clear day, you'll get outstanding views of the Wainiha Valley and the distant ocean from Kilohana Lookout. If it's raining, don't fret: search for rainbows and soak up the eerie atmosphere. Queen Emma was said to have been so moved by tales from this spiritual place that she sojourned here while chanting in reverence.

The swamp has its own unique biological rhythms and there are far more endemic birds than introduced species here – elsewhere in Hawaii the opposite is true. Many of these avian species are endangered, some with fewer than 100 birds remaining today.

Scrub jay

Na Pali Explorer   Boating

(☎303-338-9999; www.napaliexplorer.com; 9814 Kaumuali'i Hwy; raft tour adult/child $139/119, tour with beach landing $149/129) This Westside shop does it right, with small raft tours. You can choose to beach and hike up to a little village, or go for the rip-roaring experience aboard a rigid-hull inflatable boat. The larger raft has a canopy. Bring a towel to dry off after snorkeling.

Hike Kaua'i Adventures — Hiking
(☏808-639-9709; www.hikekauaiadventures. com; half-/full day up to 4 people $200/320) Longtime resident Jeffrey Courson leads guests on bespoke hiking adventures all over the island. He's hiked every trail on Kaua'i and will tailor an ideal hiking itinerary to meet your needs. He leads with knowledge of the flora and fauna and the island's deep history, and he includes door-to-door service too. You'll have a blast with Jeffrey.

Big Island Bike Tours — Cycling
(☏800-331-0159; www.bigislandbiketours. com; tours from $160; 🚲) Established by an experienced pro cyclist, this company offers various group rides, including two in the Honoka'a area. Both start in Waimea, where the company is based; one goes to the Waipi'o Valley Lookout, while the other ascends into Pa'auilo and the Hawaiian Vanilla Company.

Waimea Rivermouth — Surfing
This river break takes you both right and left. Southern swells work best here. Expect it to be crowded. And being a river break, expect the water to be dirty.

🛍 SHOPPING

Kaua'i Granola — Food
(☏808-338-0121; 9633 Kaumuali'i Hwy; ⊙10am-5pm Mon-Sat) Before you head up to Waimea Canyon and Koke'e State Parks, drop by this island bakery for snacks such as trail mix, macadamia-nut cookies, chocolate-dipped coconut macaroons and tropically flavored granola.

Aunty Lilikoi Passion Fruit Products — Food, Gifts
(☏808-338-1296, 866-545-4564; www. auntylilikoi.com; 9875 Waimea Rd; ⊙10am-6pm) Find something for almost any occasion: award-winning passion fruit–wasabi mustard, passion-fruit syrup (great for banana pancakes), massage oil (the choice for honeymooners) and a tasty lip balm (ideal for après surf), all made with at least a kiss of, you guessed it, *liliko'i* (passion fruit).

Fresh mango

MATT MUNRO/LONELY PLANET ©

⊗ EATING

This is probably the best culinary selection on the Westside. Places close early.

Ishihara Market   Supermarket, Deli **$**
(☏808-338-1751; 9894 Kaumualiʻi Hwy; ⊙6am-7:30pm Mon-Thu, to 8pm Fri & Sat, to 7pm Sun) It's an ad-hoc lesson in local cuisine shopping at this historic market (c 1934) with deli. Trusty takeout meals (get here before the lunch rush) include sushi, spicy ahi *poke* and smoked marlin. Daily specials and marinated ready-to-go meats are available for those wanting to barbecue. The parking lot is often full – it's that popular.

Yumi's   Diner **$**
(☏808-338-1731; 9691 Kaumualiʻi Hwy; mains $5-10; ⊙7:30am-2:30pm Tue-Thu, 7am-1pm & 6-8pm Fri, 8am-1pm Sat) 'Friendly, filling and reasonably priced' sums up this local institution, where you can get a plate lunch with some chicken katsu or teriyaki beef, a burger, a mini *loco moco* or a special bowl of saimin (local-style noodle soup). Be sure to order a slice of coconut pie or the pumpkin crunch for dessert.

G's Juicebar   Health Food **$**
(☏808-634-4112; 9691 Kaumualiʻi Hwy; snacks from $7; ⊙7am-6pm Mon-Fri, 9am-5pm Sat) Your quest for Kauaʻi's top acai bowl might reach the finish line inside this Rastafarian stronghold. A Marley bowl comes with kale and bee pollen; the Kauai Bowl is with mango juice and shaved coconut. Fresh tropical juice smoothies and yerba mate tea will quench your thirst.

**Jo-Jo's Anuenue Shave
Ice & Treats**   Desserts **$**
(9899 Waimea Rd; snacks from $3; ⊙10am-5:30pm; ☖) This shack delivers icy flavor: all syrups are homemade without additives and won't knock you out with sweetness. The superstar item is the *halo halo* (Filipino-style mixed fruit) with coconut.

Waimea Town Celebration

Free fun in Waimea in mid-February includes a *paniolo* (Hawaiian cowboy) rodeo; storytelling; canoe, SUP and surf-skiing races; local food vendors; carnival games; an arts-and-crafts fair; and lei-making and ukulele-playing contests.

Wrangler's Steakhouse   Steak **$$**
(☏808-338-1218; www.innwaimea.com/wranglers.html; 9852 Kaumualiʻi Hwy; mains $10-30; ⊙11am-8:30pm Mon-Thu, 4-9pm Fri & Sat, 4-8:30pm Sun; ☖) Yes, it's touristy, but this Western-style saloon dishes up plantation lunches in authentic *kaukau* (food) tins full of goodies. Sizzling dinner steaks are decent; the seafood and soup-and-salad bar less so. Save room for peach cobbler. There's atmospheric seating on the front lanai or back porch.

⊗ ENTERTAINMENT
Waimea Theater   Cinema
(☏808-338-0282; www.waimeatheater.com; 9691 Kaumualiʻi Hwy; adult/child 5-10yr $8/6) This art-deco movie theater is the place for a rainy day or for an early-evening reprieve from sun and sea. Kauaʻi is a little behind with new releases and schedules are erratic, but since this is one of only two functioning cinemas on the island (the other is in Lihuʻe), no one's complaining.

ⓘ GETTING THERE & AWAY

Waimea is easily reached by rental car. **Kauaʻi Bus** (p119) also services the village.

ⓘ GETTING AROUND

Generally speaking, you are better off with a rental car. Some car-rental agencies do not allow you to drive the road to Polihale or the backroads inland. Bike tours down Waimea Canyon are ridiculously fun.

MOLOKA'I

In this Chapter

Halawa Valley 152
Hiking Kalaupapa Trail 156
Kaunakakai.. 160
Getting There & Around................. 165

Moloka'i at a Glance...

Moloka'i is often cited as the 'most Hawaiian' of the islands, and in terms of bloodlines this is true – more than 50% of the residents are at least part Native Hawaiian.

But whether the idiosyncratic island fits your idea of 'most Hawaiian' depends on your definition. If you're after a place that best celebrates the islands' geography and indigenous culture, then Moloka'i is for you. Ancient Hawaiian sites in the island's beautiful, tropical east are jealously protected and restored, and island-wide consensus eschews development of the often sacred west.

Moloka'i in Two Days

Check out **Kaunakakai** (p160), then drive the gorgeous 27 miles east to the **Halawa Valley** (p152) and hike to the waterfall. Stop at Puko'o for lunch at **Mana'e Goods & Grindz** (p164) then snorkel at **Twenty Mile Beach** (p161). Wander Kaunakakai, gathering fare for dinner under the stars at your rental pad. On your last day let the sure-footed mules carry you to the **Kalaupapa National Historical Park** (p156).

Moloka'i in Four Days

Spend your third day in the ancient rainforests, followed by dinner at **Kualapu'u Cookhouse** (p164). On the morning of day four, stop by Kaunakakai and pick up some island books at **Kalele Bookstore** (p163), then head northwest to the beautiful West End Beaches (p161), before finding the ultimate souvenirs at Maunaloa's **Big Wind Kite Factory** (p163).

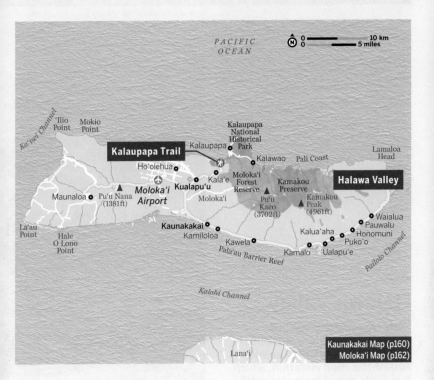

Kalaupapa Trail

Halawa Valley

| Kaunakakai Map (p160) |
| Moloka'i Map (p162) |

Arriving in Moloka'i

The Maui ferry no longer runs.

Moloka'i Airport (p313) is small; single-engine planes are the norm.

Makani Kai Air offers scheduled and charter flights to Kalaupapa and Honolulu.

Mokulele Airlines has frequent services to Honolulu and Maui.

Ohana (p197), the commuter carrier of Hawaiian Airlines, serves Honolulu, Lana'i and Maui from Moloka'i.

Sleeping

Moloka'i's one hotel is in Kaunakakai. Almost everybody stays in a B&B, cottage, condo or house. Good local sources of rental and accommodations information and reservations include www.visitmolokai.com and www. molokai.com. Quality ranges from rustic to swank. The best have private grounds on the ocean. The nicest are usually in the verdant and coastal east. There are no hostels; camping is limited to state and county parks.

View of Halawa Valley and Halawa Beach Park (p154)

Halawa Valley

With stunningly gorgeous scenery, the pristine and deeply spiritual Halawa Valley enjoys end-of-the-road isolation, which residents guard jealously with gates and 'no trespassing' signs.

Moa'ula & Hipuapua Falls

Halawa Stream

Halawa Valley

Halawa Bay

Halawa Beach Park

Kamehameha V Hwy

Great For...

❶ Need to Know

Visiting Moa'ula and Hipuapua Falls requires a guide.

★ Top Tip
Mosquitoes are voracious on the trail.
Use insect repellent.

Halawa Beach Park

Halawa Beach was a favored surfing spot for Moloka'i chiefs and remains so today for local kids, although often you won't see a soul. The beach has double coves separated by a rocky outcrop, with the north side a bit more protected than the south.

When the water is calm, there's good swimming and folks launch sea kayaks here, but both coves are subject to dangerous rip currents when the surf is heavy.

Up from the beach, Halawa Beach Park has picnic pavilions, restrooms and nondrinkable running water. Throughout the valley, there's an eerie feel that you can't quite shake, as if the generations that came before aren't sure what to make of it

all. Some locals aren't entirely welcoming of visitors.

Guides

There are several locals who offer the mandatory guiding services up the valley. Rates are usually around $40 to $75 per person, depending on how long you wish to spend in the valley. You usually meet your guide at the picnic area of **Halawa Beach Park**.

Pilipo Solatario (Halawa Valley Falls Cultural Hike; ☎808-542-1855, 808-551-1055; www. halawavalleymolokai.com; adult/child $60/35; ⊙hikes most days 9am) is a highly recommended guide who has lived most of his life in the valley along with his family. He's an amazing storyteller and he regales guests

Halawa Valley community church

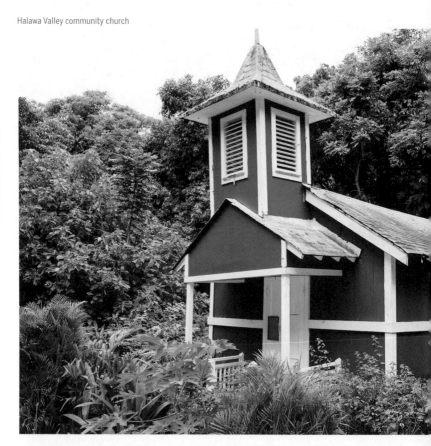

with fascinating details of local culture. The actual hike is usually led by his son.

Eddie Tanaka (☎808-658-0191, 808-558-8396; edward.tanaka@yahoo.com; hikes from $60) is a local musician and lifelong native. He'll customize a hike up Halawa Valley – make sure to spend extra time on culture and lore.

Halawa Tropical Flower Farm

Owner Pruet runs this **flower farm** (Halawa Flower Farm; www.molokaiflowers.com; PO Box 523, Kaunakakai, HI 96748; ⊙10am-4pm Tue-Fri, Sun by appointment), offers waterfall hikes and makes a mean smoothie from fruit he gathers at this lush spread of land. You can self-tour his colorful gardens or arrange in advance for a waterfall hike. Walk the dirt road in from the church, straight for about

RALF BROSKVAR/SHUTTERSTOCK ©

100ft until you reach the gate. Go around the gate continuing on another 100ft; the farm will be off to the right.

Moaʻula & Hipuapua Falls

The hike and spectacle of the 250ft, twin Moaʻula and Hipuapua Falls, which cascade down the back of the lush Halawa Valley, are a highlight of many people's Molokaʻi visit. They are reached via a straightforward 2-mile trail lined with historical sites. To protect these sites, and because the trail crosses private property, visiting the falls requires a hike with a local guide.

There are numerous cultural sites along the path. You'll pass through lush tropical foliage during the walk. Look for the bright orange blossoms of African tulip trees and the brilliant green of beach heliotrope trees. Among the sights are a burial ground that may date to AD 650 and a seven-tiered stone temple.

Walks can easily take three to five hours. Expect muddy conditions and wear stout shoes so you can navigate over river boulders. Some of the river crossings may be especially perilous. Bring water and lunch and have plenty of sunscreen. Most people thrill to a bracing plunge into the pools at the bottom of the falls. Avoid days when small cruise ships visit Molokaʻi as day-tripping crowds can lessen the experience. Rates are usually around $40 to $75 per person, depending on how long you wish to spend in the valley.

Local Church

Sunday services are still occasionally held in Hawaiian at the saintly little 1948 green-and-white church, where visitors are welcome anytime (the door remains open).

Kayaking

Kayaking from Halawa Beach is a popular way to see the northeastern shore and the world's tallest sea cliffs along the Pali Coast, although the logistics can be intimidating.

Kalaupapa Peninsula *pali*

JOHN ELK/GETTY IMAGES ©

Hiking Kalaupapa Trail

Via a twisting trail down the steep pali (cliff), the world's highest sea cliffs drop to the remote but spectacularly beautiful Kalaupapa Peninsula. Here, Hansen's disease patients were forced into isolation.

Great For...

☑ **Don't Miss**

The amazing view of Moloka'i's dramatic Pali Coast from Kalawao.

Overview of Kalaupapa Peninsula

The lush Kalaupapa Peninsula is the most remote part of Hawaii's most isolated island. The only way to reach this verdant peninsula edged with long, white-sand beaches is on a twisting trail down the steep *pali*, the world's highest sea cliffs, or by plane. This remoteness is the reason it was, for more than a century, where Hansen's disease patients were forced into isolation.

From its inception until separation ended in 1969, 8000 patients were forced to come to Kalaupapa. Less than a dozen patients (retrospectively called 'residents') remain. They have chosen to stay in the only home they have ever known and have resisted efforts to move them away. The peninsula has been designated a national historical park and is managed by the Hawaii De-

Mules, Kalalau Peninsula

partment of Health and the **National Park Service** (📞808-567-6802; www.nps.gov/kala).

Hitting the Trail

The Kalaupapa trailhead is on the east side of Hwy 470, just north of the mule stables, and marked by the Pala'au park sign and parked Kalaupapa employee cars. The 3-mile trail has 26 switchbacks, 1400 steps and drops 1664ft in elevation from start to finish.

It's best to begin hiking by 8am, before the mules start to go down, to avoid walking in fresh dung, though you have no choice on the return trip. Allow an hour and a half to descend comfortably. It can be quite an adventure after a lot of rain, though the rocks keep it from getting impossibly muddy. Many find walking sticks a huge help.

❶ Need to Know

Since visitor numbers are limited each day, you must have a reservation with **Damien Tours** (p158) to explore.

✕ Take a Break

After you climb up the steep trail, order a steak at **Kualapu'u Cookhouse** (p164).

Damien Tours

Everyone who comes to the Kalaupapa Peninsula is required to visit the settlement with **Damien Tours** (☎808-221-2153, 808-567-6171; www.damientoursllc.com; tour $60; ☺Mon-Sat). Reservations must be made in advance (call between 4pm and 8pm). Tours last 3½ hours, are done by bus and are accompanied by lots of stories about life in years past. If you're not on the mule ride or other packaged tours, bring your own lunch and a bottle of water. You must be 16 or over.

Pick-ups for the tours are at 10am, whether you arrive on the peninsula on foot, by mule or on a plane.

Hansen's Disease & the Peninsula

In 1835 doctors in Hawaii diagnosed the state's first case of leprosy, one of many diseases introduced by foreigners. Alarmed by the spread of the disease, King Kamehameha V signed a law that banished people with Hansen's disease to Kalaupapa Peninsula, beginning in 1866.

Hawaiian names for leprosy include *mai pake* (Chinese sickness) and *mai ho'oka'awale*, which means 'separating sickness,' a reference to how the disease tore families apart. Evidence suggests all patients arrived at the peninsula in boats, despite rumors that disease-fearing captains threw patients overboard to swim to land.

Once the afflicted arrived on Kalaupapa Peninsula, there was no way out, not even

Mosaic of Father Damien outside Father Damien Church, Kalaupapa Peninsula National Historic Park

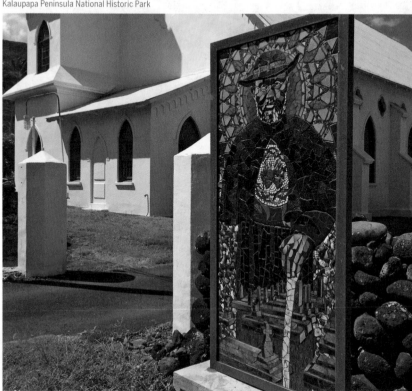

JOHN ELK/GETTY IMAGES ©

in a casket. The original settlement was in Kalawao, at the wetter eastern end of the peninsula. Early conditions were unspeakably horrible, with the strong stealing rations from the weak, and women forced into prostitution. Life spans were invariably short and desperate.

Father Damien arrived at Kalaupapa in 1873. He wasn't the first missionary to come, but he was the first to stay. What Damien provided, most of all, was a sense of hope and inspiration to others.

The same year that Father Damien arrived, a Norwegian scientist named Dr Gerhard Hansen discovered *Mycobacterium leprae,* the bacteria that causes leprosy. Hansen's disease is one of the least contagious of all communicable diseases: only 4% of human beings are even susceptible to it.

Since 1946 sulfa antibiotics have successfully treated and controlled leprosy, but the isolation policies in Kalaupapa were not abandoned until 1969, when there were 300 patients here. The last arrived in 1965 and today the few remaining residents are all in their late seventies or older.

While the state of Hawaii officially uses the term 'Hansen's disease' for leprosy, many Kalaupapa residents consider that to be a euphemism that fails to reflect the stigma they have suffered, and continue to use the old term 'leprosy.' The degrading appellation 'leper,' however, is offensive to all. 'Resident' is preferred.

★ Top Tip
Stash a container of water behind rocks at the numbered switchbacks to drink on your return.

View from Kalaupapa Lookout

NORINORI303/SHUTTERSTOCK ©

Kaunakakai

◎ SIGHTS

View a photo of Moloka'i's main town from 50 years ago and the main drag won't look much different than it does today. Worn wood-fronted buildings with tin roofs that roar in the rain seem like refugees from a Clint Eastwood western. But there's no artifice to Kaunakakai – it's the real deal. All of the island's commercial activities are here and you'll visit often – if nothing else, for its shops and services. If possible, stop by on Saturday morning when the street market draws crowds.

Kapua'iwa Coconut Grove   Historic Site

(Maunaloa Hwy) As Moloka'i was the favorite island playground of King Kamehameha V, he had the royal 10-acre Kapua'iwa Coconut Grove planted near his sacred bathing pools in the 1860s. Standing tall, about a mile west of downtown, its name means 'mysterious taboo.' Be careful where you walk (or park) when you visit, because coconuts frequently plunge silently to the ground, landing with a deadly thump.

Kaunakakai Wharf   Port

(Kaunakakai Pl) The busy commercial lifeline for Moloka'i. OK, it's not that busy... A freight barge chugs in, skippers unload catches of mahimahi (white-fleshed fish also called 'dolphin') and a buff gal practices for a canoe race. A roped-off area with a floating dock provides a kids' swim area.

One Ali'i Beach Park   Park

(Maunaloa Hwy) Three miles east of town, this park is split into two parks. One side has a coconut-palm-lined shore, a playing field, a picnic pavilion and bathrooms, and although not especially attractive, it's very popular with local families for huge weekend BBQs. The other side is a greener and more attractive picnic area. The water is shallow and silty.

Two memorials commemorate the 19th-century immigration of Japanese citizens to Hawaii.

Kapua'iwa Coconut Grove

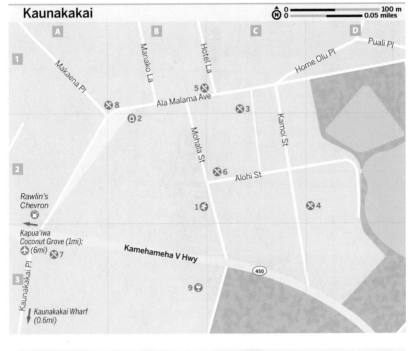

Kaunakakai

🟢 Activities, Courses & Tours
1 Moloka'i Bicycle B2

🟤 Shopping
2 Kalele Bookstore & Divine Expressions....B2

⬛ Eating
3 Friendly Market..C1

4 Kamo'i Snack-N-Go D2
5 Kanemitsu Bakery...B1
6 Maka's Korner C2
7 Moloka'i Burger A3
8 Ono Fish N' Shrimp......................................B1

🟢 Drinking & Nightlife
9 Paddler's Inn B3

🟢 ACTIVITIES

Moloka'i has wild ocean waters, rough trails, remote rainforests and the most dramatic oceanside cliffs in Hawaii. It's perfect for adventure – just don't expect to be spoon-fed.

Sea conditions are seasonal. During the summer you'll find waters are calm on the north and west shores, and made rough by the persistent trade winds on the south shore outside of the Pala'au Barrier Reef. Get out early, before the winds pick up. Winter storms make waters rough

all around the island (outside of the reef, which runs the length of the south side of the island) but, even so, the calm days between winter storms can be the best times to get out on the water.

Moloka'i has plenty of wind – advanced windsurfers can harness it in the Pailolo and Ka'iwi Channels; however, you'll need your own gear.

While activities in Kaunakakai proper are limited, it is a good place to arrange island activities. Among the activities operators and outfitters, there are three who pretty

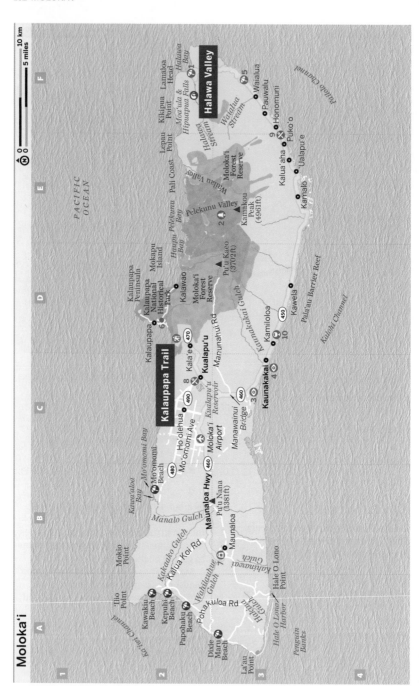

Moloka'i

Kalaupapa Trail

Halawa Valley

PACIFIC OCEAN

Ka'iwi Channel

Mokio Point

Ilio Point

Kawakiu Beach

Kepuhi Beach

Papohaku Beach

Dixie Maru Beach

La'au Point

Penguin Banks

Hale O Lono Harbor

Hale O Lono Point

Ilikipu Gulch

Wahihaunue Gulch

Pohakuloa Rd

Kolo Point

Kahinawai Gulch

Maunaloa

Maunaloa Hwy

Pu'u Nana (1381ft)

Manalo Gulch

Kaka'ako Gulch

Kalua Koi Rd

Mo'omomi Bay

Mo'omomi Beach

Kawa'aloa Bay

480

Ho'olehua

Mo'omomi Ave

490

Moloka'i Airport

460

Manawainui Bridge

Kualapu'u Reservoir

Kualapu'u

460

Kaunakakai

460

3

4

Kamiloloa

450

10

Kawela

Kaunakakai Gulch

Kaunakakai Gulch

Palā'au Channel

Palā'au Barrier Reef

Kaloko Channel

Kalaupapa

Kalaupapa Peninsula

Kalaupapa National Historical Park

Mokapu Island

Kalawao

Moloka'i Forest Reserve

Kala'e

470

Kualapu'u

Manunahui Rd

8

6

5

Pu'u Kaeo (3702ft)

Pelekunu Valley

2

Kamakou Peak (4961ft)

Moloka'i Forest Reserve

Haupu Bay

Pelekunu Bay

Wailau Valley

Pali Coast

Lepau Point

Halawa Stream

Watawa Stream

Kikipua Point

Lamaloa Head

Moa'ula & Hipuapua Falls

Halawa Bay

1

5

Waialua

Pauwalu

Honomuni

9

Puko'o

Kalua'aha

Ualapu'e

Kamalo

Waialua Channel

Palā'au Channel

5 miles

10 km

N

Moloka'i

◎ Sights
1 Halawa Beach Park.......................................F2
2 Kamakou Preserve E3
3 Kapua'iwa Coconut
   Grove C3
4 Kaunakakai Wharf.......................................C3
5 Twenty Mile Beach F3

◎ Activities, Courses & Tours
6 Damien Tours...D2

◎ Shopping
7 Big Wind Kite Factory &
   Plantation Gallery...................................B3

◎ Eating
8 Kualapu'u Cookhouse C2
9 Mana'e Goods & Grindz E3

◎ Drinking & Nightlife
10 Hale Kealoha...D3

much handle every activity on the island and at times loosely work together.

Moloka'i Bicycle   Cycling

(☎808-553-5740; www.mauimolokaibicycle.com; 80 Mohala St, Kaunakakai; bike rental per day/week from $25/75; ⊗3-6pm Wed, 9am-2pm Sat & by appointment) This shop's owner, Phillip Kikukawa, has a great depth of knowledge about biking across the breadth of the island. He'll do pick-ups and drop-offs outside his opening hours. As well as offering repairs, parts and sales, there is a selection of bikes to rent, including mountain bikes. Prices include helmet, lock, pump and maps.

Moloka'i Ocean
Tours   Boat Tour, Fishing

(☎808-553-3299; www.molokaioceantours.com; whale-watching adult/child $75/60) Offers all types of fishing charters plus coastal tours, whale-watching and snorkeling trips.

Moloka'i Outdoors   Outdoors

(☎877-553-4477, 808-553-4477; www.molokai-outdoors.com; SUP/kayak tour adult/child from $68/35, 7-8hr island tour $166/87; ⊗hours vary) Moloka'i Outdoors can custom-design adventures and arrange activities. Paddling and SUPs are its specialty and it can also arrange tours across the island. Kayak and SUP rentals (from $42 per day) can also include transport and pick-ups across the island (from $35).

Walter Naki   Cultural Tour, Boat Tour

(Molokai Action Adventures; ☎808-558-8184) Walter Naki, who is also known for his cultural tours and treks, offers deep-sea

fishing, whale-watching and highly recommended North Shore boat tours that include the Pali Coast.

◎ SHOPPING

Kalele Bookstore & Divine
Expressions   Books

(☎808-553-5112; http://molokaispirit.com; 64 Ala Malama Ave; ⊗10am-5pm Mon-Fri, 9am-2pm Sat; ⊛) New and used books, local artworks and loads of local culture and travel advice. Few locals walk past without dropping in to say hi.

Big Wind Kite Factory & Plantation
Gallery   Arts & Crafts

(☎808-552-2364; www.bigwindkites.com; 120 Maunaloa Hwy; ⊗10am-4pm Mon-Sat, 1-4pm Sun) Big Wind custom-makes kites for high fliers of all ages. It has hundreds ready to go in stock or you can choose a design and watch production begin. Lessons are

---

Snorkeling Twenty Mile Beach

Snorkeling is fantastic at Twenty Mile Beach on Hwy 450 near Waialua in East Moloka'i. Well protected by a reef, the curve of fine sand fronts a large lagoon. Near shore there are rocks and the water can be very shallow, but work your way out and you'll be rewarded with schools of fish, living sponges, octopuses and much more.

available, lest you have a Charlie Brown experience with a kite-eating tree.

There is a range of other goods to browse as well, including an excellent selection of Hawaii-themed books and artworks, clothing and crafts originating from everywhere, from just down the road to far-off Bali.

🍴 EATING

The Saturday morning market along Ala Malama Ave is a good source for local produce and prepared foods.

Maka's Korner   Cafe $
(☏808-553-8058; cnr Mohala & Alohi Sts; meals $5-10; ☺7am-9pm Mon-Fri, 8am-1pm Sat & Sun) A dead-simple corner location belies the fine yet basic fare here. Molokaʻi's best burgers come with excellent fries, although many patrons are simply addicted to the mahimahi sandwich (go nuts and order it dressed with two shrimp tempura). Pancakes are served throughout the day. Sit at the tiny counter or at a picnic table outside.

Manaʻe Goods & Grindz Hawaiian $
(☏808-558-8186; Hwy 450; meals $5-13; ☺kitchen 6:30am-4pm daily, store 6:30am-6pm Mon-Fri, to 4pm Sat & Sun; 📶) Even if it wasn't your only option, you'd still want to stop here. The plate lunches are something of

---

🍞 Hot Bread

Every night but Monday, slip down the alley to **Kanemitsu Bakery's** (☏808-553-5855; 79 Ala Malama Ave; loaf of bread $5; ☺5:30am-5pm Wed-Mon, hot bread 7:30am-11pm Tue-Sun) back door after dark and join the locals buying the seductively sweet and tasty hot loaves of bread ($7). The taciturn baker will split open your loaf and slather one of five spreads that include creme cheese and strawberry spreads. Show your real inside knowledge and ask for a fresh glazed doughnut.

---

a local legend: tender yet crispy chicken katsu (deep-fried fillets), specials such as pork stew, and standards such as excellent teriyaki burgers and fresh fish sandwiches served on perfectly grilled buns.

Kualapuʻu Cookhouse Hawaiian $$
(Kamuela Cookhouse; ☏808-567-9655; Hwy 490; mains $6-33; ☺7am-8pm Tue-Sat, 9am-2pm Sun, 7am-2pm Mon) This old roadhouse serves good lunches and is the only place for a meal west of Kaunakakai. Breakfasts feature huge omelets while plate-lunch options include excellent pork *tonkatsu* (breaded and fried cutlets). The dinner menu is more ambitious and includes ribs, steak and spicy crusted ahi (yellowfin tuna). Beer and wine can be purchased at the grocery across the street. Service is endearing. Cash only.

Ono Fish N' Shrimp   Seafood $
(☏808-553-8187; 53 Ala Malama Ave; lunches $10-12; ☺10am-2pm Wed-Sat) The best addition to the local food scene in a while, this gleaming white food truck offers up seafood tacos and shrimp plates. The preparations are creative and the fish uber fresh. End your meal with fresh mini-donuts. There's a seating area with picnic tables.

Molokaʻi Burger   Burgers $
(☏808-553-3533; www.molokaiburger.com; 20 Kamehameha V Hwy; mains $5-10; ☺7am-9pm; 📶) Molokaʻi's only drive-through restaurant is a slick operation. The burgers come in many forms but are all thick and juicy. (Try a ramen burger, which is sandwiched between squares of fried noodles.) The dining room is inoffensive; the front terrace peacefully shady. Soft serve ice cream is a treat.

Friendly Market   Supermarket $
(☏808-553-5595; 90 Ala Malama Ave; ☺8:30am-8:30pm Mon-Fri, to 6:30pm Sat) The best selection of any supermarket on the island. In the afternoon, fresh seafood from the wharf often appears.

Kamoʻi Snack-N-Go   Desserts $
(28 Kamoi St, Molokaʻi Professional Bldg; ice-cream scoops $2; ☺10am-9pm Mon-Sat,

Sea cliffs along the Moloka'i coastline

noon-9pm Sun; 🛜) This candy store is loaded with sweets and, more importantly, Honolulu-made Dave's Hawaiian Ice Cream. The banana fudge is truly a treat. Ube (purple yam) flavor is subtle and the ice cream is a beautiful purple color.

🍸 DRINKING & NIGHTLIFE

Bring games, books and a gift for gab as nighttime fun is mostly DIY on Moloka'i.

Hale Kealoha   Lounge
(📞808-553-5347; Kamehameha V Hwy, Hotel Moloka'i; mains $15-25; ⊙7am-9pm) The Hotel Moloka'i's simple waterfront bar and restaurant has waterfront views and skippable food. However, the don't-miss highlight is the local *kupuna* (elders) who gather at a long table to play Hawaiian music on 'Aloha Fridays' from 4pm to 6pm. The music always draws a crowd; the performers range from those with some languid and traditional hula moves to jam sessions with a ukulele.

It's a true community gathering with some of the people who are the heart and soul of

local culture and who delight in showing off their traditional talents. Don't miss it.

❶ GETTING THERE & AWAY

Renting a car is essential for exploring the island or if you are renting a house or condo and will need to shop. Moloka'i's highways and primary routes are good, paved roads. The free tourist map, widely available on the island, is useful. James A Bier's *Map of Moloka'i & Lana'i* ($6) has an excellent index.

A taxi from the airport costs around $30 to Kaunakakai. Many accommodations can arrange transfers.

❶ GETTING AROUND

Kaunakakai is a walking town. **Rawlin's Chevron** (cnr Maunaloa Hwy/Hwy 460 & Ala Malama Ave; ⊙office 6:30am-8:30pm Mon-Sat, 7am-6pm Sun) has credit-card-operated pumps, making it the only round-the-clock gas station on the island.

ROAD TO HANA

In this Chapter

Pi'ilanihale Heiau 170
Pi'ilani Trail 174
Ke'anae Peninsula 176
Waterfalls & Swimming Holes 178
Hana 180
Getting There & Away 185

Road to Hana at a Glance...

There's a sense of suspense you just can't shake while driving the Road to Hana, a serpentine road lined with tumbling waterfalls, lush slopes, and rugged coasts – and serious hairpin turns. Spanning the northeast shore of Maui, the legendary Hana Hwy ribbons tightly between jungle valleys, towering cliffs and powerful waterfalls. The drive is ravishingly gorgeous, but certainly not easy. As for rental cars, Jeeps and Mustangs are the ride of choice.

Road to Hana in One Day

Grab coffee early at **Huelo Lookout fruit stand**, then look for **Honomanu Bay**. Next, climb to **Wailua Valley State Wayside** (p182) for a mountain-to-sea view. Continue to **Three Bears Falls** (p179), the best in a magnificent run of roadside cascades. Slip into Hana for lunch at **Thai Food by Pranee** (p183). Visit **Pi'ilanihale Heiau** (p170) and **Kahanu Garden** (p172), the largest heiau (temple) in Polynesia. Overnight in Hana.

Road to Hana in Two Days

On day two, explore the underground wonders of the **Hana Lava Tube** (p173 then drive to Wai'anapanapa State Park to see its beautiful black-sand beach and to walk in the footsteps of early Hawaiians on the ancient coastal **Pi'ilani Trail** (p174), which leads across a high shelf of lava with wild coastal vistas. On weekends, end with a pizza from **Hana Farms Clay Oven Pizza** (p185).

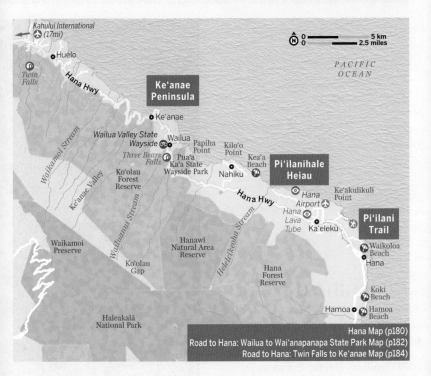

Kahului International
✈ (17mi)

Huelo

Twin
Falls

Hana Hwy

**Ke'anae
Peninsula**

Ke'anae

PACIFIC
OCEAN

0 ————— 5 km
Ⓝ 0 ————— 2.5 miles

Waikamoi Stream

Wailua Valley State
Wayside

Wailua

Three Bears
Falls

Papiha
Point

Pua'a
Ka'a State
Wayside Park

Kilo'o
Point

Kea'a
Beach

Ko'olau
Forest
Reserve

Nahiku

**Pi'ilanihale
Heiau**

Ke'akulikuli
Point

Ke'anae Valley

Waikamoi
Preserve

Waikamoi Stream

Ko'olau
Gap

Hanawi
Natural Area
Reserve

Hana Hwy

Heleleikeoha Stream

Hana
Airport ✈

Hana
Lava
Tube

Ka'eleku

Hana
Forest
Reserve

**Pi'ilani
Trail**

Waikoloa
Beach
Hana

Koki
Beach

Haleakalā
National Park

Hamoa

Hamoa
Beach

Hana Map (p180)
Road to Hana: Wailua to Wai'anapanapa State Park Map (p182)
Road to Hana: Twin Falls to Ke'anae Map (p184)

Arriving at the Road to Hana

To drive the Road to Hana at your own pace, rent a car. The drive kicks off on the eastern fringe of Haiku, near Huelo, 20 miles east of **Kahului International Airport** (p313).

Note that at the 16-mile marker on Hwy 36, the Hana Hwy becomes Hwy 360 and the mile markers begin again at zero.

Sleeping

In and around Hana you'll find resort-style hotels, condo units and a range of cottages and rooms. Many rentals have two- or three-night minimum stays, but you may be able to snag a one-night spot if it falls between longer stays, or is available at the last minute. There are campgrounds in Ke'anae and **Wai'anapanapa State Park** (p173).

Piʻilanihale Heiau

The most significant stop on the entire Road to Hana, this site combines a 294-acre ethnobotanical garden with the magnificent Piʻilanihale Heiau, the largest temple in all of Polynesia.

Great For...

❶ Need to Know

📞808-248-8912; www.ntbg.org; 650 ʻUlaʻino Rd; adult/child under 13yr $10/free, guided tour $25/free; ⊘9am-4pm Mon-Fri, 9am-2pm Sat, tours Mon-Fri; P⛾

RON DAHLQUIST/GETTY IMAGES ©

☑ **Don't Miss**

A must-do tour provides fascinating details into the extraordinary relationship between the ancient Hawaiians and their environment.

Touring the heiau is perhaps the best opportunity in all of Hawaii to really understand what traditional Hawaiian culture was like prior to contact with the West. Amazingly, very few people visit.

The History

Pi'ilanihale Heiau is an immense lava stone platform with a length of 450ft. The history of this astounding temple is shrouded in mystery, but there's no doubt that it was an important religious site. Archaeologists believe construction began as early as AD 1200 and continued in phases. The grand finale was the work of Pi'ilani (the heiau's name means House of Pi'ilani), the 14th-century Maui chief who is also credited with the construction of many of the coastal fishponds in the Hana area.

Kahanu Garden

The temple occupies one corner of Kahanu Garden, near the sea. An outpost of the National Tropical Botanical Garden, Kahanu Garden contains the largest collection of breadfruit species in the world, with over 120 varieties. Breadfruit is significant because its nutritional value makes it a dietary pillar, and hence a weapon to combat global hunger. The garden also contains a living catalog of so-called canoe plants, those essentials of traditional life brought to Hawaii in the canoes of Polynesian voyagers, along with a hand-crafted canoe house that is another step back in time.

Guided Tour

The best way to unlock the relationship between the heiau, the plants and their

Breadfruit in the Kahanu Garden

beautiful, park-like surroundings, where palms sway in the breeze, is to take a guided tour. These are given Monday through Friday at noon or 1pm and last two hours. Reserve by phone or by emailing kahanu@ ntbg.org beforehand. The only other option is a self-guided tour by brochure. The site is located 1.5 miles down 'Ula'ino Rd from the Hana Hwy.

Hana Lava Tube

One of the odder sights on the Road to Hana, this mammoth cave was formed by ancient lava flows. It once served as a slaughterhouse – 17,000lb of cow bones had to be removed before it was opened to visitors!

Winding your way through the extensive cave, which reaches heights of up to 40ft, you'll find a unique ecosystem of dripping stalactites and stalagmites. The journey is well signed, takes about 45 minutes, and is a perfect rainy-day activity. Admission includes flashlights and hard hats. If you want to lose the kids, an adjoining botanical maze made from red *ti* plants is no extra charge beyond the ticket price. Hana Lava Tube is half a mile from the Hana Hwy, and it's easy to visit it in the same day as the heiau and garden.

Wai'anapanapa State Park

Wai'anapanapa means 'glistening waters', and the clear mineral waters in the cave pools here will leave you feeling squeaky clean. There's a natural lava arch on the right side of Pailoa Bay, bordered by low rocky cliffs and a coastal trail with ancient lava stepping stones. Two impressive lava-tube caves are just a five-minute walk from the parking lot.

> ✕ **Take a Break**
>
> Savor a scoop of chili chocolate ice cream from **Coconut Glen's** (☎808-979-1168; www.coconutglens.com; Hana Hwy, Mile 27.5; scoop of ice cream $7; ⊙10:30am-5:30pm; ⌖) ✿, served in a coconut.

2P2PLAY/SHUTTERSTOCK ©

Kahanu Garden contains the largest collection of breadfruit species in the world

Monk seal on the Pi'ilani coastline

STEVE OEHLENSCHLAGER/SHUTTERSTOCK ©

Pi'ilani Trail

This gem of a coastal trail – dating back centuries – offers a private, reflective walk on top of a raw lava field several yards above the sea, with refreshing views.

Great For...

☑ **Don't Miss**

The black-sand beach in **Wai'anapana- pa State Park**.

The History

Over 300 years ago, King Pi'ilani (of heiau fame) led the construction of a path around the entire island of Maui in an effort to improve commerce between its far-flung regions. Today the King's Trail, or what's left of it, follows this ancient footpath, with some of the original worn stepping-stones still in use. The trail offers the opportunity to see the island in a unique and unforget- table way: by walking around it. The 200- mile trail skirts the coastline the entire way, providing access to remote areas where traditional Hawaiian life is still practiced.

The Hike

The trail begins along the coast just below the camping area and parallels the ocean along lava sea cliffs. Just a few minutes along you'll pass a burial ground, a natural

ℹ Need to Know

Visit the **Division of State Parks** website for more trail details (http://dlnr.hawaii.gov/dsp/hiking/maui/ke-ala-loa-o-mauipiilani-trail/).

✕ Take a Break

Re-energize with a juicy burger and a lush green view at the **Hana Burger Food Truck** (p185).

★ Top Tip

If you plan to hike the whole trail, bring water.

sea arch and a blowhole that roars to life whenever there's pounding surf. This is also the area where you're most likely to see endangered Hawaiian monk seals basking onshore.

After 0.75 miles you'll view basalt cliffs lined up all the way to Hana, and ironwood encroaching the shoreline. Round stones continue to mark the way across lava and a grassy clearing, fading briefly on the way over a rugged sea cliff. A dirt road comes in from the right as the trail arrives at Luahaloa, a ledge with a small fishing shack. Inland, stands of ironwood heighten the beauty of the scenic last mile of clifftop walking to Kainalimu Bay. Stepping-stones hasten the approach to the bay ahead, as the trail dips down a shrubby ravine to a quiet, black-cobble beach. Dirt roads lead another mile from here south to Hana.

Alternatively, walk inland to the asphalt road, and walk or hitch back to Wai'anapanapa State Park.

Trip Planning

The trail leads 3 miles south from Wai'anapanapa State Park to Kainalimu Bay, just north of Hana Bay. The hike packs a lot up front, so even if you just have time for the first mile, you won't regret it. In spots, the loose gravel path skirts sheer, potentially fatal drops into the sea – exercise caution and leave the kids behind. Wear good hiking shoes, as it gets rougher as you go along.

Ke'anae Peninsula coastline

Ke'anae Peninsula

Pull off the highway and stretch your legs for this rare slice of 'Old Hawaii,' home to an 1860s church and a wild lava coast, where families have tended stream-fed taro patches for generations.

Introduction

What awaits at the halfway point on the drive to Hana? Dramatic landscapes and the friendliest seaside village on the route. At the end of the peninsula, Ke'anae Park has a scenic coastline of jagged black lava and hypnotic white-capped waves. Plan to look but not swim – the water is rough and there's no beach. But it's oh-so photogenic.

Ke'anae Congregational Church

Marking the heart of the village is Ke'anae Congregational Church, built in 1860, and entered over the steps of the adjacent cottage. The church is made of lava rocks and coral mortar, uncovered by whitewash. It's a welcoming place with open doors and a guest book. Note the cameo portraits in the adjacent cemetery.

Great For...

☑ **Don't Miss**

A walk past a global collection of tropical trees at nearby **Ke'anae Arboretum** (https://hawaiitrails.org) 🌿.

PACIFIC OCEAN

Ke'anae
Congregational
Church

Ke'anae
Peninsula

Hana Hwy
Ko'olau
Forest
Reserve

Ke'anae

Ke'anae
Arboretum

❶ Need to Know

Access the peninsula by taking Ke'anae Rd on the *makai* (seaward) side of the highway just beyond Ke'anae Arboretum.

✕ Take a Break

Craving beef jerky or ice cream? You're in luck. Continue down the highway to **Halfway to Hana** (www.halfwaytohanamaui.com; 13710 Hana Hwy; lunch mains $7-9; ☺8:30am-4pm).

★ Top Tip

There are public restrooms (open 8am to 7pm) across from the small parking area.

Ke'anae Valley

Starting way up at the Ko'olau Gap in the rim of Haleakalā Crater and stretching down to the coast, Ke'anae Valley radiates green, thanks to the 150in of rainfall each year. At the foot of the valley lies Ke'anae Peninsula, created by a late eruption of Haleakalā that sent lava gushing all the way down Ke'anae Valley and into the ocean. Unlike its rugged surroundings, the volcanic peninsula is perfectly flat, like a leaf floating on the water.

Ke'anae Peninsula

This rare slice of 'Old Hawaii,' home to an 1860s church and a wild lava coast, is reached by taking Ke'anae Rd on the makai (seaward) side of the highway just beyond Ke'anae Arboretum.

Families have tended stream-fed taro patches here for generations.

The rock islets you see off the coast from Ke'anae Park – Mokuhala and Mokumana – are seabird sanctuaries.

Ke'anae Landing Fruit Stand

'Da best' banana bread on the entire Road to Hana is baked fresh every morning by Aunty Sandy and her crew, and is so good you'll find as many locals as tourists pulling up here. You can also get fresh fruit, hotdogs, sandwiches and drinks at this stand, located in the village center just before Ke'anae Park.

Three Bears Falls

MNSTUDIO/SHUTTERSTOCK ©

Waterfalls & Swimming Holes

Along the Road to Hana, 54 one-lane bridges mark nearly as many waterfalls, some tranquil and inviting, others so sheer they kiss you with spray as you drive past.

Great For...

☑ Don't Miss

Get up close and almost personal with a waterfall on an adventure trip with **Rappel Maui** (📞808-270-1500; www.rappelmaui.com; Hana Hwy, 10600 Hana Hwy; $200; ⊘tours 7am, 8am, 10am & 11:30am).

Twin Falls

After the 2-mile marker near the start of the drive, a parking area with a fruit stand marks the trailhead. Local kids and tourists flock to the pool beneath the lower falls, about a 10-minute walk in. If you're traveling with kids or you're up for a short, pleasant hike, this is a good one.

To get to the falls, follow the main trail across a stream. Turn left at the trail junction just ahead. Continue a short distance then climb over the aqueduct. The falls are straight ahead. You will have to do a bit of wading to get there. Turn around if the water is too high. If there's been a recent flash flood, the trail to the upper falls may close.

ⓘ Need to Know

Do not follow trails that cross private property without express permission from the owner.

✕ Take a Break

A handful of casual eateries cluster in the **Nahiku Marketplace**, serving hearty lunch plates.

★ Top Tip

Fill up the tank in Pa'ia or Ha'iku; the next gas station isn't until Hana.

Three Bears Falls

This beauty takes its name from the triple cascade that flows down a steep rockface on the inland side of the road, 0.5 miles past the 19-mile marker. Catch it after a rainstorm and the cascades come together and roar as one mighty waterfall. There's limited parking up the hill to the left after the falls. You can scramble down to the falls via a steep ill-defined path that begins on the Hana side of the bridge. The stones are moss-covered and slippery.

Pua'a Ka'a State Wayside Park

The name of this delightful park means Rolling Pig. Cross the highway from the parking area and head inland to a pair of delicious waterfalls cascading into pools.

The park is 0.5 miles after the 22-mile marker.

The best for swimming is the upper pool, visible just beyond the picnic tables. To reach it, cross the stream. Watch for falling rocks beneath the waterfall and for flash floods. To get to the lower falls, which drop into a shallow pool, walk back over the bridge and head upstream.

Wailua Falls

Beyond Hana but before you reach Kipahulu, you'll see orchids growing out of the rocks, and jungles of breadfruit and coconut trees.

Around 0.3 miles after the 45-mile marker, you'll come upon the spectacular Wailua Falls, which plunge a mighty 100ft just beyond the road. There are usually plenty of people lined up snapping photos.

Hana

BEACHES

Hana Bay Beach Park is in downtown Hana. Hamoa Beach and Koki Beach sit alongside photogenic Haneo'o Rd, which loops for 1.5 miles off the Hana Hwy just south of town.

Hamoa Beach   Beach
(Haneo'o Rd; P ⛱) With its clear water, white sand and hala-tree backdrop, this famous crescent is a little gem; author James Michener once called it the only beach in the North Pacific that actually looked as if it belonged in the South Pacific. When the surf's up, surfers and bodyboarders flock here, though beware of rip currents. When it's calm, swimming is good in the cove.

Public access is down the steps just north of the hotel's bus-stop sign; there's parking for seven or eight cars opposite. Facilities include restrooms.

Hana Bay Beach Park   Beach
(808-248-7022; www.co.maui.hi.us/Facilities; 150 Keawe Pl; P ⛱) Croquet by the beach? Why not? Welcome to Hana's version of the town plaza, a bayside park where children splash in the surf, picnickers enjoy the view from the rocky black-sand beach and musicians strum their ukuleles. And others play croquet. When water conditions are very calm, snorkeling and diving are good out past the pier. Currents can be strong, and snorkelers shouldn't venture beyond the headland. Surfers head to **Waikoloa Beach** at the northern end of the bay.

Koki Beach   Beach
(Haneo'o Rd; P) This picturesque tan beach sits at the base of red cliffs with views toward tiny 'Alau Island. Bodysurfing is excellent, as it's shallow for quite a distance, but a rip current has been known to sweep people out to sea if they go too far. Shell-picking is good along tide pools by the edge.

⊙ SIGHTS

Heavenly Hana. Is it paradise at the end of the rainbow or something a little bit different? Due to its history and its isolated location at the end of Hawaii's most famous drive, Hana has a legendary aura. But many travelers are disappointed when they arrive to find a sleepy hamlet, population 1235. But that is only because Hana takes more than an hour or two to understand.

Surprisingly, Hana does not try to maximize its benefit from the many day-trippers who arrive each afternoon. This is one of the most Hawaiian communities in the state, with a timeless rural character, and also home to many transplants willing to trade certain privations for a slow, thoughtful and personal way of life in a beautiful natural setting. Though 'Old Hawaii' is an oft-used cliché, it's hard not to think of Hana in such terms. Slow down, spend a night or two and enjoy it.

Hasegawa
General Store   Historic Site
(808-248-8231; 5165 Hana Hwy; ⊙7am-7pm; P) Need cash? Or maybe some screws? Or how about a bottle of Jim Beam? Or Ben & Jerry's Half-Baked fro yo? The Hasegawa family has operated a general store in Hana since 1910. The narrow aisles inside the tin-roof store are jam-packed with a little bit of everything. And we mean everything, from hardware to produce to tourist brochures. This icon of mom-and-pop shops is always crowded with locals picking up supplies and travelers stopping for snacks and the ATM.

✪ TOURS

Several tour companies run Road to Hana trips, with buses and shuttles pulling over for key waterfalls and other roadside attractions. **Valley Isle Excursions** (808-661-8687; www.tourmaui.com; tours adult/child 2-12yr $148/114), which includes breakfast and lunch on its Road to Hana tours, leaves Hana via the Pi'ilani Hwy, with a final stop at **Maui Wine** (808-878-6058; www.mauiwine.com; 14815 Pi'ilani Hwy; ⊙10am-5:30pm, tours 10:30am & 1:30pm) 🍴.

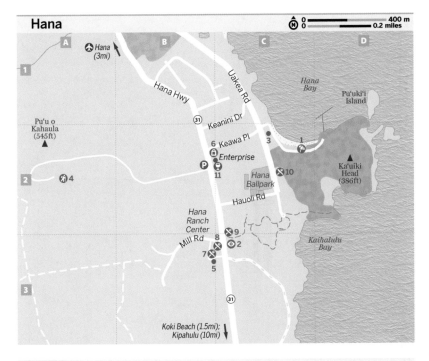

Hana

◎ Sights
1 Hana Bay Beach Park.....................C2
2 Hasegawa General
   Store...C3

✪ Activities, Courses & Tours
3 Hana-Maui Kayak &
   Snorkel......................................C2
4 Pu'u o Kahaula Hill.......................A2
5 Travaasa Hana
   Stables......................................B3

🛍 Shopping
6 Hana Coast Gallery......................B2

✖ Eating
7 Hana Ranch Restaurant.................B3
8 Shaka Pops..................................C3
9 Surfin' Burro................................C2
10 Thai Food by Pranee....................C2

✪ Drinking & Nightlife
11 Preserve Bar................................C2

✪ ACTIVITIES

Travaasa Hana organizes activities, including outrigger canoe trips and stand-up paddleboarding, for its guests. Its horseback riding tours are open to nonguests.

Skyview Soaring   Gliding

(☎808-344-9663; www.skyviewsoaring.com; Hana Airport; 30min/1hr $160/300; ☺by reservation) Haleakalā has excellent soaring conditions, and a sailplane is a unique, rewarding and safe way to see the mountain. After he cuts the engine, experienced pilot Hans Pieters will fly over the crater (weather permitting) and let you fly too, before gliding silently back to Hana Airport.

Call in advance for a reservation, or try your luck and visit the airport. Hans has clearly had his own share of luck, as he is one of the few people to have survived being struck by a propeller.

Road to Hana: Wailua to Wai'anapanapa State Park

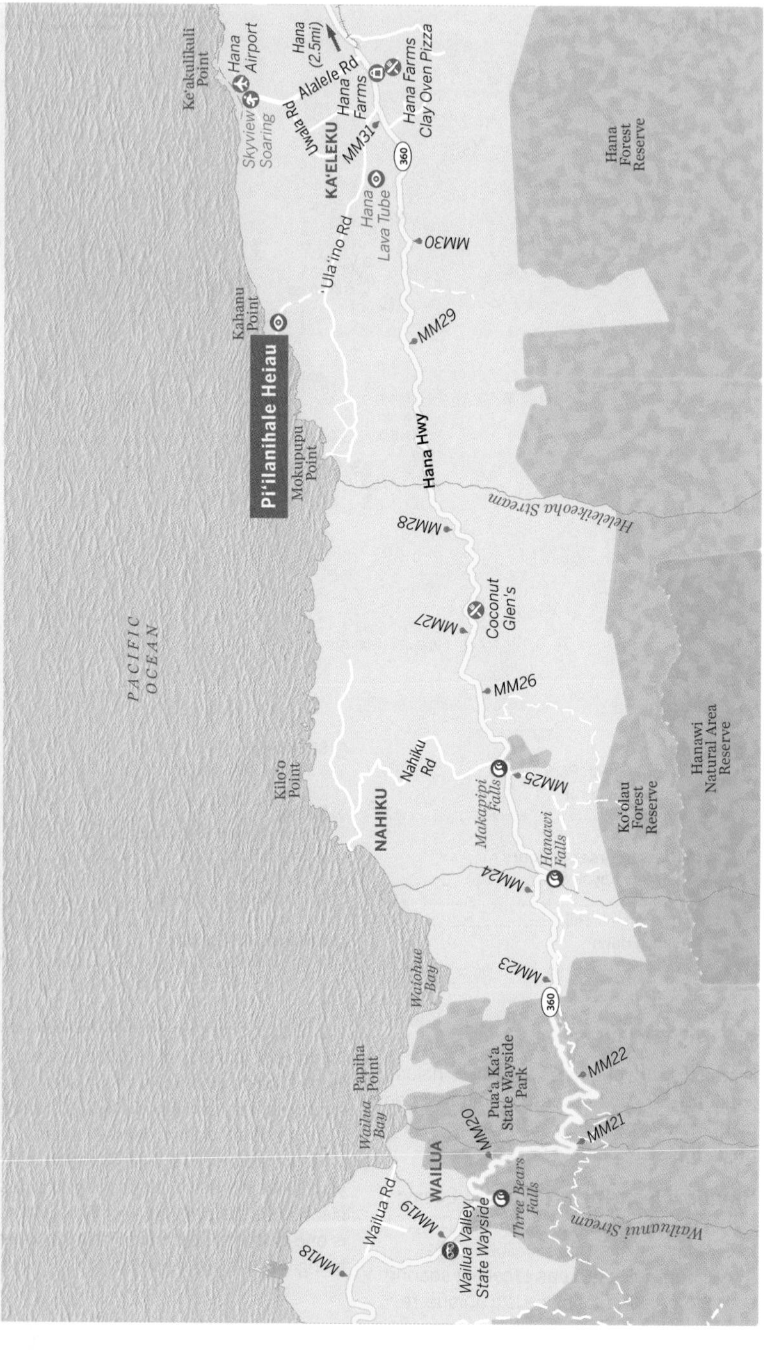

0 ——— 2 km
0 ——— 1 mile

PACIFIC OCEAN

Kerakulikuli Point

Hana Airport

Skyview Soaring

Ka'eleku Rd
Uwala Rd
Alalele Rd
Hana Rd
Hana (2.5mi)

KA'ELEKU

Hana Farms

Hana Farms
Clay Oven Pizza

MM31

360

Hana Lava Tube

Ula'ino Rd

Kahanu Point

Pi'ilanihale Heiau

Mokupupu Point

MM30

MM29

Hana Hwy

Kilo'o Point

MM28

Heleki'ekoa Stream

Coconut Glen's
MM27

MM26

Waiohue Bay

Nahiku Rd

NAHIKU

Makapipi Falls
MM25

Hanawi Falls
MM24

Ko'olau Forest Reserve

Hanawi Natural Area Reserve

Hana Forest Reserve

MM23

360

Papiha Point

Wailua Bay

WAILUA

MM20

Pua'a Ka'a State Wayside Park

MM22

MM21

Wailua Rd

MM19

Three Bears Falls

Wailua Valley State Wayside

MM18

Wailuanu Stream

Pu'u o Kahaula Hill   Hiking

(Lyon's Hill; Hana Hwy) This paved walkway up Pu'u o Kahaula Hill, behind the Travaasa Hana parking lot (take the small gate in the left corner), makes for a fine 30-minute round-trip walk. It leads to Hana's most dominant landmark, a tasteful memorial to former Hana Ranch owner Paul Fagan: like a mountaintop heiau with a huge cross. All of Hana is laid out below. Midway up the walkway you'll see a signed trail going off to your left. This leads to Koki Beach (2 miles).

Hana-Maui Kayak
& Snorkel   Cruise

(☑808-248-7711; www.hanabaykayaks.com; Hana Beach Park; snorkel trip adult/child under 11yr $99/50; 🚸) If you're an inexperienced snorkeler, or want to snorkel out beyond Hana Bay, then Kevin Coates is your man. You'll paddle beyond the pier in Hana Bay and sample the reef before rounding the corner into open sea. Kevin's been doing this since 1995, so has an endless number of stories to keep you entertained.

Travaasa Hana
Stables   Horseback Riding

(☑808-270-5276, reservations 808-359-2401; www.travaasa.com; 1hr ride $60; ⏱tours 9am & 10:30am) Enjoy a gentle trail ride through pastures and along Hana's black-lava coastline. Riders must be at least nine years old. Open to nonguests; book at the front desk.

🅐 SHOPPING

Hana Coast Gallery   Arts & Crafts

(☑808-248-8636; www.hanacoast.com; 5031 Hana Hwy; ⏱9am-5pm) Even if you're not shopping, visit this gallery at the northern side of Travaasa to browse the museum-quality wooden bowls, paintings and Hawaiian featherwork from about 40 different Hawaii artists.

Hana Farms   Food

(www.hanafarmsonline.com; 2910 Hana Hwy; ⏱8am-7pm Sun-Thu, to 8pm Fri & Sat) This small 7-acre farm grows a large variety of tropical fruits, flowers and spices, and

More Tips for Driving the Road to Hana

o Hundreds of cars are making the journey each day. To beat the crowd, get a sunrise start.

o Wear a bathing suit under your clothes so you're ready for impromptu swims.

o Bring shoes that are good for hiking as well as scrambling over slick rocks.

o Pull over to let local drivers pass – they're moving at a different pace.

o The drive can feel a bit rushed at times. Consider spending one or two nights in Hana – you can visit what you missed on the way back the next day.

transforms them into interesting products. Its well-done roadside stand offers banana breads, exotic fruit preserves, tropical hot sauces, island candies, coffee and spices. A great place to find a unique and tasty gift. The ginger lime soda is refreshing.

🅧 EATING

To the frustration of many visitors, there are only two restaurants open for dinner Sunday through Thursday (Travaasa Hana and Hana Ranch, which have the same owner) and both are pricey; the weekend adds the Hana Farms Clay Pizza Oven. Grocery stores are limited and expensive, even by Hawaii standards. So do what the locals do: load up on food in Kahului before coming to Hana.

Thai Food by Pranee   Thai $

(5050 Uakea Rd; meals $10-15; ⏱10:30am-4pm) Hana's ever-popular Thai lunch is served from an oversized mobile food truck surrounded by picnic tables. Step up to the counter for a large and tasty meal, including fiery curries with mahimahi and fresh stir-fried dishes. Get there early for the best selection. Located opposite Hana Ballpark.

Road to Hana: Twin Falls to Ke'anae

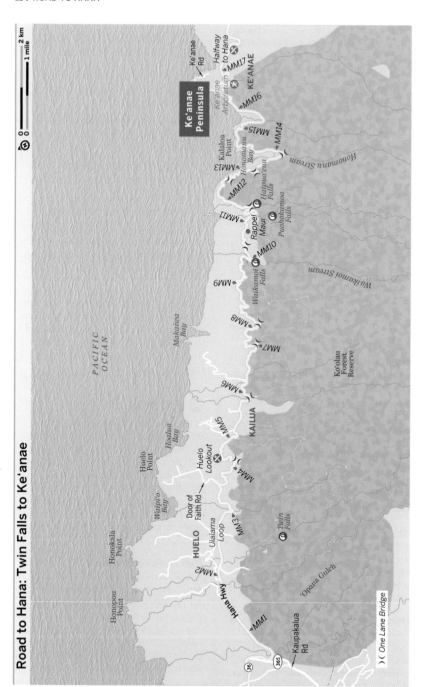

Shaka Pops   Ice Cream $

(www.shakapopsmaui.com; ice pops $4.75;
⊘11am-4pm Sun-Fri) A friendly shaka wave
greets travelers passing this happy cart,
where frozen treats-on-a-stick come in fresh,
tropical flavors. Locally made in small batch-
es, they taste great and are definitely worth
a lick. Look for the cart in front of the Hana
Ranch Center. Life is a little brighter while
slurping a Cocoa Hana Banana popsicle.

Hana Farms Clay
Oven Pizza   Pizza $$

(☎808-248-7553; www.hanafarmsonline.com;
2910 Hana Hwy; pizza $18-20; ⊘4-8pm Fri & Sat)
🍃 Located behind the Hana Farms stand,
this little gem is *the* local choice on Friday
and Saturday nights. Gourmet pizzas with
toppings sourced from the farm emerge from
clay ovens piping hot. Gas lamps light picnic
tables beneath thatched roofs. And the takea-
way pizza box is a folded palm leaf – a Hana
classic. We hear plans are afoot to open up
on more nights. Preorder by phone to avoid
waiting.

Hana Burger Food Truck   Burgers $

(☎808-268-2820; https://hanaranch.com; 5670
Hana Hwy; mains $12-16) What's that flash
of silver on the hill? Surrounded by a gorgeous field of green? If you're driving south
from Hana and you're hungry, the new
burger truck from Hana Ranch might be
the gate to heaven. Grass-fed burgers from
the ranch, picnic tables scattered across a
pasture, and Hamoa Beach down the road.
It doesn't get much better.

Surfin' Burro   Mexican $

(Hana Hwy; mains $4-8; ⊘8am-7pm) Tacos?
In Hana? Yep, and they're darn good too.
Also serves breakfast burritos and fresh-
made salsa. Look for the orange food truck
parked between the Hotel Travaasa and
Hasegawa General Store.

Hana Ranch
Restaurant   American, Hawaiian $$

(☎808-270-5280; Mill St, Hana Ranch Center;
mains $17-32; ⊘11am-8:30pm) The wall of uku-
leles is perfect for an Instagram photo at

this revamped restaurant, one of a handful
of dinner options in Hana. Enjoy the view
of the ocean from inside or from the patio.
Serves American and Hawaiian fare.

And to clear up any confusion – the Hotel
Travaasa owns this restaurant and its name.
The actual Hana Ranch runs the burger
truck down the road, which opened in 2016.

🍷 DRINKING & NIGHTLIFE

Preserve Bar   Bar

(☎808-248-8211; www.travaasa.com; 5031 Hana
Hwy, Travaasa Hana; ⊘restaurant 11:30am-9pm,
bar till later) When it comes to Hana nightlife,
this is the only game in town. Maui beers,
locally inspired cocktails and farm-to-table
bar fare is on offer. Local musicians
perform Sunday, Tuesday and Wednesday
nights, accompanied by hula dancers.
Come when there's live music, otherwise
the vibe can be eerily quiet and slow-paced.

ℹ GETTING THERE & AWAY

There are two ways to get to Hana for an
extended stay: rent a car and drive down the
winding Hana Hwy (two hours from Pa'ia), or
take a 20-minute prop-plane flight from Kahului
to **Hana Airport** (☎808-248-4861; www.hawaii.
gov/hnm; Alalele Pl) with Mokulele Airlines ($70
one way). Flights currently depart daily at 1pm
and 5pm, returning at 1:34pm and 5:35pm.
Passengers' weight cannot exceed 350lb. The
Maui Bus doesn't serve East Maui.

Several tour companies stop in Hana briefly
during their Road to Hana excursions.

Hana closes up early. The sole gas station in
all of East Maui is **Hana Gas** (☎808-248-7671;
cnr Mill Rd & Hana Hwy; ⊘7am-8pm Mon-Sat, to
6pm Sun), so plan accordingly.

ℹ GETTING AROUND

Enterprise (☎808-871-1511; www.enterprise.
com) Travaasa Hana has a very small fleet of cars
available for rent. There is no public bus service
to Hana or anywhere along the Road to Hana.

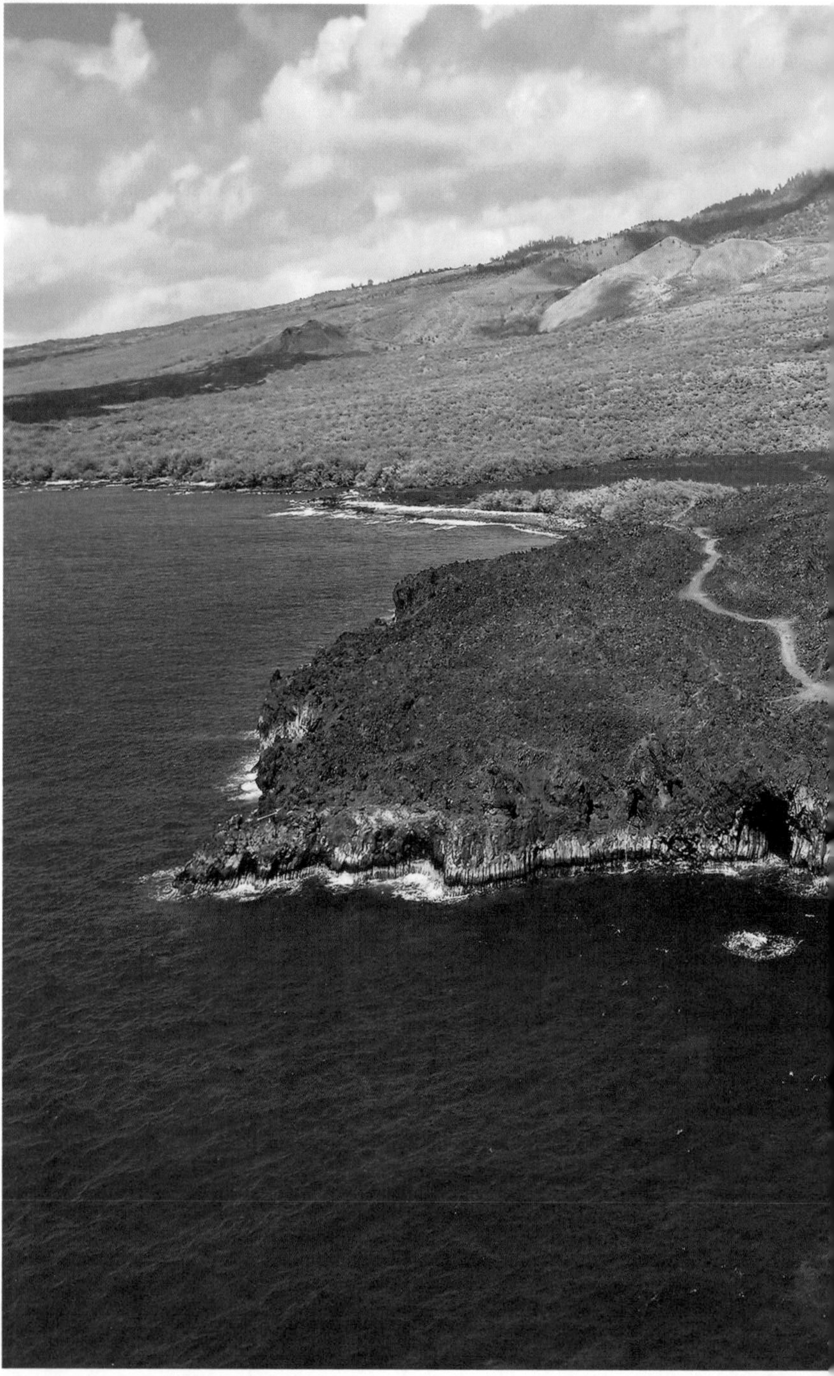

KIHEI & WAILEA

Heapili Trail (p201)

In this Chapter

Whale-Watching.............................. 190
Best Local Food 192
Beaches... 196
Activities 197
Eating 198
Drinking & Nightlife..................... 199
Getting There & Around................. 199

Kihei & Wailea at a Glance...

Sunsets are a communal affair in South Maui – just look at the throngs crowding the beach wall at Kama'ole Beach Park II in the late afternoon. It's a scene repeated up and down the coast here every day. The primary communities here – Kihei and Wailea – look pretty commercial at first glance, but dig deeper and you'll find a mixed plate of scenery and adventure that's truly unique. You can snorkel reefs teeming with turtles, kayak to remote bays or sail in an outrigger canoe. The beaches are undeniably glorious. Add reliably sunny weather, quiet coastal trails and a diverse dining scene, and South Maui's pretty irresistible.

One Day in Kihei & Wailea

The doors open early at **Kihei Caffe** (p198), a good place to fuel up before a morning of snorkeling at **Ulua Beach** (p197). Enjoy fresh fish at **Cafe O'Lei** (p199), then head to **Hawaiian Islands Humpback Whale National Marine Sanctuary Headquarters** (p191) to learn about the leviathans that breed here in winter. Grab a drink at **5 palms** (p202), then watch the sunset at **Ke-awakapu Beach** (p196).

Two Days in Kihei & Wailea

The next morning, kayak on **Makena Bay**, where green sea turtles abound. Grab delicious fresh salad at **Fork & Salad** (p202) then continue south to **La Perouse Bay**, a stunning volcanic landscape dotted with historic structures. Stop at **Big Beach** (p200) for another fine sunset. Enjoy dinner and drinks at **Monkeypod Kitchen** (p199).

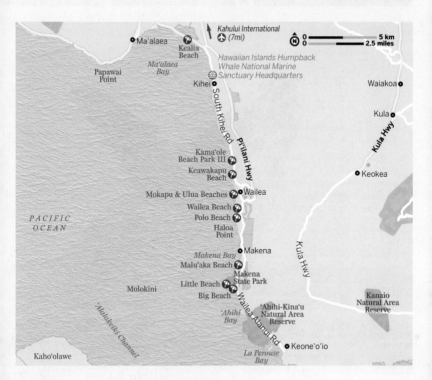

Kahului International ✈ (7mi)

Ma'alaea

Kealia Beach

Ma'alaea Bay

Papawai Point

Hawaiian Islands Humpback Whale National Marine Sanctuary Headquarters

Kihei

Waiakoa

Kula

South Kihei Rd

Pi'ilani Hwy

Kula Hwy

Kama'ole Beach Park III

Keawakapu Beach

Keokea

Mokapu & Ulua Beaches

Wailea

Wailea Beach

Polo Beach

Haloa Point

PACIFIC OCEAN

Makena

Kula Hwy

Makena Bay

Malu'aka Beach

Makena State Park

Molokini

Little Beach

Big Beach

Kanaio Natural Area Reserve

Wailea Alanui Rd

'Ahihi-Kina'u Natural Area Reserve

'Ahihi Bay

'Alalakeiki Channel

Kaho'olawe

La Perouse Bay

Keone'o'io

Arriving in Kihei & Wailea

The airport in Kahului is 10 miles from North Kihei, 16 miles from South Kihei and 18 miles from Wailea. Almost everyone rents a car at the airport. You can expect to pay about $18 to $34 for commercial shuttle service to Kihei, and $24 to $42 to Wailea. It's $30 to $45 for a taxi, depending on your destination in Kihei, and $57 for a taxi to Wailea.

Sleeping

Condos are the most common lodging option in Kihei, and complexes are scattered across the city. A handful of hotels and B&Bs are the only alternative. Wailea is known for its swanky oceanfront resorts, but you'll find a few posh condo developments as well. Wailea also has two hotels, both of them a short drive from the beach.

Humpback whale leaping out of the ocean.

IDREAMPHOTO/SHUTTERSTOCK ©

Whale-Watching

Each winter, about 12,000 graceful humpback whales – two-thirds of the entire North Pacific humpback whale population – come to the shallow coastal waters off the Hawaiian Islands to breed and give birth.

Great For...

☑ **Don't Miss**

The free 45-Ton Talks at 11am on Tuesday and Thursday at Humpback Whale National Marine Sanctuary Headquarters.

Whale Hotspots

With their tail-slaps, head lunges and spy hops, humpback whales sure know how to impress a crowd. The western coastline of the island is their chief birthing and nursing ground. Luckily for whale-watchers, humpbacks are coast-huggers, preferring shallow waters to protect their newborn calves. Along the coast there's great whale-watching at many places, especially the beach walks in Kihei and Wailea.

Hawaiian Islands Humpback Whale National Marine Sanctuary

Congress created the marine sanctuary in 1992 with a mission to protect humpback whales and their habitat. Its efforts have been a success – a majority of humpback whale populations were removed from the

❶ Need to Know

Hawaiian Islands Humpback Whale National Marine Sanctuary Head-quarters (☑808-879-2818; http://hawaii-humpbackwhale.noaa.gov; 726 S Kihei Rd; ⊙10am-3pm Mon-Fri; ᴾ☝) FREE

✕ Take a Break

The salads are fresh, locally grown and organic at Fork & Salad (p198).

★ Top Tip

Maui's peak whale-watching season is from January through March.

Whale-Watching Tours

If you want to get within splashing distance of 40-ton leviathans acrobatically jumping out of the water, take a whale-watching cruise. No one does them better than the **Pacific Whale Foundation** (☑808-249-8811; www.pacificwhale.org; 300 Ma'alaea Rd, Ma'alaea Harbor Shops; cruises adult/child 7-12yr from $35/20; ⊙schedules vary; ☝), a conservation group that takes pride in its green, naturalist-led whale-watching trips.

Trips leave from Ma'alaea Harbor and offer snorkeling lessons and wildlife talks. Snacks are provided and kids under 12 go free on certain cruises. Half-day tours concentrate on Molokini; full-day tours add Lana'i.

endangered species list in September 2016. A moratorium on whaling remains in place, however. The sanctuary extends from the shoreline to ocean depths of 600ft in the waters surrounding the Hawaiian Islands.

The sanctuary's Kihei headquarters is abuzz with cool whale happenings. The oceanfront deck, which sits just north of the ancient Ko'ie'ie Fishpond, is an ideal spot for viewing the humpback whales that frequent the bay during winter. Free scopes are set up for viewing. Inside, displays and videos provide background, and there are lots of informative brochures about whales and other Hawaiian wildlife. Swing by at 11am on Tuesday or Thursday for the free '45-Ton Talks' about whales.

Poi (mashed taro) on *ti* leaves

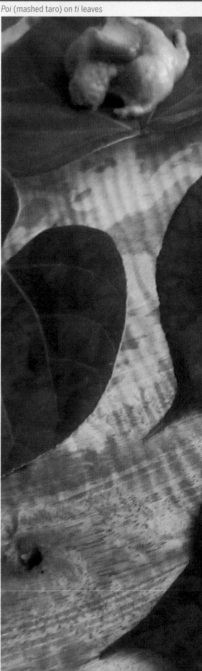

Best Local Food

We love the food in Maui because of its tasty exuberance and no-worries embrace of foreign flavors. The plate lunch. Loco moco. Even Spam musubi has a sassy – if salty – international charm. So join the fun and sample the unknown.

Great For...

✕ Take a Break
Take your plate lunch to one of the shaded picnic tables at Kama'ole Beach Park III.

★ **Top Tip**

The seafood counter at Foodland grocery store sells excellent ahi *poke* bowls to-go, with the ahi over rice.

Day-to-day eats reflect the state's multicultural heritage, with Asian, Portuguese and native Hawaiian influences the most immediately evident. Cheap, fattening and tasty, local food is also the stuff of cravings and comfort.

A Year in Food

It's always a good time to dig into produce grown in Maui's Upcountry. Due to the island's consistently warm tropical climate, most fruits and vegetables are harvested year-round.

Spring Head to Hana to celebrate taro, a unique and revered Hawaiian plant with a starchy potato-like quality. It's used in burgers, chips and mashed into a paste-like pudding called poi.

Fall To check out the range of produce grown on the island, wander the aisles at the Maui County Fair in early October in Kahului. As Halloween approaches, take the family to the pumpkin patch at Kula Country Farms, where there's also a corn maze.

Plate Lunch

The classic example of local food is the ubiquitous plate lunch. Picture this: chunky layers of tender *kalua* pork, a dollop of smooth, creamy macaroni and two hearty scoops of white rice. Yum, right? The pork can be swapped for other proteins like fried mahimahi (fish) or teriyaki chicken. The plate lunch is often served on disposable plates and eaten using chopsticks. A favorite breakfast combo includes fried egg and spicy Portuguese sausage (or bacon, ham, Spam etc) and, always, two scoops of rice.

Poke

Top spots for plate lunches in South Maui are Kihei Caffe (p198) and Da Kitchen Express (p198).

Poke

Raw fish marinated in *shōyu* (soy sauce), oil, chili peppers, green onions and seaweed, *poke* comes in many varieties. Sesame ahi (yellowfin tuna) is particularly delicious and goes well with beer. Top spots for trying poke in South Maui are **Foodland** (808-879-9350; www.foodland.com; 1881 S Kihei Rd, Kihei Town Center; 5am-1am), **Eskimo Candy** (808-879-5686; www.eskimocandy. com; 2665 Wai Wai Pl; mains $9-18; 10:30am-7pm Mon-Fri;) and **Tamura's Fine Wine &**

Liquors (808-891-2420; www.tamurasfinewine.com; 91 E Lipoa St; fresh poke per lb $18.99; 9:30am-9pm Mon-Sat, to 8pm Sun).

Pupu

The local term used for all kinds of munchies or 'grazing' foods is *pupu*. Much more than just cheese and crackers, pupu represent the ethnic diversity of the islands and might include boiled peanuts in the shell, edamame (boiled fresh soybeans in the pod) and universal items such as fried shrimp.

Shave Ice

Ignore those joyless cynics who'll tell you that shave ice is nothing more than a snow cone. Shave ice is not just a snow cone. It's a tropical 21-gun salute – the most spectacular snow cone on earth. The specifics? The ice is shaved as fine as powdery snow, packed into a paper cone and drenched with sweet fruit-flavored syrups in dazzling hues. For added decadence, add Kaua'i cream, azuki beans and ice cream. Give it a try at Local Boys Shave Ice (p199).

> ☑ **Don't Miss**
>
> Breakfast with the crowds and the birds at **Kihei Caffe** (p198).

MARIDAV/SHUTTERSTOCK ©

> 🍴 **Seafood**
>
> Locals eat twice as much seafood as the per-capita national average. *Ahi* is the local favorite, but *mahimahi* and *ono* are also very popular. Browse the Hawaii Seafood website (www.hawaii-seafood.org) to find out more about local fish, including sustainability, fishing methods, seasonality, nutrition and cooking tips
>
> The free Seafood Watch (www.seafoodwatch.org) guide, provides at-a-glance information about ocean-friendly seafood, including sustainability specifics for Hawaii's fish. Download the free smartphone app or print a pocket guide from the website.

> ℹ **Need to Know**
>
> If you're invited to someone's home, bring a dish – preferably homemade, but a cake from a bakery is great too.

🌏 BEACHES

The further south you travel, the better the beaches.

Big Beach   Beach

(Oneloa Beach; http://dlnr.hawaii.gov/dsp/parks/maui; Makena Rd; ⏰6am-6pm; Ⓟ) The crowning glory of Makena State Park, this untouched beach is arguably the finest on Maui. In Hawaiian it's called Oneloa, literally 'Long Sand.' And indeed the golden sands stretch for the better part of a mile and are as broad as they come. The waters are a beautiful turquoise. When they're calm you'll find kids boogie-boarding here, but at other times the shorebreaks can be dangerous, suitable for experienced bodysurfers only, who get tossed wildly in the transparent waves.

Keawakapu Beach   Beach

(☎808-879-4364; www.mauicounty.gov/Facilities; Ⓟ) From break of day to twilight, this sparkling stretch of sand is a showstopper. Extending from south Kihei to Wailea's Mokapu Beach, Keawakapu is set back from the main road and is less visible than

Kihei's main roadside beaches just north. It's also less crowded, and is a great place to settle in and watch the sunset.

Wailea Beach   Beach

(☎808-879-4364; www.mauicounty.gov/Facilities; access road off Wailea Alanui Dr; Ⓟ🚻) To strut your stuff celebrity-style, make a beeline to this sparkling strand, which fronts the Grand Wailea and Four Seasons resorts and offers a full menu of water activities. The beach slopes gradually, making it a good swimming spot. When it's calm, there's decent snorkeling around the rocky point on the southern end. Most afternoons there's a gentle shorebreak suitable for bodysurfing. Divers entering the water at Wailea Beach can follow an offshore reef that runs down to Polo Beach.

Kama'ole Beach Park III   Beach

(☎808-879-4364; www.mauicounty.gov/Facilities; 2800 S Kihei Rd; Ⓟ🚻) A pretty, golden-sand beach with full facilities and lifeguards, plus a playground and parking lot. Great spot for a beach day. The shaded picnic tables start filling up early on week-

From left: Triopical reef fish; Hammock in Wailea; Wailea Beach walk

DARREN J. BRADLEY/SHUTTERSTOCK ©

MATT MUNRO/LONELY PLANET ©

ends. Also has ADA parking, pathways and beach access.

Mokapu & Ulua Beaches Beach
(☑808-879-4364; www.mauicounty.gov/Facilities; Haleali'i Pl; P) With the opening of the Andaz Maui resort, the scene has gotten busier at these two beaches, which are a few steps away from the resort. The lovely **Mokapu Beach** is behind the Andaz, on the northern side of a small point between the beaches. Snorkelers should head straight for **Ulua Beach** to the south of the point.

✪ ACTIVITIES

Hawaiian Sailing
Canoe Adventures Canoeing
(☑808-281-9301; www.mauisailingcanoe.com; adult/child 4-14yr $179/129; ⊗tours 9am; 🚣) Learn about native traditions and snorkel beside sea turtles on a three-hour trip aboard a Hawaiian-style outrigger canoe. Tours depart from Polo Beach.

Wailea Beach Walk Walking
For the perfect sunset stroll, take the 1.3-mile shoreline path that connects Wailea's beaches and the resort hotels that front them. The undulating path winds above jagged lava points and back down to the sandy shore. In winter this is a fantastic location for spotting humpback whales. On a good day you may be able to see more than a dozen of them frolicking offshore.

Hoapili Trail Hiking
From La Perouse Bay, this section of the ancient King's Trail follows the coastline across jagged lava flows. The first part of the trail is along the sandy beach at La Perouse Bay. Be prepared: wear hiking boots, bring plenty to drink, start early and tell someone where you're going. It's a dry area with no water and little vegetation, so it can get very hot.

Right after the trail emerges onto the lava fields, it's possible to take a spur trail for 0.75 miles down to the light beacon at the tip of Cape Hanamanioa. Alternatively, walk inland to the Na Ala Hele sign and turn right onto the King's Hwy as it climbs

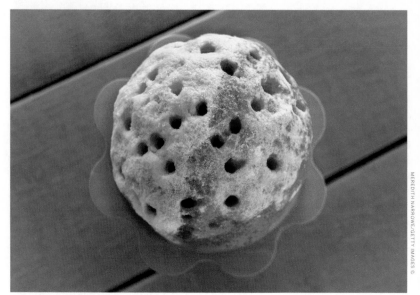

MEREDITH NARROWE/GETTY IMAGES ©

Shave ice

through rough 'a'a lava inland before coming back to the coast to an older lava flow at Kanaio Beach. Although the trail continues, it becomes harder to follow and Kanaio Beach is the recommended turn-around point. If you don't include the lighthouse spur, the round-trip distance to Kanaio Beach is about 4 miles.

For more details and a very basic map, visit www.hawaiitrails.org, the state's trail and access website.

EATING

From food trucks to farm-to-table eateries to chef-driven hot spots, South Maui has it all.

Fork & Salad   Health Food $

(☑808-879-3675; www.forkandsaladmaui.com; 1279 S Kihei Rd, Azeka Mauka Shopping Center; mains $9-17; ☺10:30am-9pm; 🖋) Local farms strut their stuff at this glossy new salad emporium winning raves across Kihei. Step up to the counter, choose a classic or signature salad – or build your own – then add a deliciously seasoned protein, from

organic chicken to sustainable shrimp to seared ahi. Ooh and ahh as staff toss it with Hawaiian-inspired dressings. Creamy *liliko'i* (passion fruit), anyone?

Kihei Caffe   Cafe $

(☑808-879-2230; www.kiheicaffe.com; 1945 S Kihei Rd, Kihei Kalama Village; mains $7-13; ☺5am-2pm) Maybe it's the sneaky birds on the patio, or the quick-to-arrive entrées, but dining at this busy Kihei institution is not exactly relaxing. But you know what? That's part of the quirky charm. Order at the inside counter, fill your coffee cup at the thermos, snag a table on the patio then watch the breakfast burritos, veggie scrambles and loco moco (rice, fried egg and hamburger patty) flash by. Solos, couples, families – everyone's here or on the way. Cash only.

Da Kitchen Express   Hawaiian $

(☑808-875-7782; www.dakitchen.com; 2439 S Kihei Rd, Rainbow Mall; breakfast $11-15, lunch & dinner $11-18; ☺9am-9pm) Da Kitchen is da bomb. Come to this no-frills eatery for Hawaiian plate lunches done right. The local favorite is Da Lau Lau Plate (with steamed pork wrapped in taro leaves), but you won't go wrong with any choice, from charbroiled teriyaki chicken to the gravy-laden loco moco. We particularly liked the spicy kalua pork.

Local Boys Shave Ice   Sweets $

(☎808-344-9779; www.localboysshaveice. com; 1941 S Kihei Rd, Kihei Kalama Village; shave ice from $4.50; ☺10am-9pm) Load up on napkins at Local Boys, where they dish up hearty servings of shaved ice drenched in a rainbow of sweet syrups. We like it tropical (banana, mango and 'shark's blood') with ice cream, *kauai* cream and azuki beans. Cash only.

Monkeypod Kitchen   Pub Food $$

(☎808-891-2322; www.monkeypodkitchen.com; 10 Wailea Gateway Pl, Wailea Gateway Center; lunch $15-27, dinner $15-41; ☺11:30am-11pm, happy hour 3-5:30pm & 9-11pm;) ✔ Happy hours are crowded but convivial at Chef Peter Merriman's latest venture, where the staff, your fellow drinkers and the 36 craft beers on tap keep the alohas real. But microbrews are not the only draw. Gourmet pub grub takes a delicious Hawaiian spin and is typically sourced from organic and local ingredients, with Maui Cattle burgers and plenty of Upcountry veggies.

Café O'Lei   Hawaiian $$

(☎808-891-1368; www.cafeoleirestaurants.com; 2439 S Kihei Rd, Rainbow Mall; lunch $8-16, dinner $17-29; ☺10:30am-3:30pm & 4:30-9:30pm) This strip-mall bistro looks ho-hum at first blush. But step inside. The sophisticated atmosphere, innovative Hawaii Regional Cuisine, honest prices and excellent service knock Café O'Lei into the fine-dining big leagues. For a tangy treat, order the blackened mahimahi with fresh papaya salsa. Look for unbeatable lunch mains, with salads, for under $10, and a sushi chef after 4:30pm (Tuesday to Saturday).

🍷 DRINKING & NIGHTLIFE

Most bars in Kihei are across the street from the beach and have nightly entertainment. Kihei Kalama Village, aka the Bar-muda Triangle (or just the Triangle), is a lively place at night, packed with buzzy watering holes.

5 Palms   Cocktail Bar

(☎808-879-2607; www.5palmsrestaurant. com; 2960 S Kihei Rd, Mana Kai Maui; ☺8am-11pm, happy hour 3-7pm & 9-11pm) For sunset cocktails beside the beach, this is the place. Arrive an hour before the sun goes down because the patio bar, just steps from stunning Keawakapu Beach, fills quickly. During happy hour, sushi and an array of delicious appetizers are half-price, with a one drink minimum, while mai tais and margaritas are $5.75. Popular with tourists and locals.

ⓘ GETTING THERE & AWAY

A few rental car agencies can be found along North and South Kihei Rds. These are good options if you're looking for lower rates or a day-trip rental. **Kihei Rent A Car** (☎808-879-7257; www.kiheirentacar.com; 96 Kio Loop; per day/week from $35/175; ☺7:30am-9pm) rents cars and 4WDs to those aged 21 and over, and includes free mileage. Uber is available, and rates currently seem to run higher than taxis, ranging from $53 to $101 per ride from the airport, depending on Kihei destination.

ⓘ GETTING AROUND

The **Maui Bus** (808-871-4838; www.mauicounty.gov/bus; single ride $2, day pass $4) serves Kihei with two routes. One route, the Kihei Islander, connects Kihei with Wailea and Kahalu. The other route, the Kihei Villager, primarily serves the northern half of Kihei. Both routes operate hourly from around 6am to 8pm and cost $2.

Mouflon ram on Lana'i

JOE WEST/SHUTTERSTOCK ©

A Day on Lana'i

Lana'i is the most central of the Hawaii islands, but it's also the least 'Hawaiian'. Now-closed pineapple plantations are its main historic legacy. Locals are a mix of people descended from immigrant field workers from around the world.

Great For...

☑ Don't Miss

Cathedrals (p202), the island's most spectacular dive site, features arches and grottoes amid a large lava tube.

Ferry from Maui

Worth it just for the ride, the **Expeditions Maui–Lana'i Ferry** (☎800-695-2624; www.go-lanai.com; adult/child 1 way $30/20) links Lahaina Harbor (Maui) with Manele Bay Harbor on Lana'i (one hour) several times daily. In winter there's a fair chance of seeing humpback whales; spinner dolphins are a common sight all year, especially on morning sails. Hulopo'e Beach is near the dock; Lana'i tour and activity operators will meet the ferries if you call ahead. Day-trip packages from Maui are popular.

Itinerary

Take the early morning ferry from Lahaina on Maui; keep an eye out for schools of dolphins as the boat approaches Manele Bay. Catch the shuttle into Lana'i City and pour your own coffee for breakfast at

Rock formations, Garden of the Gods

LYNN Y/SHUTTERSTOCK ©

❶ Need to Know

Air service is limited to several flights daily on **Ohana** (☏800-367-5320; www. hawaiianairlines.com), linking Lana'i to Honolulu. There is also usually one flight to/from Moloka'i.

★ Top Tip

Lana'i City is laid out in a simple grid pattern, and almost all of the shops and services border **Dole Park**.

Blue Ginger Café (☏808-565-6363; www. bluegingercafelanai.com; 409 7th St; mains $5-15; ⊘6am-8pm Thu-Mon, to 2pm Tue & Wed) before strolling the town's shops and superb **Culture & Heritage Center** (www.lanaichc. org; 111 Lana'i Ave; ⊘8:30am-3:30pm Mon-Fri, 9am-1pm Sat) **FREE**. In the afternoon, snorkel at Hulopo'e Beach (p203) or dive at Manele Bay before heading back to Maui on the sunset ferry.

Life with Larry

Decades of sleepy seclusion for Lana'i were interrupted in 2012 when the fabulously wealthy co-founder of Oracle, the huge software developer, Larry Ellison, bought out the island's longtime owner Castle & Cooke (which once ran the ubiquitous pineapple plantations under the Dole name). For his estimated $600 million purchase

price, Ellison got 98% of Lana'i (the rest is private homes or government land) and a bevy of businesses, such as the resorts.

The Garden of the Gods

Strange rock formations, views that would overexcite a condo developer and more deserted beaches are the highlights of northwestern Lana'i.

Reached via the unpaved Polihua Rd, the stretch leading to Kanepu'u Preserve and the Garden of the Gods is fairly good, although often dusty. It generally takes about 30 minutes from town. To travel onward to Polihua Beach, though, is another matter: depending on when the road was last graded, the trip could take anywhere from 20 minutes to an hour, as you descend 1800ft down to the coast.

Beautiful Beaches

Lana'i's finest beach (and one of the best in Hawaii) is the golden crescent of sand at **Hulopo'e Bay** (off Hwy 440; 🚻). Enjoy snorkeling in a marine preserve, walking to

Wind the Windows Down

The best drive on Lana'i, Keomuku Rd (Hwy 44) heads north from Lana'i City into cool upland hills, where fog drifts above grassy pastures. Along the way, impromptu overlooks offer straight-on views of the southeast shore of Moloka'i and its tiny islet Mokuho'oniki, in marked contrast to Maui's sawtooth high-rises in Ka'anapali off to your right.

The 8-mile road gently slopes down to the coast in a series of switchbacks, through a mostly barren landscape punctuated by eccentrically shaped rocks.

Keep your eyes open – sightings of wild mouflon sheep on the inland hills are not uncommon. Males have curled-back horns, and dominant ones travel with a harem. You may also see white-spotted axis deer.

Luahiwa Petroglyphs

Lana'i's highest concentration of ancient petroglyphs are carved into three dozen boulders spread over three dusty acres on a remote slope overlooking the Palawai Basin.

Many of the rock carvings are quite weathered, but you can still make out linear and triangular human figures, dogs and a canoe. Other than gusts of wind, the place is eerily quiet. You can almost feel the presence of the ancients here – honor their spirits and don't touch the fragile carvings.

To get to this seldom-visited site, head south from Lana'i City along tree-lined Manele Rd. After 2 miles, look for a cluster of six trees on the left and turn on to the wide dirt road. Stay on this road for 1.2 miles. When you see a house and gate, take

a fabled archaeological site or just relaxing in the shade of palms. Nearby, Manele Harbor provides a protected anchorage for sailboats, other small craft and the Maui ferry, just a 10-minute walk from Hulopo'e Beach.

Manele and Hulopo'e Bays are part of a marine-life conservation district that prohibits the removal of coral and restricts many fishing activities, all of which makes for great snorkeling and diving. Spinner dolphins seem to enjoy the place as much as humans. During wintertime *kona* (leeward) storms, strong currents and swells enliven the calm and imperil swimmers.

Cathedrals Diving

Diving in and around the bay is excellent. Coral is abundant near the cliffsides, where the bottom quickly slopes off to about 40ft. Beyond the bay's western edge, near Pu'u Pehe rock, is Cathedrals, the island's most spectacular dive site, featuring arches and grottoes amid a large lava tube that is 100ft in length.

Coastline near La Perouse Bay

a very sharp turn left onto a grass and dirt track for 0.3 miles. The large boulders will be on your right up the hill and there will be a turnout and small stone marker.

Lana'i for Children

The kids will love **Hulopo'e Beach**, where there are some cool tide pools filled with colorful little critters that will thrill the little ones; older kids will enjoy the great snorkeling. Overall, however, Lana'i is not an island where children in need of complex diversions will thrive.

Kapiha'a Village Interpretive Trail

This ancient trail makes for a fine and refreshing walk with superb coastal views. It begins on the coast just beneath the Four Seasons Resort Lana'i; you'll see a sign as you walk up from the beach. Other signs point out history along the way.

The trail is mostly flat, but dips down into gulches with wisps of beach, and gets very hot at midday. A spur leads to the site of an ancient village, Kapiha'a, and on to the golf clubhouse.

✖ Take a Break

Enjoy top-notch sushi at the newly revamped **Nobu** (☎808-565-2832; www. noburestaurants.com/lanai; off Hwy 440, Four Seasons Resort Lana'i; meals $50-200; ⊙dinner 6-9:30pm, bar 4:30-10:30pm) **at the Four Seasons.**

HALEAKALĀ NATIONAL PARK

In this Chapter

Hiking the Summit Area 208
Hiking the Kipahulu Area 210
Experiencing Sunrise 212
Kula 217
Getting There & Away 219

Haleakalā National Park at a Glance...

To peer into the soul of Maui, make your way to the summit of Haleakalā. There, the huge crater opens beneath you, in all its raw volcanic glory, caressed by mist and, in the experience of a lifetime, bathed in the early light of sunrise. Lookouts provide breathtaking views of the moonscape below, dotted with cinder cones.

The rest of this park, which is divided into two distinct sections, is all about interacting with this mountain of solid lava and the rare lifeforms here. You can hike down into the crater, follow lush trails on the slopes, or put your mountain bike through its paces.

Haleakalā National Park in One Day

Begin at the **visitor center** at the summit. Next, take an invigorating hike on the sun-warmed cinders of the unearthly **Keonehe'ehe'e (Sliding Sands) Trail** (p208).

Once done, continue to Maui's highest point, **Pu'u'ula'ula (Red Hill) Overlook** (p216). Descend to the **Kalahaku Overlook** (p216), on the crater rim. Then stroll on the **Hosmer Grove Trail** (p209), in forest brimming with birdsong.

Haleakalā National Park in Two Days

Start day two in the wet and wild Kipahulu section. Stroll the **Kuloa Point Trail** (p211), savoring the ocean view. Join the Pipiwai Trail for a 10-minute hike to view the 200ft **Makahiku Falls** (p210) followed by the magical bamboo forest. End at the 400ft cascade of **Waimoku Falls** (p210). Pitch a tent at **Kipahulu Campground** (p216), once an ancient Hawaiian settlement.

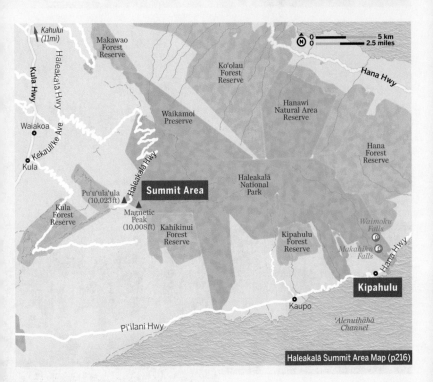

Haleakalā Summit Area Map (p216)

Arriving in Haleakalā National Park

To explore the park in-depth, you will need to rent a car. The summit is 40 miles from Kahului, just over an hour's drive. Kipahulu is 55 miles from Kahului via the Road to Hana. Expect the drive to take at least two hours. Guided tours also stop at both sections of the park.

Sleeping

There are basic campsites and cabins in the Summit Area. Campsites and cabins in the crater must be reserved. The campground in Kipahulu is first-come, first-served.

Kula is close to Haleakalā National Park. If you want to get a jump on the drive to the summit for the sunrise, choose to stay here. Choices are rustic cabins and a handful of B&Bs and rentals.

Native silversword plants in Haleakalā National Park

MICHAEL SCHWAB/GETTY IMAGES

Hiking the Summit Area

There's a trail for every type of hiker in this otherworldly place, from short nature walks ideal for families to hardy two-day treks.

Great For...

❶ Need to Know

Haleakalā National Park (☏808-572-4400; www.nps.gov/hale; Summit District: Haleakalā Hwy, Kipahulu District: Hana Hwy; 3-day pass car $20, motorcycle $15, individual on foot or bicycle $10; P 🚻)

Keonehe'ehe'e (Sliding Sands) Trail

This stunner starts at the southern side of the Haleakalā Visitor Center at 9740ft and winds down to the crater floor. There is no shade, so bring water and a hat.

The path descends gently into an unearthly world of stark lava sights and ever-changing clouds. The only sound is the crunching of volcanic cinders beneath your feet. If you're pressed for time, just walking down 20 minutes will reward you with an into-the-crater experience and fabulous photo opportunities. The climb out takes nearly twice as long.

The full trail leads 9.2 miles to the Paliku Cabin & Campground, passing the Kapalaoa cabin at 5.6 miles after roughly four hours. The first 6 miles follow the southern wall. There are great views, but virtually no

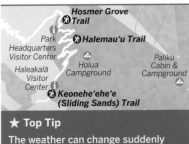

Hosmer Grove
🚶 Trail

Park
Headquarters
Visitor Center

🚶 Halemau'u Trail

Haleakalā
Visitor
Center ℹ

Holua
Campground

Paliku
Cabin &
Campground

🚶 Keonehe'ehe'e
(Sliding Sands) Trail

★ Top Tip

The weather can change suddenly from dry, hot conditions to cold, wind-swept rain. Dress in layers and bring extra clothing.

vegetation. Four miles down, after an elevation drop of 2500ft, Keonehe'ehe'e Trail intersects with a spur that leads north into the cinder desert, where it connects with the Halemau'u Trail after 1.5 miles.

Continuing on Keonehe'ehe'e, you head across the crater floor for 2 miles to Kapalaoa. Verdant ridges rise on your right, giving way to ropy *pahoehoe* (smooth-flowing lava). From Kapalaoa cabin to Paliku, the descent is gentle and the vegetation gradually increases. Paliku (6380ft) is beneath a sheer cliff at the eastern end of the crater. In contrast to the crater's barren western end, this area receives heavy rainfall, with ohia forests climbing the slopes.

Hosmer Grove Trail

Anyone who is looking for a little greenery after hiking the crater will enjoy this shaded woodland walk, as will birders. The half-mile loop trail starts at Hosmer Grove campground, 0.75 miles south of the Park Headquarters Visitor Center, in a forest of lofty trees.

The exotics here were introduced in 1910 in an effort to develop a lumber industry in Hawaii. Species include fragrant incense cedar, Norway spruce, Douglas fir, eucalyptus and various pines. Although the trees adapted well enough to grow, they didn't grow fast enough at these elevations to make tree harvesting practical.

After the forest, the trail moves into native shrubland, with *'akala* (Hawaiian raspberry), *māmane, pilo,* kilau ferns and sandalwood. The *'ohelo*, a berry sacred to the volcano goddess Pele, and the *pukiawe*, which has red and white berries and evergreen leaves, are favored by nene (native Hawaiian geese).

Halemau'u Trail

With views of crater walls, lava tubes and cinder cones, the **Halemau'u Trail** (www.nps.gov/hale; off Haleakalā Hwy) down to the Holua campground and back – 7.4 miles round-trip – can be a memorable day hike. Just be sure to start early before the afternoon clouds roll in and visibility vanishes. The first mile is fairly level and offers a fine view of the crater with Ko'olau Gap to the east.

MICHAEL GORDON/SHUTTERSTOCK ©

Hiking the Kipahulu Area

The crowning glory of the Kipahulu section of the park is 'Ohe'o Gulch, with its magnificent waterfalls and wide pools, each one tumbling into the next one below.

Great For...

Don't Miss

The magic bamboo grove on the Pipiwai Trail.

Pipiwai Trail

This fun trail (www.nps.gov/hale; Kipahulu Area, Haleakalā National Park) ascends alongside the 'Ohe'o streambed, rewarding hikers with picture-perfect views of waterfalls and an otherworldly trip through a bamboo grove. The trail starts on the *mauka* (inland) side of the visitor center and leads up to Makahiku Falls (0.5 miles) and Waimoku Falls (2 miles). To see both falls, allow about two hours return.

Along the path, you'll pass large mango trees and patches of guava before coming to an overlook after about 10 minutes. Makahiku Falls, a long bridal-veil waterfall that drops into a deep gorge, is just off to the right. Thick green ferns cover the sides of 200ft basalt cliffs where the water cascades.

Continuing along the main trail, you'll walk beneath old banyan trees, cross

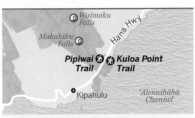

❶ Need to Know

Haleakala National Park (📞808-572-4400; www.nps.gov/hale; Kipahulu District: Hana Hwy; 3-day pass car $20, motorcycle $15, individual on foot or bicycle $10)

✕ Take a Break

Drive to Hana for a grass-fed hamburger from **Hana Burger Food Truck** (p185).

★ Top Tip

Wear your grippiest water shoes for the slippery Pipiwai Trail.

Palikea Stream (killer mosquitoes thrive here) and enter the wonderland of the Bamboo Forest, where thick groves of bamboo bang together musically in the wind. The upper section is muddy, but boardwalks cover some of the worst bits. Beyond the bamboo forest is Waimoku Falls, a thin, lacy 400ft waterfall dropping down a sheer rock face. Forget swimming under Waimoku Falls – its pool is shallow and there's a danger of falling rocks.

Kuloa Point Trail

Even if you're tight on time, take this 20-minute stroll! The **Kuloa Point Trail** (www.nps.gov/hale; Kipahulu Area, Haleakalā National Park), a half-mile loop, runs from the visitor center down to the lower pools and back. A few minutes down, you'll reach a broad grassy knoll with a gorgeous view

of the Hana coast. On a clear day you can see Hawai'i, the Big Island, 30 miles away across 'Alenuihaha Channel. The large freshwater pools along the trail are terraced one atop the other and connected by gentle cascades. Flash floods have taken several lives here, so the Park Service does not recommend swimming in them.

Best Day Hikes

Ten hours If you're planning a full-day outing, and you're in good physical shape, the 11.2-mile hike that starts down Keonehe'e-he'e (Sliding Sands) Trail and returns via Halemau'u Trail is the prize. It crosses the crater floor, taking in both a cinder desert and a cloud forest, showcasing the park's amazing diversity.

Three hours For a half-day experience that offers a hearty serving of crater sights, follow Keonehe'ehe'e (Sliding Sands) Trail down to where it goes between two towering rock formations, before dropping steeply again.

One hour Take to the forest on the Hosmer Grove Trail and see the green side of Haleakalā National Park.

Sunrise over Haleakalā

Experiencing Sunrise

Haleakalā means 'House of the Sun', so it's no surprise that since the time of the first Hawaiians, people have been making pilgrimages up to Haleakalā to watch the sun rise.

Great For...

☑ **Don't Miss**

A sunrise look at Science City, whose domes turn a blazing pink.

★ **Top Tip**

The best photo opportunities occur before the sun rises. Once the sun is up, the silvery lines and the subtleties often disappear.

Above and below: Sunrise over Haleakalā Crater

The Sunrise Experience

Watching the sunrise is an experience that borders on the mystical. Mark Twain called it the 'sublimest spectacle' that he had ever seen.

Plan to arrive at the summit an hour before the actual sunrise; that will guarantee you time to see the world awaken. Around that point the night sky begins to lighten and turn purple-blue, and the stars fade away. Ethereal silhouettes of the mountain ridges appear. The gentlest colors show up in the fragile moments just before dawn. The undersides of the clouds lighten first, accenting the night sky with pale silvery slivers and streaks of pink.

About 20 minutes before sunrise, the light intensifies on the horizon in bright oranges and reds. For the grand finale, the moment when the disk of the sun appears, all of Haleakalā takes on a fiery glow. It feels like you're watching the earth awaken.

Come prepared – it's going to be c-o-l-d! Temperatures hovering around freezing and a biting wind are the norm at dawn and there's often a frosty ice on the top layer of cinders. If you don't have a winter jacket or sleeping bag to wrap yourself in, bring a warm blanket from your hotel. However many layers of clothes you can muster, it won't be too many.

One caveat: a rained-out sunrise is an anticlimactic event, but stick around. Skies may clear and you can enjoy a fantastic hike into the crater. If you just can't get up that early, sunsets at Haleakalā have inspired poets as well.

Sunrise Viewing Reservations

Due to severe overcrowding at the summit in recent years, the park now requires advance reservations for sunrise viewing. Reservations can be made at www.rec-reation.gov; the cost is $1.50 per car. You can make a reservation up to 60 days in advance. To enter the park, the reservation holder must present the reservation receipt and a photo ID.

Visiting the Park

Pack plenty of snacks, especially if you're going up for the sunrise. No food or bottled water is sold anywhere in the park. You don't want a growling stomach to send you back down the mountain before you've had a chance to see the sights.

PIERRE LECLERC/SHUTTERSTOCK ©

✕ Take a Break

After the sunrise and bit of exploring, grab a late breakfast at **Kula Bistro** (p218).

❶ Need to Know

The park now requires advance reservations for sunrise viewing plus a $1.50 fee.

Haleakalā Summit Area

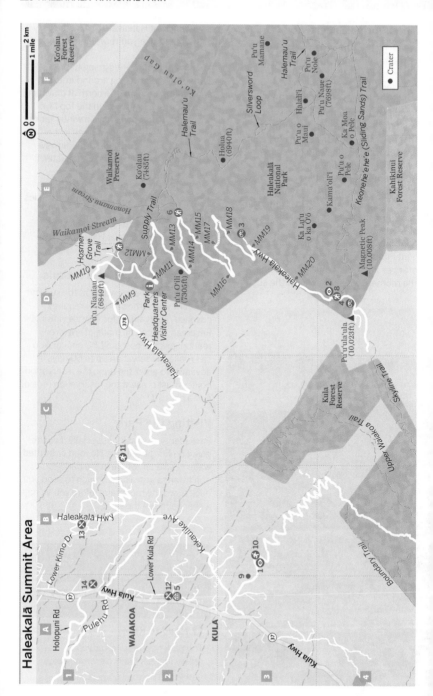

Korolau Forest Reserve

Waikamoi Preserve

Ko'olau (7435ft)

Kohau

Halemau'u Trail

Ko'olau Gap

Silversword Loop

Halemau'u Trail

Pu'u Mamane

Pu'u Nole

Pu'u Naue (7698ft)

Ka Moa o Pele

Halalii

Pu'u o Maui

Pu'u o Pele

Kama'oli'i

Keonehe'ehe'e (Sliding Sands) Trail

Holua (6940ft)

Haleakalā National Park

Kahikinui Forest Reserve

Ka Lu'u o ka O'ō

Magnetic Peak (10,008ft)

Hanamanu Stream

Waikamoi Stream

Supply Trail

Hosmer Grove Trail

MM12

MM10

MM9

Pu'u Nianiau (6849ft)

Park Headquarters Visitor Center

Pu'u O'ili (7305ft)

MM11

MM13

MM14

MM15

MM16

MM17

MM18

MM19

MM20

Haleakalā Hwy

Pu'u'ula'ula (10,023ft)

Kula Forest Reserve

Skyline Trail

Upper Waiakoa Trail

Boundary Trail

Kula Hwy

Haleakalā Hwy

378

Lower Kimo Dr

Haleakala Hwy

Kekaulike Ave

Lower Kula Rd

WAIAKOA

KULA

Pulehu Rd

Kula Hwy

Holopuni Rd

37

37

• Crater

0 ⌒N

0 2 km

0 1 mile

Haleakalā Summit Area

◎ **Sights**
1 Aliʻi Kula Lavender B3
2 Haleakalā Visitor Center D4
3 Kalahaku Overlook E3
4 Puʻuʻulaʻula (Red Hill) Overlook D4
5 Worcester Glassworks A2

⊕ **Activities, Courses & Tours**
6 Halemauʻu Trail E2
7 Hosmer Grove Trail D1

8 Keoneheʻeheʻe (Sliding Sands)
   Trail D4
9 Oʻo Farm A3
10 Proflyght Paragliding B3
11 Skyline Eco-Adventures C2

⊗ **Eating**
12 Kula Bistro A2
13 Kula Lodge Restaurant B1
14 La Provence A1

Kula

◎ SIGHTS

Aliʻi Kula Lavender　　　Gardens
(☏808-878-3004; www.aklmaui.com; 1100 Waipoli Rd; $3; ⏰9am-4pm) Perched on a broad hillside with panoramic views of the West Maui Mountains and the central Maui coast, this charming lavender farm is a scenic place to relax. Distractions include fragrant pathways, a gift shop with lavender products, and a lanai (veranda) with sweeping views where you can enjoy a scone and a cup of lavender tea.

Worcester Glassworks　　　Gallery
(☏808-878-4000; www.worcesterglassworks.com; 4626 Lower Kula Rd; ⏰10am-5pm Mon-Sat) This family-run working studio and gallery produces some amazing pieces, particularly the sand-blasted glass in natural forms (eg seashells). Visitors are welcome to watch the artists and their solar-powered furnaces at work. The adjacent store offers gorgeous pieces for sale. Call ahead to confirm it's open. Look for the small sign at the house just south of Kula Bistro. Very welcoming.

⊕ ACTIVITIES

Oʻo Farm　　　Food & Drink
(☏808-667-4341; www.oofarm.com; 651 Waipoli Rd; tours $58; ⏰farm tour 10:30am-2pm Mon-Fri, coffee tour 8:30-10:30am Wed & Thu) Whether a gardener or a gourmet, you're going to love a tour of this Upcountry farm, which supplies Pacifico restaurant and the Feast at Lele. Where else can you help harvest your meal, give the goodies to a gourmet chef and feast on the bounty? On the new 'Seed to Cup' Coffee Tours you'll learn about coffee cultivation.

The coffee tour is also interactive. You'll tour the fields where the coffee is grown, sip French-press coffee and savor a garden frittata along with jam and homemade bread.

Proflyght Paragliding　　　Paragliding
(☏808-874-5433; www.paraglidemaui.com; Waipoli Rd; paraglide 1000ft $115, 3000ft $225; ⏰office 7am-7pm, flights 2hr after sunrise) Strap into a tandem paraglider with a certified instructor and take a running leap off the cliffs beneath Polipoli Spring State Recreation Area. The term 'bird's-eye view' will never be the same. Must be at least eight years old and under 230lb.

Want to watch the gliders and their colorful chutes float on the breeze? Drive up Waipoli Rd just beyond Aliʻi Kula Lavender in the morning, pull over and look up. Gorgeous!

Skyline Eco-Adventures　　　Adventure Sports
(☏808-878-8400; www.zipline.com; 18303 Haleakalā Hwy; zipline tour adult/child under 18yr $120/60; ⏰8:30am-2pm) Maui's first zipline has a prime location on the slopes of Haleakalā. The five lines are relatively short (100ft to 850ft) compared with the competition, although a unique 'pendulum zip' adds some spice. Good for newbies. Feeling *really* adventurous? Try its new Haleakalā Hike & Bike tour ($250). It includes a summit sunrise, biking down the volcano, and then ziplining. Up at 2am!

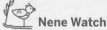
Nene Watch

The native nene, Hawaii's state bird, is a long-lost cousin of the Canada goose. By the 1950s, hunting, habitat loss and predators had reduced its population to just 30. Thanks to captive breeding and release programs, it has been brought back from the verge of extinction and the Haleakalā National Park's nene population is now about 200.

Nene nest in shrubs and grassy areas from 6000ft to 8000ft, surrounded by rugged lava flows with sparse vegetation. Their feet have gradually adapted by losing most of their webbing. The birds are extremely friendly and love to hang out where people do, anywhere from cabins on the crater floor to the Park Headquarters Visitor Center.

Their curiosity and fearlessness have contributed to their undoing. Nene don't fare well in an asphalt habitat and many have been run over by cars. Others have been tamed by too much human contact, so no matter how much they beg for your peanut butter sandwich, don't feed the nene. It only interferes with their successful return to the wild.

The nonprofit Friends of Haleakalā National Park runs an Adopt-a-Nene program. For $30 you get adoption papers, information about your nene, a certificate and postcard. The money funds the protection of nene habitat.

Hawaiian nene (native goose)
GMOFOTO/SHUTTERSTOCK ©

🅖 TOURS

A number of tour-bus companies operate half-day and full-day sightseeing tours on Maui, covering the national park and other island destinations.

Polynesian Adventure Tours
(☑808-833-3000; www.polyad.com; tours adult from $114, child 3-11yr from $69) Part of Gray Line Hawaii, it's a big player among Hawaiian tour companies; offers tours to Haleakalā National Park, Central Maui and 'Iao Valley State Monument, and the Road to Hana. Also runs short trips from Maui to Pearl Harbor in O'ahu (from adult/child $378/357).

Roberts Hawaii
(☑800-831-5541; www.robertshawaii.com; tours adult/child 4-11yr $108/79) In operation for more than 70 years, Roberts Hawaii runs three tours: Hana, 'Iao Valley and Lahaina, and Haleakalā National Park.

⊗ EATING

Kula Lodge
Restaurant   Hawaiian $$$
(☑808-878-1535; www.kulalodge.com; 15200 Haleakalā Hwy; breakfast $12-27, lunch $18-42, dinner $26-42; ☺7am-9pm) Assisted by its staggering view, perhaps the best of any Maui restaurant, Kula Lodge has reinvented itself to great effect. Inside, veteran Chef Marc McDowell has the kitchen humming to a farm-to-table variety menu. Locally sourced salads are delicious. Outside, brick ovens provide build-your-own pizzas served under cabanas (11am to 8pm). A spectacular sunset here is the perfect ending to a day on the summit.

Don't spend too long looking over the dessert menu – the upside-down pineapple cake sells out. Reserve on holidays.

Kula Bistro   Italian $$$
(☑808-871-2960; www.kulabistro.com; 4566 Lower Kula Rd; breakfast $9-17, lunch & dinner $12-39; ☺7:30-10:30am Tue-Sun, plus 11am-8pm daily) Is everyone in town here or what? Yup, sure looks like it. And we think we know

why. This superb family-owned bistro offers a friendly dining room, sparkling service and delicious home cooking, including fabulous pizza and huge servings of coconut cream pie (enough for two). BYO wine from Morihara Store across the street. No corkage fee.

La Provence
Cafe $

(☏808-878-1313; www.laprovencekula.com; 3158 Lower Kula Rd, Waiakoa; pastries $3-6, lunch $11-14, crepes $4-13; ⌚7am-2pm Wed-Sun) One of Kula's best-kept secrets, this little courtyard restaurant in the middle of nowhere is the domain of Maui's finest pastry chef. Popular offerings include ham-and-cheese croissants, chocolate-filled pastries, and filled crepes. Weekends offer a brunch menu that draws patrons from far and wide. Try the warm goat cheese and Kula greens salad. Hours may fluctuate so call before driving here. Cash and check only.

Dinner is served second and fourth Fridays of the month (6pm to 9pm, mains $26 to $33).

INFORMATION

No food or beverages are sold in either section of the park. Pick up picnic supplies on the way or grab a meal before you visit. Stock up in Kula or another town in the Upcountry.

GETTING THERE & AWAY

Summit Area

Getting to Haleakalā is half the fun. Snaking up the mountain, it's sometimes hard to tell if you're in an airplane or a car – all of Maui opens up below you, with sugarcane and pineapple fields creating a patchwork of green on the valley floor. The highway ribbons back and forth, and in some places as many as four or five switchbacks are in view all at once.

Haleakalā Hwy (Hwy 378) twists and turns for 11 miles from Hwy 377 near Kula up to the park entrance, then another 10 miles to Haleakalā summit. It's a good paved road, but it's steep and winding. You don't want to rush, especially when it's dark or foggy. Watch out for cattle wandering freely across the road.

The drive to the summit takes about 1½ hours from Pa'ia or Kahului, two hours from Kihei and a bit longer from Lahaina. If you need gas, fill up the night before, as there are no services on Haleakalā Hwy.

On your way back downhill, be sure to put your car in low gear to avoid burning out your brakes.

There is no public bus service to the park.

Kipahulu Area

The Kipahulu Area is on Hwy 31, 10 scenic miles south of Hana. There's no direct road access from here to the rest of Haleakalā National Park; the summit must be visited separately. There is no public bus service to the park. Don't feel like driving? Check for guided day tours that stop at the park.

GETTING AROUND

There is no public bus service inside the park. You will need a car to explore in-depth.

WAIPI'O VALLEY

In this Chapter

Muliwai Trail 224
Honoka'a 228
Getting There & Away 229

Waipi'o Valley at a Glance...

Looking like an enormous scoop that was scalloped from the emerald coastline, Waipi'o Valley is a spectacular natural amphitheater. Waipi'o ('curving water') is one of seven valleys carved into the windward side of the Kohala Mountains. The valley goes back 6 miles, its flat floor an emerald patchwork of jungle, huts and taro patches. Hidden (and inaccessible without crossing private property) is Hi'ilawe, a distant ribbon of white cascading 1450ft, the longest waterfall in the state. The water flows into a river that ends at Waipi'o's black-sand beach, a rugged beauty surrounded by dramatic running cliffs that disappear around the corner of the island.

Waipi'o Valley in One Day

Eat breakfast at **Gramma's Kitchen** (p228) then check out the view of the valley from the **Waipi'o Valley Lookout**. (p229) Spend the day **walking** (p226) the steep path to the beach or, for deeper appreciation, joining a guided tour into the valley. After your hike, eat a plate lunch followed by dessert at **Tex Drive-In** (p228).

Waipi'o Valley in Two Days

On the second day, tour a boutique **farm** (p228). Take your pick of mushrooms, vanilla, tea or coffee. Dig into pasta at **Cafe il Mondo** (p229) then see what's playing at **Honoka'a People's Theatre** (p229).

Arriving in Waipi'o Valley

From Honoka'a, Hwy 240 runs just under 10 miles to the Waipi'o Valley Lookout. The turnoff onto Kukuihaele Rd is around the 8-mile marker, and it connects again with Hwy 240 near the lookout. There is no bus service here.

Sleeping

You'll find memorable options in Kukuihaele, the residential community at the rim of the valley, including clifftop properties with spectacular views. In general, rates reflect the premium location.

If you plan on camping in Waimanu Valley, apply for a permit online through the **Division of Forestry & Wildlife** (p226), which is based in Hilo.

Camping along the Muliwai Trail

Muliwai Trail

For expert trekkers only, this 8.5-mile backcountry trail goes from Waipiʻo Valley to Waimanu Valley, traversing steep, slippery and potentially treacherous ground. But it is lovely, with little waterfalls and icy pools for swimming.

Great For...

☑ **Don't Miss**

Waimanu Valley is a mini Waipiʻo, minus the tourists.

Hike Overview

It takes 6½ to eight hours one way and crosses 13 gulches – brutal to ascend and descend. Plan on camping in Waimanu Valley for at least two nights. For safety reasons, do not attempt this hike during or after rains. For detailed hiking information, contact Na Ala Hele (www.hawaiitrails.org/trails) in Hilo.

Trailhead & the Z Trail

The Muliwai Trail begins at the base of the cliffs on the far side of the valley. A shaded path at the end of the beach takes you to a dual trailhead: head right and up for Muliwai (straight ahead leads to the King's Trail). The ancient Hawaiian footpath now rises over 1200ft in a mile of hard laboring back and forth up the cliff face; it's nicknamed 'Z Trail' for the killer switchbacks.

ⓘ Need to Know
Information Booth (Waipi'o Valley;
⊗8am-dusk)

✕ **Take a Break**

After your hike order a *kalua loco moco*
at **Waipi'o Cookhouse** (☑808-775-1443;
48-5370 Honoka'a-Waipi'o Rd; mains $12-14;
⊗7:30am-6pm) 🍴.

★ **Top Tip**

Park your car at the signposted
24-hour parking area.

Hunters still use this trail to track feral pigs.
The hike is exposed and hot, so cover this
stretch early.

The Hike

The trail moves into ironwood and Norfolk
pine forest, and tops a little knoll before
gently descending and becoming muddy
and mosquito-ridden. The view of the
ocean gives way to the sounds of a rushing
stream. The trail crosses a gulch and
ascends past a sign for Emergency Helipad
No 1. For the next few hours the trail finds
a steady rhythm of gulch crossings and
forest ascents. A waterfall at the third gulch
is a source of fresh water; treat it before
drinking. For a landmark, look for Emergency Helipad No 2 at about the halfway point
from Waipi'o Beach. Beyond that, there's

an open-sided emergency shelter with pit
toilets and Emergency Helipad No 3.

Rest at Helipad No 3 before making the
final difficult descent. Leaving the shelter,
hop across three more gulches and pass
Emergency Helipad No 4, from where it's
less than a mile to Waimanu Valley. This
final section of switchbacks starts out
innocently enough, with some artificial and
natural stone steps, but over a descent of
1200ft the trail is poorly maintained and
hazardous later.

A glimpse of Wai'ilikahi Falls (accessible
by a 45-minute stroll) on the far side of the
valley might inspire hikers to press onward,
but beware: the trail is narrow and washed
out in parts, with sheer drop-offs into the
ocean and no handholds apart from mossy
rocks and spiny plants. If the descent is
questionable, head back to the trail shelter
for the night.

Waimanu Valley is...well, this is as good
as God's green Earth gets. There was once

a sizable settlement here, and the valley contains many ruins, including house and *heiau* (ancient stone temple) terraces, stone enclosures and old *lo'i* (taro fields). In the early 19th century an estimated 200 people lived here, but the valley was abandoned by its remaining three families after the 1946 tsunami. Today you'll bask alone amid a stunning deep valley framed by cliffs, waterfalls and a boulder-strewn beach.

From the bottom of the switchbacks, Waimanu Beach is 10 minutes past the camping regulations signboard. To ford the stream to reach the campsites on its western side, avoid the rope strung across the water, which is deep there. Instead, cross closer to the ocean entry where it is shallower. Camping requires a state permit from the **Division of Forestry & Wildlife** (☑808-973-9778; http://dlnr.hawaii.gov/do-faw/; 2135 Makiki Heights Dr, Greater Honolulu; ⓧ7:45am-4:30pm Mon-Fri) for a maximum of six nights.

There are nine campsites: recommended are No 2 (full valley views, proximity to stream, grassy spots), No 6 (view of Wai'ilikahi Falls, access to the only sandy beach) and No 9 (very private at the far end of the valley, lava-rock chairs and a table). Facilities include fire pits and composting outhouses. There's a spring about 10 minutes behind campsite No 9, with a PVC pipe carrying water from a waterfall; all water must be treated.

Return Hike

On the return trip, be careful to take the correct trail. Walking inland from Waimanu Beach, don't veer left on a false trail-of-use that attempts to climb a rocky stream bed.

Instead keep heading straight inland past the camping regulations sign to the trail to the switchbacks. It takes about two hours to get to the trail shelter, and another two to reach the waterfall gulch: refill your water here (again, treat before drinking). Exiting the ironwood forest soon after, the trail descends back to the floor of Waipi'o Valley.

★ Waipi'o Valley Hike

To reach the valley floor and Waipi'o Beach, you must walk or drive (only with 4WD) the incredibly steep road from the lookout. Walking is recommended for those with the leg power to hike down- and uphill. If not, join a guided tour that transports you into the valley. Driving is risky: the road is not only steep but narrow and winding; at the bottom, the muddy, puddle-strewn unpaved road is a quagmire during rain.

If the parking lot near the Information Booth is full, park along the road leading there. Lock your car.

King's Trail

If hiking to Waipi'o Beach is too civilized for you, take it up a notch with this trail. From the beach, cross the stream (only if safe) to the far western end. This trail goes inland for about 45 minutes to Nanaue Falls, a stepped series of three pools, which are a popular swimming hole for residents.

The trail parallels the valley walls and passes through a natural botanic garden. You'll encounter coffee plants, *liliko'i* (passion fruit), massive monkeypods, papaya, elephant ear, avocado and lots more, making you realize what a cornucopia the valley really is. You'll also come across small groups of friendly wild horses, the descendants of domesticated animals left behind after the tsunami.

this is as good as God's Green Earth gets

Waterfall in Waipi'o Valley

Honoka'a

SIGHTS

Honoka'a's slow-paced main street belies the town's former importance as the third-largest town in the Hawaiian Islands, after Honolulu and Hilo. Once a major hub for the dominant cattle and sugar industries, it was forced to reinvent itself when those industries crashed. By the time Honoka'a Sugar Company processed its last harvest in 1993, the town had dwindled in size and was struggling to find new economic niches. Eventually, new farmers found success with niche edibles, such as the Hamakua mushrooms now prized by gourmet chefs.

Today Honoka'a town remains a lively, if tiny, hub, as the only actual town along the Hamakua Coast. It serves the rural residents and farmers of Pa'auilo and Ahualoa, as well as tourists on their way to Waipi'o Valley, 10 miles west. The town's retro buildings have a jaunty western vibe, which bursts into full glory during Honoka'a Western Week.

ACTIVITIES & TOURS

Although nearby Waipi'o Valley is better known for activities, the back roads in Pa'auilo and Ahualoa make for terrific cycling. If hesitant to explore on your own, book a tour. Big Island Bike Tours (p146), based in Waimea, offers a couple of group rides in the Honoka'a area.

If you're interested in food, local agriculture or nature and the outdoors, visit one of the small, family-run farms in pastoral Pa'auilo or Ahualoa, on the *mauka* (inland) side of the highway. They are working farms so you absolutely must book visits in advance.

Mauna Kea Tea   Farm

(☎808-775-1171; www.maunakeatea.com; 46-3870 Old Mamalahoa Hwy, Ahualoa; 1½hr tour per 2/3/4 plus people $30/25/20; ⊙tours 10am Mon, Wed & Thu) ✿ If you're into tea, organic farming and philosophical inquiry, arrange a tour at this family-run 2-acre plantation. Its green and oolong teas are intended to represent the inherent 'flavor' of the land rather than the artificial fertilizers of mass-produced teas. Tours must be booked in advance.

Hawaiian Vanilla Company   Food

(☎808-776-1771; www.hawaiianvanilla.com; 43-2007 Pa'auilo Mauka Rd, Pa'auilo; tour $25, afternoon tea $34, lunch per adult/child $39/19; ⊙tour 1pm Mon-Fri, afternoon tea 3pm Sat, lunch 12:30pm Mon-Fri; ⊕) ✿ The first commercial vanilla operation in the US, this family-run farm is an agritourism success story. The foodie tours (lunch or afternoon tea) are pricey crowd-pleasers, but the farm tour is too superficial to warrant the price.

Long Ears Coffee   Farm

(☎808-775-0385; www.longearscoffee.com; tour $35) ✿ Try unique three-year-old 'aged' Hamakua coffee at this family farm. Wendell and Irmanetta Branco process their own and other Hamakua farms' beans, creating a sustainable agricultural economy for farmers. On tour you'll see the entire process: growing trees, harvesting cherries, pulping, drying, husking and roasting. Directions to the farm are given upon booking a tour.

⊗ EATING

Gramma's Kitchen   American $

(☎808-775-9943; www.facebook.com/grammaskitchenhonokaa; 45-3625 Mamane St; mains $12-20; ⊙8am-3pm daily, plus 5-8pm Fri & Sat) The restaurant's storefront sign states 'Very homestyle cooking.' And it's true. Gramma's is your ticket for local dishes, such as hearty Portuguese bean soup, teriyaki cheeseburgers (with pineapple and bacon) and a perfectly seared and crusted ahi roll. Expect a casual diner setting, cheerful staff and small-town aloha.

Tex Drive-In   Bakery $

(☎808-775-0598; www.texdriveinhawaii.com; 45-690 Pakalana St; malasadas $1.20, mains $5-10; ⊙6am-8pm) A *malasada* is just a doughnut, but Tex is famous for serving them hot and fresh. They come plain or filled; either way, folks drive across the island to devour them. Tex also serves decent plate lunches and *loco moco* (rice, fried egg and hamburger patty or other main dish topped with gravy) and seasonal taro burgers. Go elsewhere for health food; come here for local color.

Adjacent to the drive-in, the Tex store (9am to 5pm) sells a variety of locally made gifts, from toiletries to T-shirts.

Hamakua Harvest
Farmers Market   Market

(www.hamakuaharvest.org; cnr Hwys 19 & 240; ⊗9am-2pm Sun) 🍴 Featuring over 35 vendors, live music and talks, this market is worth checking out. Everything is locally grown or made, including produce, honey, goat cheese, coconut-milk gelato, smoked fish and much more. To get here, turn *makai* (seaward) off Hwy 19 at the eastern end of Mamane St.

Cafe il Mondo   Italian $$

(808-775-7711; www.cafeilmondo.com; 45-3580 Mamane St; calzones $14, pizzas $15-20; ⊗11am-2pm & 5-8pm Mon-Sat) Honoka'a's fanciest restaurant is this longtime Italian spot, specializing in thin-crust pizzas, pastas and enormous calzones packed to bursting point. With a grand stone-tiled patio, gleaming wood furnishings, sleek bar and live music, the vibe is romantic. But the crowd is refreshingly informal, convivial and diverse.

✪ ENTERTAINMENT
Honoka'a People's
Theatre   Theater

(📞808-775-0000; http://honokaapeople. com; 45-3574 Mamane St; movie tickets adult/ child/senior $6/3/4; ⊗typical showtimes 5pm & 7pm Tue-Sun) There's something wonderful about watching a movie in a huge,

👓 Waipi'o Valley Lookout

Located at the end of Hwy 240, this lookout offers a jaw-dropping view of Waipi'o's emerald amphitheater, black-sand beach and pounding surf. Feast your eyes on one of Hawaii's iconic images.

FOMINAYAPHOTO/SHUTTERSTOCK ©

old-fashioned theater – like this one, with a 50ft screen and over 500 seats. Built in 1930, this theater still shows movies and hosts special events. For a bargain movie and a way to immerse yourself with locals, you can't go wrong coming here. Check the website and call to confirm show times.

ℹ GETTING THERE & AROUND

From Hwy 19, there are several turnoffs toward Honoka'a town, including Plumeria Rd on the western end and Mamane St on the eastern end. A handy landmark is Tex Drive-In; the road just east of the drive-in leads into town. The drive from Hilo should take around an hour.

You can catch **Hele-On Bus** (📞808-961-8744; www.heleonbus.org; per trip adult/senior & student $2/1, 10-ride ticket $15, monthly pass $60) to Honoka'a from Hilo or Kailua-Kona, but service is infrequent. Check the website for details.

In and around Honoka'a, you'll need a car.

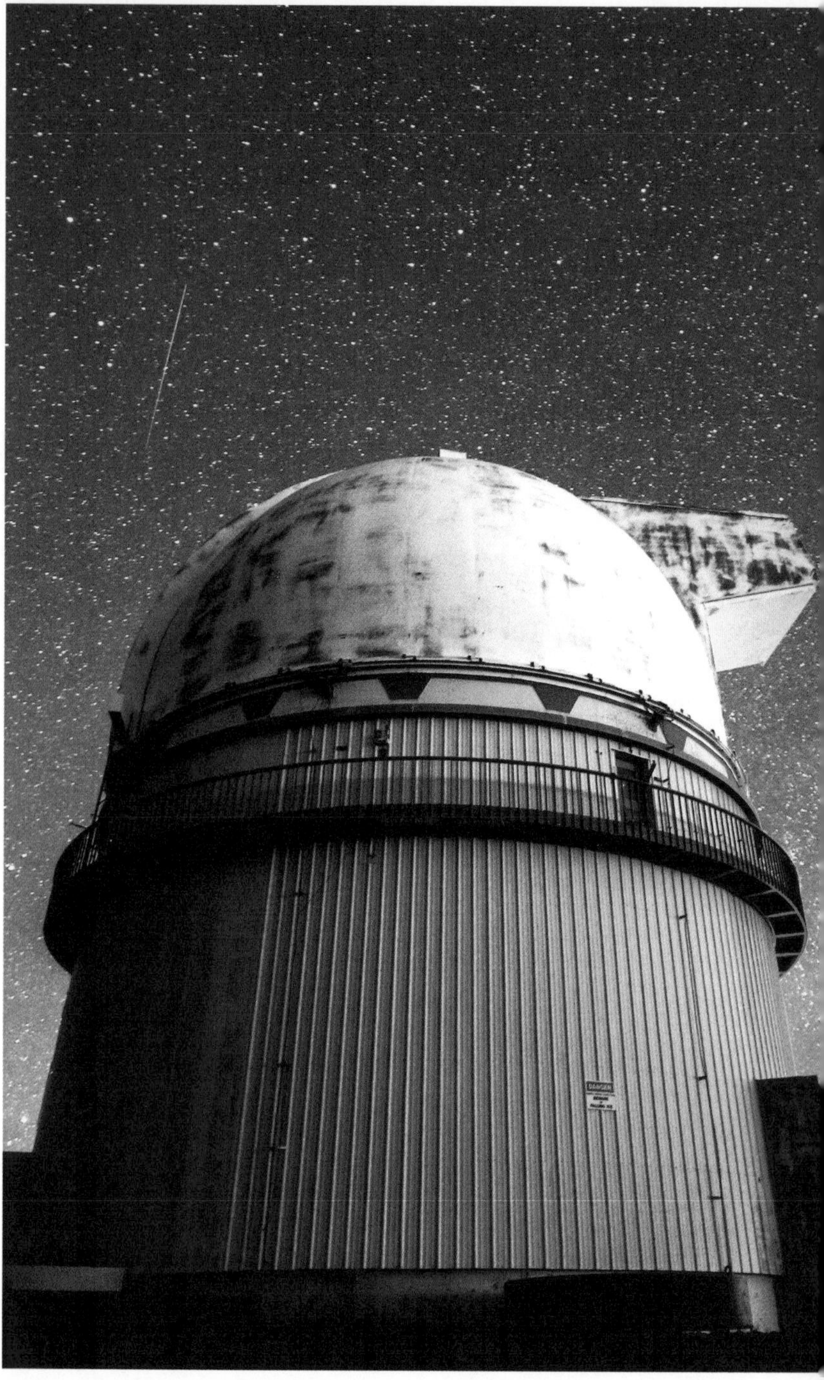

MAUNA KEA

In this Chapter

Mauna Kea Summit Area 234
Humuʻula—Mauna Kea
Summit Trail 238
Stargazing 240
Mauna Loa Observatory Trail 242
Kona 244
Getting There & Away 249

Mauna Kea at a Glance...

Mauna Kea (White Mountain) is called Mauna O Wakea by Hawaiian cultural practitioners. While all of the Big Island is considered the first-born child of Wakea (Sky Father) and Papahanaumoku (Earth Mother), Mauna Kea has always been the sacred piko (navel) connecting the land to the heavens.

For the scientific world, it began in 1968 when the University of Hawaiʻi (UH) began observations from the mountain. The summit is so high and pollution-free that it allows investigation of the furthest reaches of the observable universe. The summit is home to 13 observatories.

Mauna Kea in Two Days

Start in Kailua-Kona, where the sunshine will switch your body clock to local time. Spend two days enjoying ocean sports, such as bodyboarding at **Magic Sands Beach** (p244), snorkeling at Kahaluʻu Beach, diving or deep-sea fishing. Between dips, ground yourself in island history at **Huliheʻe Palace** (p244), where Hawaiian royalty vacationed.

Mauna Kea in Three Days

On day three begin with brunch and an ocean view at **Daylight Mind** (p248) in Kona, then spend an afternoon ascending **Mauna Kea** (p234), where you'll witness an unforgettable sunset and then enjoy amazing stargazing.

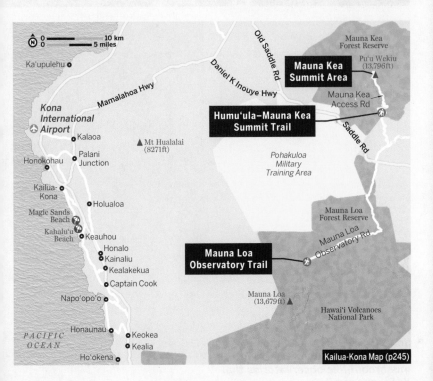

Arriving in Mauna Kea

From Waimea or Kona take Saddle Road (Hwy 200) or the Daniel K Inouye reroute. From Hilo, drive *mauka* (inland) on Kaumana Dr (Hwy 200) or Puainako Extension (Hwy 2000), both of which become Saddle Road. Start with a full tank of gas – there are no service stations out here.

Sleeping

The closest accommodations are the cabins at Mauna Kea Recreation Area on Saddle Road. Beyond those, look for lodging in Waimea and Hilo.

Observatories on Mauna Kea at sunset

Mauna Kea Summit Area

At 13,796ft in the air, you are above 40% of the atmosphere and 90% of its water vapor – perfect conditions for the giant mushroom-like observatories that dot the summit.

Great For...

☑ Don't Miss

Off the visitor center parking lot is an enclosed area where rare and endangered silversword plants grow.

ⓘ Need to Know

Mauna Kea Visitor Information Station (MKVIS; ☎808-961-2180; www.ifa. hawaii.edu/info/vis; ⊙9am-10pm)

Mauna Kea Visitor Information Station

Modestly sized MKVIS packs a punch with astronomy and space-exploration videos and posters galore, and information about the mountain's history, ecology and geology. Budding scientists of all ages revel in the gift shop, while knowledgeable staff help you pass the time acclimatizing to the 9200ft altitude. Check the website for upcoming special events, such as lectures about science and Hawaiian culture, typically held on Saturday nights.

Excellent free stargazing programs happen from 6pm until 10pm nightly, weather permitting.

Inside the gift shop you can buy hot chocolate, coffee, packets of instant noodles and freeze-dried astronaut food to munch on; hoodies, hats and gloves to stay warm; and books about science and Hawaiian culture.

Sunset View from the Summit

Across from MKVIS, a 15-minute uphill hike crests Pu'u Kalepeamoa (9394ft), a cinder cone offering glorious sunset views.

Subaru Telescope

When it came online in 1999, Japan's 8.2m (29.6ft) Subaru Telescope was the most expensive observatory ever constructed. The 22-ton mirror is one of the largest optical mirrors in existence. The telescope recently helped create a 3D map of 3000 galaxies that shows Einstein's theory of relativity

View from Mauna Kea Summit

MARISA ESTIVILL/SHUTTERSTOCK ©

still holds true. Observatory tours (which, sadly, don't include looking through the telescope) are given in Japanese or English, but not both; they fill up fast so register online early.

Children under 16 years old are not allowed on tours and there are no public restrooms.

Incidentally, Subaru is the Japanese word for the Pleiades (Seven Sisters) constellation.

WM Keck Observatory

Mirrors larger than 8m (26.2ft) are so heavy that gravity distorts them as they move. Keck's breakthrough design overcame that limitation in 1993 by using a series of 36 hexagonal mirror segments mounted and independently adjusted that function as a single piece of glass 10m (32.8ft) in diameter. The results were so good, they built Keck II next door in 1996. Visitors are welcome into the gallery, which has brief displays, public restrooms and views inside the Keck I dome.

★ Top Tip

Visit this sacred area with respect, and pack out your trash.

✕ Take a Break

After sunset, drive down to **Kona Brewing Company** (p249) for a beer and fish tacos.

Mauna Kea Summit Observatory

BENNY MARTY/SHUTTERSTOCK ©

Humu'ula–Mauna Kea Summit Trail

This daunting, all-day hike on an exposed trail is a journey into the sky. The trail starts at 9200ft, then climbs almost 4600ft over the next 6 miles to Mauna Kea's summit.

Great For...

☑ Don't Miss

A stop at the visitor center for more background about mountain history and geology.

Trailhead

Prepare for serious weather. Snow and 100mph winds are possible. Park at the Visitor Information Station and walk 1000ft up the road toward the **Onizuka Center for International Astronomy** where visiting researchers and observatory staff reside. Where the pavement ends, go left on the dirt road, following several 'Humu'ula Trail' signs to the trail.

The Climb

Reflective T-posts and cairns mark the route as the trail traverses up above the 10,000ft vegetation zone. As you weave around cinder cones and traipse over crumbled 'a'a lava and slippery scree, you pass various spur trails – all lead back to the access road.

Silversword

ⓘ Need to Know

Register at the Visitor Information Station where you can also get advice from the staff.

✕ Take a Break

Before you hike, fuel up with coffee and pancakes at **Evolution Bakery & Cafe** (p248) in Kona.

★ Top Tip

Start by 6am if possible. It typically takes five hours to reach the summit, half as long to return.

Return to the four-way junction and head north (uphill) for the final push to the Mauna Kea Summit Rd at a parking area. The trail officially ends at the access road's mile marker 7, but the true summit still snickers at you another 1.5 miles away.

The Return

The return route is via the same way you came up, only this time the sprawling vistas will be in your face; but so will the breeze. As an alternative, return along the shoulder of the access road rather than retracing the trail. The road is 2 miles longer but is smoother.

Respecting the Summit

For Native Hawaiians, the summit is a region, a realm, not a point on a map. But if you really need to place a boot toe on Puʻu Wekiu, Mauna Kea's true summit, soldier on till you reach the UH 2.2m Telescope, where the short spur trail to the summit begins. However, consider that this is a sacred mountain, which some believe has already suffered enough disrespect from the development here.

Most of the way you will be passing through the Mauna Kea Ice Age Natural Area Reserve. Much of Mauna Kea was once covered with glaciers, which were responsible for much of the unique lava and erosion patterns.

At Mile 3.1, begin looking for outcroppings of dark gray or black stone. When eruptions occur underneath ice, the rapid cooling can result in a dense, fine-grained basalt forming. Ancient Hawaiians established a major mining operation to make adze heads. The trail passes just to the west of an impressive pile of flakes accumulated over hundreds of years.

Slow exposure of stars above Mauna Kea

Stargazing

Studying the stars atop Mauna Loa is unique and profoundly memorable. On an average night you might move from the Ring Nebula to the Andromeda Galaxy to a galactic cluster to Jupiter's moons.

Great For...

☑ Don't Miss

At sunset, look east to see 'the shadow' – the gigantic silhouette of Mauna Kea looking over Hilo.

MKVIS Stargazing Program

The Mauna Kea Visitor Information Station offers a terrific free nightly stargazing program. The program begins at 6pm with the film *First Light,* a documentary about Mauna Kea as both a cultural and an astronomical entity. How much you'll see through the telescopes depends on cloud cover and moon phase; call ahead if you want to double check. The busiest nights are Friday and Saturday, there are no reservations, and lines can get long. Special scope attachments accommodate visitors in wheelchairs.

During big meteor showers, the station staffs its telescopes for all-night star parties. On many weekends it hosts special guests and lecturers.

ⓘ Need to Know

The public may drive to the summit in the daytime, but you must descend 30 minutes after sunset.

✕ Take a Break

After a chilly evening, warm up with pho at **Ba-Le Kona** (p248).

★ Top Tip

There are no restaurants, gas stations or emergency services on Mauna Kea or along Saddle Road.

seemingly close enough to touch (though it pretty much kills the stargazing).

To Buy a Summit Tour or Not

Tours have many positives: transportation from other parts of the island to the visitor station, 4WD to the summit, warm clothing, a box dinner, excellent guides with deep knowledge of astronomy, and the ease of it all. The negatives to consider include the considerable cost (around $200 per individual), a fixed and limited schedule, and the herd factor.

Itinerary-wise, a typical sunset tour starts in the early afternoon, stops for dinner, arrives at the summit just before sunset, stays about 40 minutes, descends to the visitor station area for private star-gazing with a single telescope, and gets you home after 9pm.

Now assess the DIY alternative. If you have the proper vehicle you can hike on your own, poke into the Keck observatory, and experience a sacred mountain at your own pace. Finally, you can access the visitor station for a smorgasbord of stargazing amid multiple telescopes. The total cost is zero, apart from the car.

Stargazing Planner

Here are some tips from the experts about the best times – celestially speaking – to visit Mauna Kea.

● Lunar eclipses and meteor showers are special events in this rarefied air; the Leonides in November are particularly impressive. Check StarDate (http://stardate.org/nightsky/meteors) for meteor showers, eclipses, moon phases and more.

● The Milky Way streaks the night sky bright and white between January and March.

● Don't forget the monthly full moon. It's simply spectacular as it rises over you,

Mauna Loa Observatory Trail

The 6.4-mile, 2500ft climb to the top of Mauna Loa starts from Mauna Loa Observatory. It's a steep, exhausting, all-day adventure, but also an exceptional one.

Great For...

☑ Don't Miss

Driving Mauna Loa Observatory Rd, which punches through piles of *'a'a* (rough, jagged type of lava).

Trail Details & Weather Conditions

Start early; you want to be off the mountain or descending if afternoon clouds roll in. Depending on how far you go, prepare for a seven- to 10-hour round-trip hike. The trail is marked by *ahu* (cairns), which disappear in the fog. If fog does roll in, stop hiking; find shelter in one of several small tubes and hollows along the route until you can see again, even if this means waiting till morning – it's dangerously easy to get turned around up here. There are no visitor facilities or toilets at the trailhead or Mauna Loa Observatory.

The Trail

It is nearly 4 miles to the trail junction with the Mauna Loa Trail. Allow three hours for this gradual ascent of nearly 2000ft.

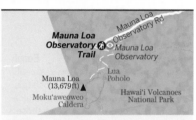

Mauna Loa
Observatory 🅰
Trail

Mauna Loa
Observatory Rd

Mauna Loa
Observatory

Lua
Poholo

Mauna Loa
(13,679ft) ▲
Mokuʻaweoweo
Caldera

Hawaiʻi Volcanoes
National Park

ⓘ Need to Know

Prepare for snow at any time, and take a flashlight; it'll take longer than you think.

✕ Take a Break

Refuel after your climb with an **Ultimate Burger** (p248) back in Kona.

★ Top Tip

Bring copious amounts of water, food, a flashlight and rain gear. Wear boots, a winter coat and cap.

If it weren't for the altitude, this would be a breeze. Proceed slowly but steadily, keeping breaks short. If you feel the onset of altitude sickness, descend. About two hours along, you enter Hawaiʻi Volcanoes National Park, and the old lava flows appear in a rainbow of sapphire, turquoise, silver, ocher, orange, gold and magenta.

At the trail junction, the majesty of the summit's Mokuʻaweoweo Caldera overwhelms you. Day hikers have two choices: proceed another 2.6 miles (about three hours) along the Summit Trail to the top at 13,677ft (visible in the distance), or explore the caldera by following the 2.1-mile Mauna Loa Cabin Trail. If you can stand not summiting, the second option is extremely interesting, leading to even grander caldera views and a vertiginous peek into the awesome depths of Lua Poholo (Falling Pit) – a pit crater that collapsed inward when lava left the summit. To do both would be an exhausting feat; choose wisely.

Camping Permit

If you would like to overnight at Mauna Loa Cabin, obtain a permit ($10 per group) the day before at Hawaiʻi Volcanoes National Park's Backcountry Office, where rangers can inform you about current trail conditions and water-catchment levels at the cabin.

Kona

◉ SIGHTS

Magic Sands Beach — Beach

(La'aloa Beach Park; Ali'i Dr; ⊙sunrise-sunset;
P⃞ ⬥) This small but gorgeous beach (also
called White Sands and, officially, La'aloa
Beach) has turquoise water, great sunsets,
little shade and possibly the best bodysurfing and bodyboarding on the Big Island.
Waves are consistent and just powerful
enough to shoot you across the water into
a sandy bay (beware: the north side of the
bay has more rocks). During high winter
surf the beach can vanish literally overnight, earning the nickname 'Magic Sands.'
The park is about 4 miles south of central
Kailua-Kona.

When the rocks and coral located past
the disappearing sands are exposed, the
beach becomes too treacherous for most
swimmers. Gradually the sand returns,
transforming the shore back into its former
beachy self. Facilities include restrooms,
showers, picnic tables and a volleyball
court; a lifeguard is on duty.

White Sands is almost always packed,
but there's little proprietary attitude from
locals. Sunsets here will get you all the likes
on social media.

Hulihe'e Palace — Historic Building

(📞808-329-1877; http://daughtersofhawaii.org;
75-5718 Ali'i Dr; adult/child $10/1; ⊙9am-4pm
Mon-Sat, 10am-3pm Sun) ✎ This palace is
a fascinating study in the rapid shift the
Hawaiian royal family made from Polynesian god-kings to Westernized monarchs.
Here's the skinny: Hawai'i's second
governor, 'John Adams' Kuakini, built a
simple two-story, lava-rock house as his
private residence in 1838. After Kuakini's
death, the house became the favorite
vacation getaway for Hawaiian royalty. The
palace contains Western antiques collected
on royal jaunts to Europe and ancient
Hawaiian artifacts, most notably several of
Kamehameha the Great's war spears.

Ahu'ena Heiau — Temple

(http://ahuenaheiau.org; 75-5660 Palani Rd; ⬥)
After uniting the Hawaiian Islands in 1810,
Kamehameha the Great established the
kingdom's royal court in Lahaina on Maui,
but he continued to return to the Big Island.
After a couple of years, he restored this sacred site as his personal retreat and temple
(which now sits adjacent to a hotel). Notice
the towering carved *ki'i* (deity) image with
a golden plover atop its helmet: these
long-distance flying birds may have helped
guide the first Polynesians to Hawaii.

✪ ACTIVITIES

Many activity outfitters and tour companies are based either here or in Keauhou,
about 5 miles south of Kailua-Kona.

Kailua Bay Charter Company — Cruise

(📞808-324-1749; www.konaglassbottomboat.
com; Kailua-Kona Pier; 50min tour adult/child under 12yr $50/25; ⊙11am & 12:30pm; ⬥) Gain a
new perspective on Kailua-Kona's coastline,
its underwater reef and sea life from a 36ft
glass-bottomed boat with a cheery crew and
onboard naturalist. Easy boarding is available for passengers with mobility issues.
Times vary; check the website or call ahead.

Paradise Sailing — Boating

(www.paradisesailinghawaii.com; Honokohau
Marina; $94) The beauty of the Big Island can
be hard to appreciate when you're scream-
ing past it with an outboard motor ringing
in your ears, and as such, Paradise Sailing
offers a nice alternative: true wind-pow-
ered sailing aboard a 36ft catamaran, with
a small number of passengers as your
companions. Guests are given the chance
to operate the boat themselves.

SUP at Kona Boys Beach Shack — SUP

(Kona Boys; 📞808-329-2345; www.konaboys.
com; Kamakahonu Beach; surfboard/SUP rental
from $29, SUP lesson & tours per person group/
private $99/150; ⊙8am-5pm) The Kona Boys
Beach Shack organizes SUP lessons as well
as more ambitious coastal paddling tours,

and rents SUP sets and surfboards right on Kamakahonu Beach – which, sheltered as it is, is perfect for learning SUP basics. Call in advance to arrange group or private surfing or SUP lessons. You can also book through the shop in **Kealakekua** (☑808-328-1234; www.konaboys.com; 79-7539 Mamalahoa Hwy; single/double kayak per day $54/74, tours $139-189; ☺7:30am-5pm).

HYPR Nalu Hawaii   Surfing

(☑808-960-4667; www.hyprnalu.com; 75-5663A Palanai Rd; semi-private/private surfing lessons $120/175) While this is primarily a surf and SUP gear shop, the folks at HYPR Nalu also offer respectable surfing lessons. Rather than throwing you right onto the water, they're big on prior preparation: this outfit makes a point of observing your technique in store, all while giving feedback that incorporates the physics and philosophy of surfing.

Kona Coast by Air   Scenic Flights

(☑808-646-0231; http://konacoastbyair. com; 73-200 Kupipi St, Airport; 45/75min flight $230/330; ☺6:30-11am & 5-6:30pm) You can see the Big Island while hiking, and you can see it underwater, but what about seeing it from the sky? That's the promise of Kona Coast by Air, which leads powered hang-glider trips through the clouds. You get to operate the flying tri-cycle (yup, that's what you're piloting), which is pretty damn exhilarating.

Kona Brewing Company   Tours

(☑808-334-2739; http://konabrewingco.com; 74-5612 Pawai Pl; ☺30min tours 10:30am & 3pm) ✏ **FREE** Since 1994, this eco-conscious company has anchored Hawai'i's micro-brewery scene. The once-small, family-run operation is now one of the nation's fast-est-growing microbreweries – from Maine to California, you can sip 'liquid aloha,' which circulates throughout 4000 kegs in Hawaii alone. Complimentary tours include tasting samples; note that kids under 15 are not allowed to tag along.

Kona Boys Beach Shack (p244), Kona

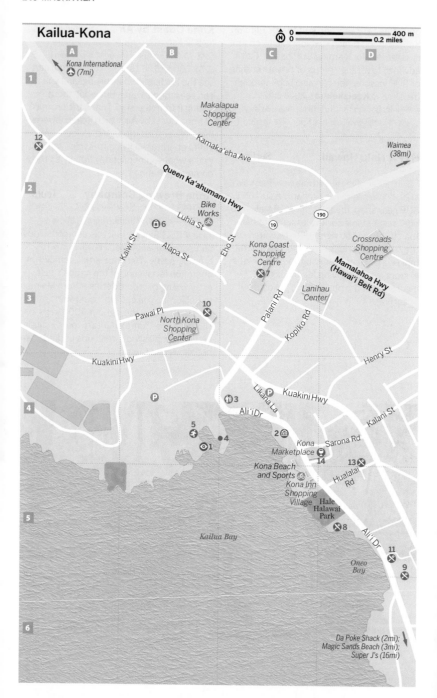

Kailua-Kona

N
0   400 m
0   0.2 miles

Kona International ✈ (7mi)

Waimea (38mi)

Makalapua Shopping Center

Kamaka'eha Ave

Queen Ka'ahumanu Hwy

⊗12

Bike Works ☜

🔒6   Luhia St

Kaiwi St

Alapa St

Eho St

19

190

Kona Coast Shopping Centre

⊗7

Crossroads Shopping Centre

Mamalahoa Hwy (Hawai'i Belt Rd)

Lanihau Center

Palani Rd

Kopiko Rd

⊗10

Pawai Pl

North Kona Shopping Center

Kuakini Hwy

Henry St

Ⓟ

Likana La

Kuakini Hwy

Kalani St

🅿

🍴3

Ali'i Dr

5
✚

⊙1   ●4

2🏛

Kona Marketplace

Sarona Rd

14

⊗13

Hualalai Rd

Kona Beach and Sports ☜

Kona Inn Shopping Village

Hale Halawai Park

⊗8

Ali'i Dr

Kailua Bay

Oneo Bay

⊗11

⊗9

Da Poke Shack (2mi);
Magic Sands Beach (3mi);
Super J's (16mi)

Kailua-Kona

◎ **Sights**
1 Ahu'ena Heiau B4
2 Hulihe'e Palace C4

⊕ **Activities, Courses & Tours**
3 HYPR Nalu Hawaii C4
4 Kailua Bay Charter Company C4
   Kona Brewing Company .... (see 10)
5 SUP at Kona Boys Beach Shack B4

⑥ **Shopping**
6 Kona Bay Books B2

⊗ **Eating**
7 Ba-Le Kona C3
8 Daylight Mind D5
9 Evolution Bakery & Cafe D5
10 Kona Brewing Company B3
11 Sushi Shiono D5
12 Ultimate Burger A2
13 Umekes D4

⊙ **Drinking & Nightlife**
14 Sam's Hideaway D4

TOURS

Mauna Kea Summit Adventures
Tours

(☏808-322-2366; www.maunakea.com; tours per person $212) The granddaddy of Mauna Kea tours has been taking folks to the summit for over 30 years. A hot dinner outside MKVIS, cold-weather parkas to borrow and stargazing through an 11in Celestron telescope are included. Pick-ups from Kailua-Kona, Waikoloa and Hwys 190/200 junction. Children must be at least 13 years old.

🅰 SHOPPING

Kona Bay Books
Books

(☏808-326-7790; http://konabaybooks.com; 74-5487 Kaiwi St; ⊙10am-6pm) The Big Island's largest selection of used books, CDs and DVDs, including Hawaiiana titles, is piled floor to ceiling in this warehouse-sized bookstore.

⊗ EATING

Da Poke Shack
Seafood $

(☏808-329-7653; http://dapokeshack.com; 76-6246 Ali'i Dr, Castle Kona Bali Kai; mains & meals $5-12; ⊙10am-6pm; ⋔) Poke is a local specialty that blends ceviche and sushi: raw, marinated cubes of fish mixed with soy sauce, sesame oil, chilies, seaweed and... well, really, the sky's the limit. The point is, poke is wonderful, and Da Poke Shack is

the spot to get it. You'll be eating at a picnic table or, better, bring it to the beach.

Umekes
Hawaii Regional $

(☏808-329-3050; www.umekespoke808.com; 75-143 Hualalai Rd; mains $5-14; ⊙10am-7pm Mon-Sat; ⋔⋔) Umekes takes island-style food to the next level. Local ingredients such as ahi tuna, spicy crab salad and salted Waimea beef are served plate-lunch style with excellent, innovative sides such as seasoned seaweed and cucumber kimchi (along with heaped scoops of rice). It's some of the best-value grinds on the island. There's another location at 74-5563 Kaiwi St.

Sushi Shiono
Japanese $$$

(☏808-326-1696; www.sushishiono.com; 75-5799 Ali'i Dr, Ali'i Sunset Plaza; à la carte dishes $4-18, lunch plates $10-19, dinner mains $20-40; ⊙11:30am-2pm Mon-Sat, 5:30-9pm Mon-Sat, 5-9pm Sun) Inside a mini mall, wickedly fresh sushi and sashimi are complemented by a sake list that's as long as Honshu. The joint is owned by a Japanese expat, who employs an all-star, all-Japanese cast of sushi chefs behind the bar. Dinner reservations recommended.

Super J's
Hawaiian $

(Ka'aloa's Super J's; ☏808-328-9566; 83-5409 Mamalahoa Hwy; plates $8-12; ⊙10am-6:30pm Mon-Sat; 🅿⋔) The full title of this place is 'Ka'aloa's Super J's Hawaiian Food,' but everyone calls it Super J's. They also call it freakin' delicious. The laulau (pork, chicken or fish wrapped inside taro or ti leaves) is

From left: Gecko; Tropical fish; Ahu'ena Heiau (p244), Kona Bay

steamed until it's so tender it melts under your fork, the *lomilomi* salmon is perfectly salty – you'll even want second helpings of poi (mashed taro). Best of all is the setting: you're basically eating in a welcoming Hawaiian family's kitchen. It's on the *makai* (seaward) side of Hwy 11, between Miles 106 and 107.

Ba-Le Kona   Vietnamese $
(☎808-327-1212; 74-5588 Palani Rd, Kona Coast Shopping Center; mains $5-12; ⏰10am-9pm Mon-Sat, to 4pm Sun; 🖋) Don't let the fluorescent-lit dining room and polystyrene plates fool you: Ba-Le serves the sort of Vietnamese that makes you want to pack it all up and move to Hanoi. Flavors are simple, refreshing and bright, from the green-papaya salad to traditional pho (noodle soup), and rice plates of spicy lemongrass chicken, tofu, beef or roast pork.

Ultimate Burger   Burgers $
(www.ultimateburger.net; 74-5450 Makala Blvd; burgers $6-15) 🖋 Kailua-Kona is likely your introduction to the Big Island; with this in mind, let Ultimate Burger be your introduction to the wonderful world of Big Island

beef. There's a big focus on organic ingredients and local sourcing, and we commend such efforts, but also: these burgers are *delicious*. Wash them down with some homemade lemonade.

Daylight Mind   Fusion $$$
(☎808-339-7824; http://daylightmind.com; 75-5770 Ali'i Dr; brunch $10-18, dinner $15-38; ⏰8am-9pm) A pretty perch over the water and an airy dining space is complemented by fare that runs the gamut from Hawaii Regional (short ribs braised in local coffee) to Pacific fusion (Hamakua mushroom polenta). It's all delicious, but the morning brunch stands out as a particularly excellent start to a Kona day.

Evolution Bakery & Cafe   Bakery $
(☎808-331-1122; www.evolutionbakerycafe.com; 75-5813 Ali'i Dr; mains $5-10; ⏰7-11:30am; 🛜🖋) 🖋 Kailua-Kona has always had room for a spot that's hip enough for a MacBook, and crunchy enough for dreadlocks. Enter Evolution. There's wi-fi, smoothies, vegan bagels, pancakes and sandwiches, Kona coffee and some seriously good mac nut (served to the Mac nuts, get it? Never

STEVE BOWER/SHUTTERSTOCK ©

mind) banana bread. Much of the menu is vegan friendly and gluten free.

🍸 DRINKING & NIGHTLIFE

Kailua-Kona's bar scene is pretty touristy, but there are a handful of places for a cocktail or a beer. Always a good fallback, **Kona Brewing Company** (☏808-334-2739; http://konabrewingco.com; 75-5629 Kuakini Hwy; mains $13-25; ⊗11am-10pm; 🖢) 🍴 usually has live Hawaiian music from 5pm to 8pm on Sundays.

Sam's Hideaway   Bar
(☏808-326-7267; 75-5725 Ali'i Dr; ⊗9am-2am) Sam's is a dark, cozy (OK, maybe 'dank') little nook of a bar. You'll rarely find tourists but there are always locals, especially on karaoke nights. Trust us: you haven't done Kailua-Kona until you've seen a 7ft Samoan guy tear up as he belts out 'The Snows of Mauna Kea.'

ⓘ GETTING THERE & AWAY

A car is almost a necessity on Hawai'i, but for those who are not renting one upon arrival at **Kona International Airport** (p313), taxis are

available curbside (book late-night pick-ups in advance). Taxi fares average $25 to Kailua-Kona or $35 to Keauhou, plus tip.

Speedi Shuttle (☏877-242-5777, 808-329-5433; www.speedishuttle.com; airport transfer Kailua Kona shared/private $32/124, Mauna Lani $59/186; ⊗9am-last flight) is economical if you're in a group. Book in advance, and beware, they've been known to run on island time.

ⓘ GETTING AROUND

At the time of research, a **bike share** ($3.50 per half hour) program was just getting off the ground. Kiosks are located at Hale Halawai Park, Huggo's On the Rock's and Courtyard King Kamehameha's Kona Beach Hotel. The kiosks accept credit cards. **Bike Works** (☏808-326-2453; www.bikeworkskona.com; 74-5583 Luhia St, Hale Hana Center; bicycle rental per day $40-60; ⊗9am-6pm Mon-Sat, 10am-4pm Sun) rents high-quality mountain and road-touring bikes. You can also try **Kona Beach and Sports** (☏808-329-2294; www.konabeachandsports.com; 75-5744 Ali'i Dr, Kona Inn Shopping Village; bicycle rental per day $25-30; ⊗9:30am-8pm).

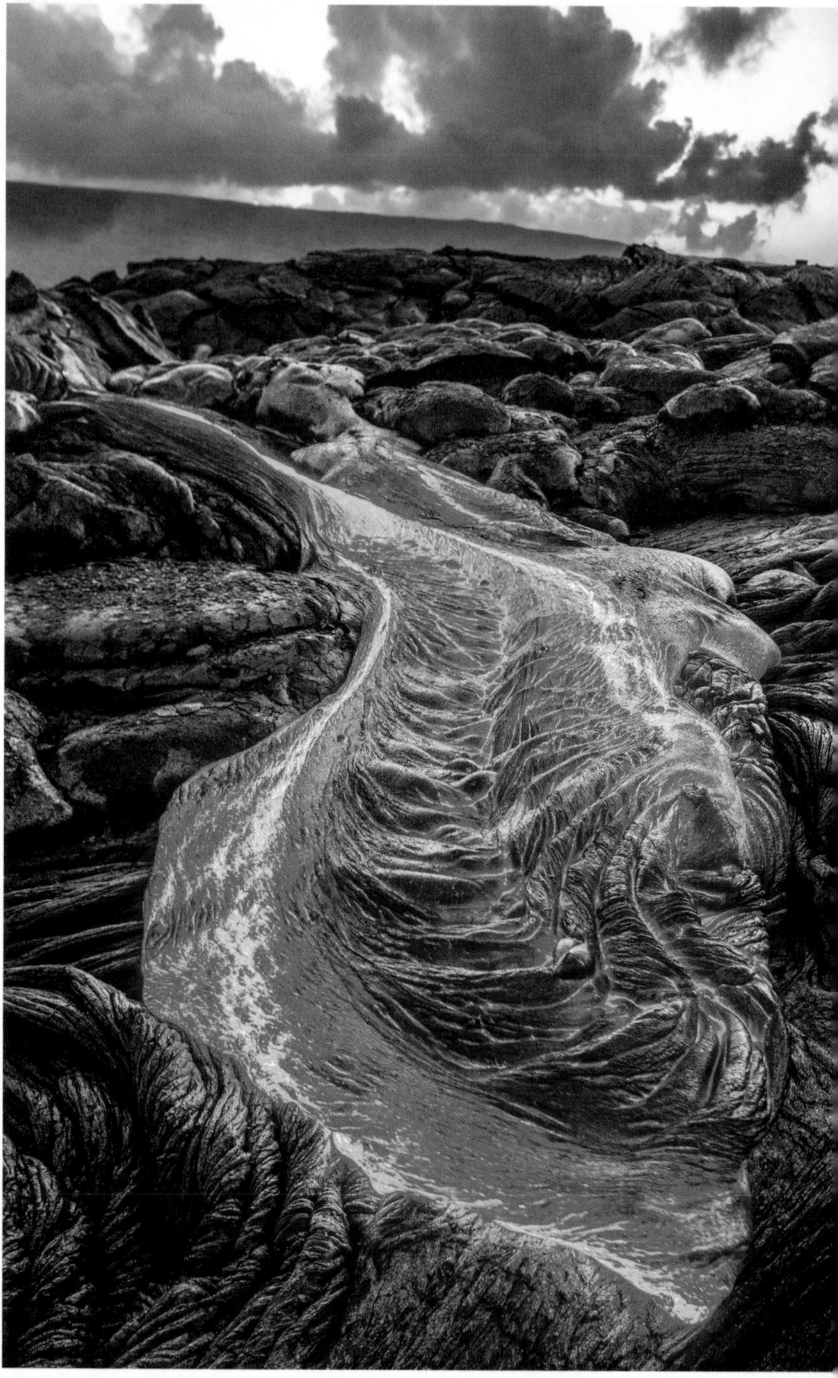

HAWAI'I VOLCANOES NATIONAL PARK

In this Chapter

Kilauea Iki Overlook & Trail............ 254
Halema'uma'u Viewpoint............... 256
Top Day Hikes 258
Crater Rim Drive............................. 262
Hilo.. 266
Getting There & Away 275

Hawai'i Volcanoes National Park at a Glance...

From the often-snowy summit of Mauna Loa, the world's most massive volcano, to the boiling coast where lava pours into the sea, Hawai'i Volcanoes National Park is a micro-continent of thriving rainforests, volcano-induced deserts, high-mountain meadows, coastal plains and plenty of geological marvels in between.

At the heart of it all is Kilauea – the earth's youngest and most active shield volcano. Since 1983 Kilauea's East Rift Zone has been erupting almost nonstop from the Pu'u 'O'o vent, adding nearly 500 acres of new land to the island.

Hawai'i Volcanoes National Park in One Day

Get up to speed at **Kilauea Visitor Center & Museum** (p255), then take in the sights around the Kilauea Caldera on the Crater Rim Dr. Hike across a crater on the **Kilauea Iki Trail** (p255). Eat and spend the night in Volcano. Don't miss the hot lava view from **Halema'u-ma'u Viewpoint** (p264).

Hawai'i Volcanoes National Park in Two Days

Start day two with two easy day hikes, **Pu'u Loa Petroglyphs** (p258) and **Footprints** (p260). Attend a ranger talk or two then check out the art in the **Volcano Arts Center** (p260). Eat dinner with a fantastic view of the crater as a backdrop at the **Rim Restaurant** and then attend **Art After Dark in the Park** (p255).

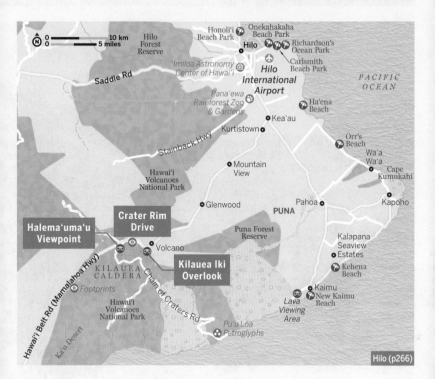

Arriving in Hawai'i Volcanoes National Park

The park is 30 miles (45 minutes) from Hilo and 95 miles (2¾ hours) from Kailua-Kona via Hwy 11. The turnoffs for Volcano Village are a couple of miles east of the main park entrance.

Sleeping

The park's two vehicle-accessible campgrounds are relatively uncrowded outside of summer months. Nights can be crisp and cool and wet. Campsites are first-come, first-served (with a seven-night limit). Nearby Volcano Village has the most variety for those who prefer a roof over their heads.

Hiking in Kilauea Iki Crater

TOMMAYAPHOTO/SHUTTERSTOCK ©

Kilauea Iki Overlook & Trail

On Crater Rim Drive, this overlook perches beside a steaming 1-mile crater. The Kilaueu Iki Trail far below is as astonishing as it looks.

Great For...

☑ **Don't Miss**

Fascinating and informative talks with **Art After Dark in the Park** in the Visitor Centre.

Kilauea Visitor Center & Museum

Stop here first. Extraordinarily helpful (and remarkably patient) rangers and volunteers can advise you about volcanic activity, air quality, road closures, hiking-trail conditions and how best to spend however much time you have. Interactive museum exhibits are small but family friendly, and will teach even science-savvy adults about the park's delicate ecosystem and Hawaiian heritage. All of the rotating movies are excellent. Pick up fun junior ranger program activity books for your kids before leaving.

A well-stocked nonprofit bookstore inside the center sells souvenirs, rain ponchos, walking sticks and flashlights. Wheelchairs are free to borrow. There are also restrooms, a pay phone, and a place to fill up your water bottles.

Kilauea Iki Trail

MNSTUDIO/SHUTTERSTOCK ©

ⓘ Need to Know

Kilauea Visitor Center & Museum
(☏808-985-6000; www.nps.gov/havo;
Crater Rim Dr; ⊙9am-5pm, film screenings
hourly 9am-4pm; ⛾) ✿

✕ Take a Break

Savor the rich Special Curry at **Thai
Thai Restaurant** (☏808-967-7969;
19-4084 Old Volcano Rd; mains $15-26;
⊙11:30am-9pm; ✎) after your hike.

★ Top Tip

Check the outdoor signboards by the
Kilauea Visitor Center entrance for
upcoming talks and ranger-led hikes.

The Crater

When 'Little Kilauea' burst open in a fiery
inferno in November 1959, it filled the
crater with a roiling lake of molten rock fed
by a 1900ft fountain that lit up the night sky
with 2 million gushing tons of lava per hour
at its peak. The lake took more than 30
years to completely solidify.

Kilauea Iki Trail

If you can only do one day hike, make it this
one. Do the 4.5-mile loop counterclockwise
through an astounding microcosm of the
park that descends through fairy-tale ohia
forests to a mile-wide, still-steaming lava
lake that was filled relatively recently by a
fiery fountain spewing 403 million gallons
of lava per second (that's a lot of lava).

Kilauea Iki erupted for five weeks at the
end of 1959, alternately filling the crater

with several meters of lava that washed
against its walls like ocean waves and then
drained back into the fissure. The lava
fountain that formed the cinder pile above
reached 1900ft, the highest ever recorded
in Hawaii. This awesome sight suddenly
turned terrifying when boulders blocked
the passage like your thumb on a garden
hose, sending a jet of lava shooting across
the crater toward crowds of visitors.

Hit the trail before 8am to beat the
crowds. The faint footpath across the crater
floor is marked by *ahu* (stone cairns) to aid
navigation. Follow them; the crust can be
thin elsewhere.

Art After Dark in the Park

Experts in science, conservation, art or
history unlock the mysteries of the park in
this award-winning lecture series. In our
experience, they're so fascinating we would
go even if there was more of a nightlife
around here.

Lava lake from Halemaʻumaʻu Viewpoint.

Halemaʻumaʻu Viewpoint

There's absolutely nothing like watching a gaping crater full of roiling hot lava send a billowing column of steam into the sky. There's never a wrong time to visit.

Great For...

☑ Don't Miss

The history and geology exhibits inside the **Jaggar Museum** (☎808-985-6051; Crater Rim Dr; ⏰10am-8pm daily; ♿).

History & Geology

Halemaʻumaʻu is really a crater within the crater of Kilauea Caldera. The name means 'house of the ʻamaʻu fern,' though ancient songs also refer to it as Halemaumau without the okina (glottal stops), or 'house of eternal fire.'

In 1823, missionary William Ellis first described the boiling goblet of Halemaʻumaʻu to a wide audience, and his fantastic account attracted travelers from all over the world. Looking in, some saw the fires of hell, others primeval creation, but none left the crater unmoved. Mark Twain wrote in 1866 that he witnessed: '[C]ircles and serpents and streaks of lightning all twined and wreathed and tied together...I have seen Vesuvius since, but it was a mere toy, a child's volcano, a soup kettle, compared to this.' Then, in 1924, the crater floor subsided rap-

VOLCANO

Halema'uma'u Viewpoint

KILAUEA CALDERA

❶ Need to Know

Kilauea Visitor Center & Museum

(☏808-985-6000; www.nps.gov/havo; Crater Rim Dr; ⊗9am-5pm, film screenings hourly 9am-4pm; ▣) ✿

✕ Take a Break

Enjoy margherita pizza at **'Ōhelo Café** (☏808-339-7865; www.ohelocafe.com; 19-4005 Haunani Rd, cnr Old Volcano Rd; pizza $12-15, mains $21-40; ⊗11:30am-2:30pm & 5:30-9:30pm, closed 1st Tue of the month) in Volcano after admiring the crater.

★ Top Tip

Best viewing is on a clear night after sunset.

idly, touching off a series of explosive eruptions. Boulders and mud rained for days. When it was over, the crater had doubled in size – to about 300ft deep and 3000ft wide. Lava activity ceased and the crust cooled. But not for long. Since then, Halema'uma'u has erupted 18 times, making it the most active area on Kilauea's summit.

How active Kilauea Volcano will be when you visit is subject to the whims of Pele, the Hawaiian goddess of fire and volcanoes, so set expectations low, and hope to be pleasantly surprised. Best viewing is on a clear night after sunset, though a break in thunderclouds can create an otherworldly frame for Pele's fire.

All of Hawai'i is the territory of Pele, goddess of fire and volcanoes, but Halema'uma'u is her home, making it a sacred site for Hawaiians.

What's New: Lava Lake

In April 2015, the lava lake in Pele's home overflowed onto the crater floor, adding an approximately 30ft layer of fresh lava. If the lake level remains high, molten lava is visible from the Jaggar Museum overlook (p263).

Lake of Fire

On March 19, 2008, Halema'uma'u Crater shattered a quarter-century of silence with a huge steam-driven explosion that scattered rocks and Pele's hair (strands of volcanic glass) over 75 acres. A series of explosions followed, widening a 300ft vent in the crater floor which has continued to spew a column of gas and ash across the Ka'u Desert. If you are lucky, Pele may be in a rare mood, sending spatter and rocks shooting up to the now-closed section of Crater Rim Dr.

Puʻu Loa Petroglyphs

GEORGEBURBA/GETTY IMAGES ©

Top Day Hikes

Although staring into the Halemaʻumaʻu crater after a 200ft walk from your car is amazing, the real magic of Hawaiʻi Volcanoes National Park can only be found while exploring its 150 miles of trails.

Great For...

☑ **Don't Miss**

Footprints preserved in fragile sediment and continually revealed and reburied by windblown sand on the Footprints Trail.

Mauna Iki Trail

For solitude in a mesmerizing lava landscape, head 2 miles across the Kaʻu Desert to our favorite viewpoint: the barren summit of Mauna Iki (3032ft). Take in sprawling Mauna Loa and steaming Kilauea, while the vast Kaʻu Desert appears to melt into the ocean. The trail's north end is sometimes referred to as Footprints Trail.

If you continue past the summit, it's 7 miles to Hilina Pali Rd past craggy cinder cones, fissures and chasms. Take note of sulfur dioxide levels as you'll be smack in the fallout zone – hence the distinct lack of vegetation.

Puʻu Loa Petroglyphs

The gentle, 1.3-mile round-trip to Puʻu Loa (roughly, 'hill of long life') leads to one of Hawaiʻi's largest concentrations of ancient

❶ Need to Know

Stop by the **Kilauea Visitor Center & Museum** (📞808-985-6000; www.nps.gov/havo; Crater Rim Dr; ⏰9am-5pm, film screenings hourly 9am-4pm; 👶) 🐾 before you set off to check for road closures.

✂ Take a Break

Pick up a grab-and-go wrap for a picnic at **Eagle's Lighthouse Café** (📞808-985-8587; www.eagleslighthouse. com; 19-4005 Haunani Rd; mains $5-11; ⏰7am-5pm Mon-Sat; 📶🐾).

petroglyphs, some over 800 years old. Here Hawaiians chiseled more than 23,000 drawings into *pahoehoe* (smooth-flowing lava) with adze tools quarried from Keanakako'i. Stay on the boardwalk – not all petroglyphs are obvious, and you might damage some if you walk over the rocks. The trailhead parking is signed between Miles 16 and 17 on Chain of Craters Road.

There are abstract designs, animal and human figures, as well as thousands of dimpled depressions (or cupules) that were receptacles for *piko* (umbilical cords). Placing a baby's *piko* inside a cupule and covering it with stones bestowed health and longevity on the child. Archaeologists believe a dot with a circle around it was for a firstborn, while two circles were reserved for the firstborn of an *ali'i* (chief).

Napau Crater Trail

This 7-mile (one-way) undulating hike over rugged terrain begins with the excellent Mauna Ulu Eruption Trail before continuing across acres of *pahoehoe* to the edge of the mile-long Makaopuhi Crater. There it heads into the muddy fern forest past the Old Pulu Factory to the edge of Napau Crater with Pu'u 'O'o steaming silently on the horizon.

We have a love-hate relationship with this trail, which can be grueling at times, but pays big dividends in terms of diversity and views.

Pu'u Huluhulu Trail

Technically just the first part of the Napau Crater Trail, this mellower 3-mile hike starts with a closeup inspection of the multicolored 1969 fissure eruption that destroyed Chain of Craters before the road reached its 10th birthday. The trail ends atop Pu'u Huluhulu (shaggy hill) with a commanding view of Mauna Ulu: the ultimate result of that eruption.

It's easy to miss the fissure, the hike's most unique feature. At the self-registration box, don't take off across the *pahoehoe*, but instead turn right and look across the old road for the start of the 0.5-mile loop.

After that, continue toward the *kipuka* (oasis) besieged by clinkery *'a'a* and an army of lava trees as tall as you are. Lava trees form when a shell of lava cools around a tree while the rest of the molten rock drains away, leaving behind a hollowed rock pillar.

Following Ancient Footprints

In 1782, Kilauea belched a massive cloud of steam, hot sand, suffocating gas, rocks and ash that swept across the Ka'u Desert on hurricane-force winds. Warriors and civilians were caught in the sticky, wet hellstorm. As they gasped for breath, stumbling to their deaths, their feet left ghostly footprints in the muck. That muck dried, preserving the gory moment for all eternity. Or at least that's how famed geologist Dr Jaggar imagined it.

A short, 0.8-mile walk down the Mauna Iki trail from the Ka'u Desert trailhead on

Gecko on black lava stone

Hwy 11 brings you to a field of scattered footprints preserved in fragile sediment and continually being revealed and reburied by windblown sand.

Kipuka Puaulu

A shady, 1.2-mile hike easy enough for young kids loops through a rainforest *kipuka* that has rebounded after years of intensive grazing turned it into a grassland. Now, thanks to fencing and aggressive restoration, this parcel has more native tree species per acre than anywhere else in the park, making it a haven for birds and birdwatchers.

> ★ **Top Tip**
> Dress for rapidly changing weather: a hot sunny stroll can turn cold and wet in an instant.

LUC KOHNEN/SHUTTERSTOCK ©

The trailhead is 1.5 miles up Mauna Loa Rd at the turnaround. Do it early morning or at dusk, when you'll be enveloped by the songs of honeycreepers – the *'amakihi* (yellow-green honey creeper), *'apapane* (bright red Hawaiian honeycreeper) and possibly *'i'iwi* (scarlet Hawaiian honeycreeper) – plus the inquisitive *'elepaio* (Hawaiian monarch flycatcher). A small lava tube is enticing, but the park discourages exploration to protect unique species of big-eyed hunting spider and lava-tree cricket.

Halema'uma'u Trail

Once traversed by the likes of Mark Twain, the caldera-crossing portion of this trail has been closed for several years due to the explosive activity at the other end. What is open is a pleasant path between the forested terraces descending beneath Volcano House to the bottom of Kilauea Caldera.

Drinking Water

Despite being bordered by rainforest, this is a surprisingly dry area and dehydration comes easily. No drinking water is available, except possibly at primitive campgrounds (where it must be treated before drinking), so pack at least three quarts of water per person per day.

 Hike with New Friends

If you prefer to join a group, the nonprofit Friends of Hawai'i Volcanoes National Park leads weekend hikes and field trips, and organizes volunteer activities including native forest restoration.

Entrance to the Thurston Lava Tubes (p264)

BILDAGENTUR ZOONAR GMBH/SHUTTERSTOCK ©

Crater Rim Drive

This incredible 11-mile paved loop road starts at Kilauea Visitor Center and skirts the rim of Kilauea Caldera, passing steam vents and rifts, hiking trailheads and amazing views of the smoking crater.

Great For...

ⓘ Need to Know

The park is typically open 24 hours a day.

Volcano Arts Center

Near the visitor center, this sharp local art gallery spotlights museum-quality pottery, paintings, woodwork, sculpture, jewelry, Hawaiian quilts and more in a series of rotating exhibits. The nonprofit shop, housed in the historic 1877 Volcano House hotel, is worth a visit just to admire its construction. Ask about upcoming art classes and cultural workshops, including the Aloha Fridays weekly immersive experiences (11am to 1pm Friday).

Sulfur Banks

A wooden boardwalk weaves between misty, rocky vents stained chartreuse, yellow, orange and other psychedelic colors by tons of sulfur-infused steam rising from deep within the earth. Once frequented by rare birds (hence the Hawaiian name,

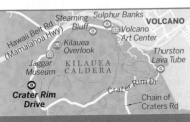

★ **Top Tip**

Get an early start. The tour buses and crowds start arriving around 10am.

a convenient drive-up photo op. Hot rocks below the surface boil rainwater as it percolates down, producing the steam. While the vents at the parking area are perfectly fine, even more evocative is Steaming Bluff, found along a short walk out to the rim. Here, curtains of steam frame the cliffs above a post-apocalyptic view.

Kilauea Overlook

A pause-worthy panorama, most remarkable for the 6-ton volcanic bomb sitting defiantly on the rim daring you to take eruptions lightly. There is no view from the covered picnic tables, but there is shelter from wind and rain.

Jaggar Museum

There's plenty packed into this small one-room geology museum (p256) including real-time seismographs and tiltmeters recording earthquakes inside the park (and under your feet). Other exhibits introduce Hawaiian gods and goddesses and give a short history of the neighboring Hawai'i Volcano Observatory (closed to visitors), founded by famed volcanologist Dr Thomas A Jaggar. Park rangers frequently give geology talks inside the museum, while visitors pack the porch outside for the best view of the lava lake in Halema'uma'u Crater.

The museum and observatory sit high on the Kilauea's rim above the sacred cliffs of Uwekahuna (wailing priests). These terraces formed when the caldera collapsed

Ha'akulamanu), invasive plants and other changes to the environment have made it less hospitable to *nene* (native Hawaiian goose)and *kolea* (Pacific golden plover). The easy 0.7-mile one-way trail connects to Crater Rim Dr near the parking lot for Steaming Bluff. Wheelchair-accessible.

About 500 years ago, Kilauea's summit collapsed inward, leaving a series of concentric cliffs stepping down towards its center. These sulfur banks are on the outermost ring and formed due to deep cracks along the fault that allow gases to escape the magma pocket below. This potent gas creates the small crystalline structures that give the rocks their hue.

Steam Vents & Steaming Bluff

Creating impressive billowing plumes in the cool early morning, these vents make

inward forming a 1600ft-deep hole, which has since been filled with 1200ft of lava.

Halemaʻumaʻu Viewpoint

The original Halemaʻumaʻu Overlook off Crater Rim Dr has been closed since 2008 due to volcanic activity and the very real threat of death (ie don't even think about sneaking out there). Fortunately, the next-closest view from the Jaggar Museum patio is also extraordinary.

There's absolutely nothing like watching a gaping crater full of roiling hot lava send a billowing column of steam into the sky – especially after dark when the flickering spotlights of creation set everything aglow

Thurston Lava Tube

On Kilauea's eastern side, Crater Rim Dr passes through a rainforest thick with tree ferns and ohia trees to the overflowing parking lot for ever-popular **Thurston Lava Tube** (Nahuku; off Crater Rim Dr; 🚻). A 0.3-mile loop walk starts in an ohia forest filled with birdsong before heading underground through a gigantic (but short) artificially lit lava tube. For a more memorable experience, visit the glowing maw after dark.

Lava tubes form when the outer crust of a lava river hardens while the liquid beneath the surface continues to flow through. When the eruption stops, the flow drains out, leaving only that hard shell behind. Nahuku, as this tube is called in Hawaiian, was 'discovered' by controversial figure Lorrin Thurston, the newspaper baron (and patron of famed volcanologist Dr Jaggar) who was instrumental in overthrowing the Kingdom of Hawaii.

Viewing the Lava Up Close

Lucky travelers may be able to view liquid rock making the 6.4-mile journey from the Puʻu Oʻo Vent to the ocean: a journey of pure creation, and sometimes destruction. If the show is really on, there will be surface flows, lava 'skylights' and flaming trees. When the flow mellows or changes course, you may be able to see a steam plume during the day, or an unearthly red glow

after dark – even more ominous when it's coming from a crack between your feet.

Where the lava will be flowing when you visit and whether or not you can reach it are impossible to predict. Ask at the Kilauea Visitor Center, call the park or check the NPS website (www.nps.gov/havo) for updates, but know that sometimes it can be an arduous 10-mile round-trip hike or more from the end of Chain of Craters Rd. Staying informed about the flow helps manage expectations (especially those of kids).

Lava entering the ocean is wondrous but extremely dangerous. The explosive clash between seawater and 2100°F lava can spray scalding water and poisonous steam hundreds of feet into the air and throw flaming lava chunks well inland. Unstable

Lava flowing into the ocean from Kilauea

ledges of lava crust (called lava benches) sometimes collapse without warning. Several observers have been injured, some fatally, over the past decade. Stay well inland from the lava flow and heed all official warnings.

It may be easier to hike to the flow from the other side at the county-run **lava viewing area** (www.hawaiicounty.gov/lava-viewing/; end of Hwy 130; ⊙3-9pm) at the end of Hwy 130 in Puna. There, locals often rent time-saving bicycles, and guides are plentiful.

No matter where you begin, bring a flashlight and plenty of water, and plan to stick around after sunset.

Chain of Craters Road

This is it: possibly the most scenic road trip on an island packed with really scenic road

trips. Heading south from Crater Rim Dr, paved Chain of Craters Rd winds almost 19 miles and 3700ft down the southern slopes of Kilauea, ending abruptly at rivers of lava making their way to the coast.

✕ Take a Break

Enjoy a world-class view with your meal at the spectacularly situated **Rim Restaurant** (www.hawaiivolcanohouse.com/dining; Volcano House, Crater Rim Dr; lunch $14-20, dinner $20-40; ⊙7-10am, 11am-2pm, 5:30-8:30pm 🚻🖉).

★ Top Tip

Drive slowly, especially in rainy or foggy conditions, and watch out for endangered birdlife.

Hilo

Most sights are found in downtown Hilo, where historic early-20th-century buildings overlook the coast, which locals call 'bayfront.' Further east sits Hilo's landmark dock, Suisan Fish Market (p273), and the **Keaukaha neighborhood**, where all of Hilo's beaches are located, except for Honoli'i Beach Park. On weekends, expect jammed parking lots and steady traffic along Kalaniana'ole Ave. Otherwise parking is readily available, whether on the street or in a lot.

🏖 BEACHES

Carlsmith Beach Park   Beach
(Kalaniana'ole Ave; 🚻) Although this beach may look rocky, the swimming area is protected by a reef, making it family friendly. The anchialine ponds, which flow to the ocean, are ideal for kids. Snorkeling is decent during calm water conditions. There are lifeguards on weekends and holidays, plus restrooms, showers and picnic areas.

Onekahakaha Beach Park   Beach
(Kalaniana'ole Ave; ⏰7am-9pm; 🚻) Perfect for kids, this spacious beach has a broad, shallow, sandy-bottomed pool, protected by a boulder breakwater. The water is only 1ft to 2ft deep in spots, creating a safe 'baby beach.' An unprotected cove north of the kiddie pool is deeper but can be dangerous due to rough surf and needle-sharp *wana* (sea urchins). Surrounding grassy lawns shaded by trees are ideal for picnicking. There are lifeguards on weekends and holidays, plus restrooms, showers, covered pavilions and picnic areas.

Richardson's Ocean Park   Beach
(Kalaniana'ole Ave; ⏰7am-7pm; 🚻) Near the end of Kalaniana'ole Ave, this little pocket of black sand is a favorite all-round beach. When calm, the protected waters are popular for swimming and snorkeling, with frequent sightings of sea turtles (keep your distance; at least 50yd in the water). High surf, while welcome to local bodyboarders, can be hazardous. Bring water shoes for

protection from rocks. There are lifeguards every day, plus restrooms, showers, picnic areas and a parking lot.

◉ SIGHTS

Pacific Tsunami Museum   Museum
(📞808-935-0926; www.tsunami.org; 130 Kamehameha Ave; adult/child $8/4; ⏰10am-4pm Tue-Sat) You cannot understand Hilo without knowing its history as a two-time tsunami survivor (1946 and 1960). This seemingly modest museum is chock-full of riveting information, including a section on the Japanese tsunami of 2011, which damaged Kona. Allow enough time to experience the multimedia exhibits, including chilling computer simulations and heart-wrenching first-person accounts.

Pana'ewa Rainforest Zoo & Gardens   Zoo
(📞808-959-9233; www.hilozoo.com; off Hwy 11; ⏰9am-4pm, petting zoo 1:30-2:30pm Sat; 🚻) **FREE** Hilo's 12-acre zoo is a terrific family-friendly freebie. Stroll through tropical gardens to see a modest but interesting collection of monkeys, reptiles, sloths, parrots and more. The star attraction? A pair of Bengal tigers: Sriracha (orange female) and Tzatziki (white male). Two play structures and a shaded picnic area are perfect for kids. Generally uncrowded and wheelchair accessible.

To get here, turn *mauka* (inland) off the Volcano Hwy onto W Mamaki St, just past the 4-mile marker.

'Imiloa Astronomy Center of Hawai'i   Museum
(📞808-969-9700; www.imiloahawaii.org; 600 'Imiloa Pl; adult/child 6-17yr $17.50/9.50; ⏰9am-5pm Tue-Sun; 🚻) 'Imiloa, which means 'exploring new knowledge,' is a $28 million museum and planetarium complex with a twist: it juxtaposes modern astronomy on Mauna Kea with ancient Polynesian ocean voyaging. It's a great family attraction and the natural complement to a summit tour. One planetarium show is included with admission. On Friday catch special evening

Hilo

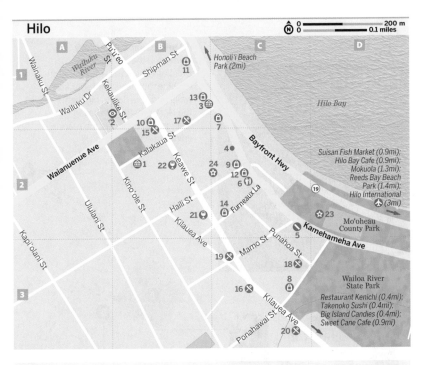

Hilo

◉ Sights
1 East Hawai'i Cultural Center/HMOCA......B2
2 Federal Building B1
3 Pacific Tsunami Museum B1

⊕ Activities, Courses & Tours
4 Hawaii Forest & Trail C2
5 Nautilus Dive Center C2
6 Orchidland Surfboards C2

⊕ Shopping
7 Basically Books C1
8 Bryan Booth Antiques..............................C3
9 Extreme Exposure Fine Art Gallery C2
10 Local Antiques & Stuff B1
11 Locavore Store B1
12 Most Irresistible Shop in Hilo C2
13 Sig Zane Designs B1

14 Still Life Books C2

⊗ Eating
15 Bears' Coffee B2
16 Hawaiian Crown Plantation &
     Chocolate Factory.................................C3
17 Moon & Turtle B1
18 Paul's Place..C3
19 Pineapples..C3
20 Two Ladies Kitchen.................................C3

⊙ Drinking & Nightlife
21 Bayfront Kava Bar....................................B2
22 Hilo Town Tavern B2

⊙ Entertainment
23 Mo'oheau Bandstand D2
24 Palace Theater C2

programs, including a mind-blowing Led Zeppelin planetarium rock show.

ACTIVITIES

While Hilo's coast is lined with reefs rather than sand, its gentle waters are ideal for stand up paddle surfing (SUP) – launch

Historic Downtown Hilo

Explore the town's history on this stroll through downtown Hilo, the charming heart of the town. You'll find parks, beaches and open space along Kamehameha Ave, plus historic buildings and bustling local life.

Start Mo'oheau Bandstand
Distance 1 mile
Duration half day

4 Mokupapapa Discovery Center, in the FW Koehnen Building (1910) with its eye-catching blue facade with interior koa walls and ohia floors, highlights the Northwestern Hawaiian Islands and their pristine marine environment.

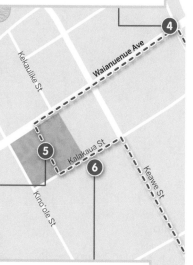

5 Walk through the small but lovely green space of **Kalakaua Park**, where a bronze statue of King David Kalakaua (the 'Merrie Monarch') stands in the center. The lily-filled pool honors Korean War veterans, and buried under the grass is a time capsule, sealed on the last total solar eclipse (July 11, 1991), to be opened on the next one.

6 Next door is the notable **Hawaiian Telephone Company Building**, designed in the 1920s by CW Dickey with Spanish, Italian and Californian mission influences. Note the high-hipped, green tile roof and the brightly colored terracotta tiles set in the building.

2 The **S Hata Building** is a 1912 example of renaissance revival architecture with a distinctive row of arched windows on the 2nd floor. The US government seized this building from its original Japanese owner during WWII. After the war, the owner's daughter bought it back for $100,000.

0 —— 100 m
0 —— 0.05 miles

3 Tour the **Pacific Tsunami Museum**, which brings to life the two catastrophic tsunami of 1946 and 1960. It's located in the old First Hawaiian Bank building, with its parapet, fluted columns and wrought-iron features; it was designed by renowned Honolulu architect CW Dickey in 1930.

Hilo Bay

1 The **Mo'oheau Bandstand** (c 1905) is a rare survivor of the 1946 tsunami. If you're lucky, the county band will be performing their monthly concert.

Kamehameha Ave

Bayfront Hwy

Halii St

Furneaux La

Punahoa St

Kilauea Ave

Mamo St

START **1**

19

2

7

FINISH

Mo'oheau County Park

Wailoa River State Park

7 The **Hilo Farmers Market** is jammed from daybreak on Wednesday and Saturday, when locals and tourists alike meander around a dazzling array of fresh produce, flowers, and other locally made goods. Bring cash and a bag.

Take a Break Try the island-grown, island-made chocolate at Hawaiian Crown.

Carlsmith Beach Park (p266)

from **Reeds Bay Beach Park** (251 Banyan Dr; 🏊) or **Mokuola** (Coconut Island; 🏊). For surfing, head to **Honoli'i Beach Park** (180 Kahoa St), but only if you're an experienced surfer.

Diving is best on the Kona side but there are decent shore-diving spots in or near Hilo; inquire at Nautilus Dive Center.

Hawaii Forest & Trail   Hiking
(☎808-331-3657; www.hawaii-forest.com; 224 Kamehameha Ave; Mauna Kea summit tour $215; ⊙9am-5pm Mon-Fri, to 4pm Sat) Reliable guided-tour company offers island-wide adventures: hiking, ziplining, swimming, birding and more. The Mauna Kea summit tour includes dinner and use of hooded parkas and gloves. This office is the departure point for all Hilo-based tours. Friendly staff can advise on various tours.

Hilo Bayfront Trails   Walking
(www.hilobayfronttrails.org) Walk or cycle from downtown Hilo to Banyan Dr along a paved coastal path. While it doesn't overlook the ocean throughout, it's still very scenic. Park at either end, downtown or Lili'uokalani

Park, and enjoy a leisurely loop, stopping for shave ice or lunch along the way.

Nautilus Dive Center   Diving
(☎808-935-6939; www.nautilusdivehilo.com; 382 Kamehameha Ave; intro charter dive $85; ⊙9am-5pm Mon-Sat) Hilo's go-to dive shop offers guided dives, PADI certification courses and general advice on shore diving.

Orchidland Surfboards   Surfing
(☎808-935-1533; www.orchidlandsurf.com; 262 Kamehameha Ave; ⊙9am-5pm Mon-Sat, 10am-3pm Sun) Board rentals, surf gear and advice from owner Stan Lawrence, who opened the Big Island's first surf shop in 1972.

🔒 SHOPPING

While locals flock to chain-store-heavy **Prince Kuhio Plaza** (☎808-959-3555; www.princekuhioplaza.com; 111 E Puainako St; ⊙10am-8pm Mon-Thu, to 9pm Fri & Sat, to 6pm Sun) south of the airport, downtown is far better for unique shops, including a few top-notch antique collections. Be careful to distinguish between products genuinely made in Hawaii and cheap imports.

Basically Books   Books

(☎808-961-0144; www.basicallybooks.com; 160 Kamehameha Ave; ☺9am-5pm Mon-Sat, 11am-3:30pm Sun) A browser's paradise, this shop specializes in maps, travel guides and books about Hawaii, including a wide selection for children. Also find gifts, from toys to CDs. Staff are helpful and know their stuff.

Still Life Books   Books

(☎808-756-2919; stilllife@bigisland.com; 58 Furneaux Lane; ☺11am-3pm Tue-Sat) Bibliophiles and audiophiles should set aside ample time to browse this hand-picked inventory of secondhand books and LPs. Expect literature, history, art, travel and philosophy. No potboilers. This cozy basement space is filled with great finds, including the owner, a true book and music aficionado.

Extreme Exposure Fine Art Gallery   Photography

(☎808-936-6028; www.extremeexposure.com; 224 Kamehameha Ave; ☺10am-8pm Mon-Sat, 11am-5pm Sun) At this unpretentious gallery, find excellent nature photography – featuring Hawaii's wildlife, seascapes, landscapes and lava displays – by photographers Bruce Omori and Tom Kuali'i. There's something for all budgets, from framed prints to greeting cards.

Local Antiques & Stuff   Antiques

(104 Keawe St; ☺10:30am-4:30pm Tue-Sat) This teeming display of local artifacts and memorabilia is a must-see. There's something for every budget: retro glass bottles, plantation-era housewares, Japanese *kokeshi* dolls, vintage aloha shirts, knickknacks galore and valuable koa furniture. A real mom-and-pop operation run by a local couple who amassed their eclectic collection over many years.

Bryan Booth Antiques   Furniture

(☎808-933-2500; www.bryanboothantiques. com; 94 Ponahawai St; ☺10am-5pm Mon-Sat) Transporting a rocking chair or dining table home might be a deal breaker. But Bryan Booth's expertly restored wood furniture might convince you otherwise. In his spacious showroom, find exquisite pieces from

the late 1800s and early 1900s, along with antique lamps, framed art and china. Expect prices from about $500 to $5000-plus.

Sig Zane Designs   Clothing

(☎808-935-7077; www.sigzane.com; 122 Kamehameha Ave; ☺9:30am-5pm Mon-Fri, 9am-4pm Sat) Legendary in the hula community, Sig Zane creates iconic custom fabrics, marked by rich colors and graphic prints of Hawaiian flora. You can spot a 'Sig' a mile away.

Most Irresistible Shop in Hilo   Gifts & Souvenirs

(☎808-935-9644; www.facebook.com/mostirresistibleshop; 256 Kamehameha Ave; ☺9am-6pm Mon-Fri, to 5pm Sat, 10:30am-3:30pm Sun) True to its name, this shop is filled with quality treasures: jewelry, Japanese dishware, children's games and toys, clothing, home textiles, Hello Kitty items and random cute stuff. Staff are friendly and discreet, letting you browse in peace.

Big Island Candies   Sweets

(☎800-935-5510, 808-935-8890; www.bigislandcandies.com; 585 Hinano St; ☺8:30am-5pm) Once a mom-and-pop shop, this wildly successful confectioner is now a full-fledged destination. In an immaculate showroom-factory, enjoy generous samples, fantastic displays and beautifully packaged candies and cookies. Expect crowds of locals and Japanese tourists. Don't miss the signature macadamia-nut shortbread.

✖ EATING

Two Ladies Kitchen   Sweets $

(☎808-961-4766; 274 Kilauea Ave; 8-piece box $6; ☺10am-5pm Wed-Sat) This hole-in-the-wall is famous statewide for outstanding Japanese *mochi* (sticky rice cake) in both traditional and island-inspired flavors such as *liliko'i* (passion fruit) and *poha* (gooseberry). They're sold in boxes of six to eight pieces. Study the flavor chart on the wall before ordering.

Ahi (tuna) *poke*

Paul's Place   Cafe $

(☑808-280-8646; http://paulsplcafe.wixsite.
com/paulsplacecafe; 132 Punahoa St; mains
$8-12; ⊘7am-3pm Tue-Sat) In a six-seat dining
room, Paul serves exquisite renditions
of the classics, including light and crispy
Belgian waffles, robust salads and his
signature eggs Benedict with smoked
salmon, asparagus and a unique sauce.
Everything's healthy, served with lots
of fresh fruit and veggies. Reservations
strongly recommended.

Suisan Fish Market   Seafood $

(☑808-935-9349; 93 Lihiwai St; takeout poke
$10-12, poke per lb $18; ⊘8am-6pm Mon-Fri,
to 4pm Sat, 10am-4pm Sun) For a fantastic
variety of freshly made *poke* (cubed raw
fish mixed with shōyu, sesame oil, salt, chili
pepper, 'inamona or other condiments; sold
by the pound), Suisan is a must. Buy a bowl
of takeout *poke* and rice and eat outside
the shop or across the street at Lili'uokalani
Park. Could life be any better?

KTA Super Store – Puainako   Supermarket

(☑808-959-9111, pharmacy 808-959-8700; 50
E Puainako St, Puainako Town Center; ⊘grocery
5:30am-midnight, pharmacy 8am-7pm Mon-Fri,
9am-7pm Sat) ✔ An outstanding family-owned company, KTA's flagship store
includes a bakery, pharmacy and deli, and a
fantastic selection of fresh *poke* (arguably
the best in Hilo). Look for the Mountain
Apple house label for locally sourced milk,
produce and prepared products. Don't miss
the takeout bento box meals, which sell out
by mid-morning.

Hawaiian Crown Plantation & Chocolate Factory   Sweets $

(☑808-319-6158; www.hawaiiancrown.com; 160
Kilauea Ave; chocolates $6.50-8.50; ⊘8:30am-
5:30pm Tue-Sat, 11:30am-4pm Sun) ✔ Locally
grown and locally made, these chocolate
bars and 'turtles' (up to 80% cocoa) make a
perfect gift or treat for yourself. Cacao fans
can also buy nibs, either unsweetened or
agave sweetened, and learn about this crop
from the welcoming proprietor. The shop

also offers hot or iced Big Island coffee, sat-
isfying smoothies and healthy açai bowls.

Hilo Bay Cafe   Hawaii Regional Cuisine, Sushi $$

(☑808-935-4939; www.hilobaycafe.com; 123
Lihiwai St; mains $18-32; ⊘11am-9pm Mon-Thu,
to 9:30pm Fri & Sat; ⏵) With sweeping bay
views and great Hawaii Regional Cuisine,
this casually sophisticated restaurant could
be stuffy. But it's not. Here you'll find a diverse crowd feasting on an eclectic omnivo-
rous menu, including gourmet versions of
comfort food, such as Hamakua mushroom
pot pie. The sushi is fresh, with creative
rolls and a vibrant sashimi salad featuring
generous slabs of ahi.

Moon & Turtle   Hawaii Regional Cuisine $$

(☑808-961-0599; www.facebook.com/
moonandturtle; 51 Kalakaua St; tapas $8-22;
⊘11:30am-2pm & 5:30-9pm Tue-Sat) ✎ A hit
among foodies, this tapas-style restaurant
specializes in local seafood, meat and produce prepared in startlingly creative ways.
The ever-changing menu is short, but each
dish is meticulously sourced and prepared.
You'll surely remember (and crave) the
smoky sashimi, crispy brussels sprouts
and wild boar fried rice. Save room for the
heavenly sweet-tart *liliko'i* pie.

Pineapples   Hawaii Regional Cuisine $$

(☑808-238-5324; www.pineappleshilo.com; 332
Keawe St; mains $14-24; ⊘11am-9:30pm Sun &
Tue-Thu, to 10pm Fri & Sat; ⏵) On any given
day, Pineapples' open-air dining room is
jammed with a convivial crowd, mostly
visitors but locals too. The food features
island-sourced ingredients and caters to all
palates: island tacos stuffed with *kalua* pig,
grass-fed beef burger topped with grilled
pineapple, and lusciously smooth and rich
pumpkin curry. Local art lines the wall;
nightly live music features local musicians.

Restaurant Kenichi   Japanese $$

(☑808-969-1776; www.restaurantkenichi.com;
684 Kilauea Ave; mains $13-15; ⊘10am-2pm &
5-9pm Mon-Sat; ⏶) For delicious, untouristy

From left: Green sea turtle; Native Hawaiian ki'i; Richardson's Ocean Park (p266)

dining, Kenichi has it all: Japanese comfort food, high-volume flavor, cheerful staff and a simple dining room crowded with locals. Favorites include steaming ramen bowls made with house *dashi* (broth), succulent grilled *saba* (mackerel), boneless Korean chicken and rib-eye steak, rushed to your table, aromatic and sizzling. Save room for nostalgic desserts like banana cream pie.

Sweet Cane Cafe Health Food $

(📞808-934-0002; www.sweetcanecafe.com; 48 Kamana St; mains $7.50-9, fruit bowls $8-10; ⏰8am-6pm Mon-Sat; 🅿) 🍃 Everything is fresh, locally sourced and vegetarian at this casual cafe. Sandwiches are stuffed with roasted veggies or an ulu jalapeno patty, while the Pesto Zoodles (raw zucchini noodles) are perfectly textured and immersed in succulent macnut pesto. Smoothies and açai or pitaya bowls are popular and healthy mini meals. Limited parking.

Takenoko Sushi Sushi $$$

(📞808-933-3939; 681 Manono St; nigiri $2.50-8, chef's choice $40; ⏰11:30am-1:30pm & 5-9pm Thu-Mon) Reserve a spot at this superb eight-seat sushi bar a year in advance.

For the long wait, you're treated to the upper echelon of Japanese cuisine, with top-quality fish (mostly flown fresh from Japan), a spotlessly clean setting, expert sushi chef and gracious service. Each bite is a memorable experience. The three dinner seatings are at 5pm, 7pm and 9pm.

🍷 DRINKING & NIGHTLIFE

Hawai'i Nui Brewing Brewery

(📞808-934-8211; www.hawaiinuibrewing.com; 275 E Kawili; ⏰noon-5pm Mon, Tue & Thu, to 6pm Wed & Fri, to 4pm Sat) This microbrewery has a small tasting room where you can sample excellent craft beer, including brews originated by Mehena Brewing, Hilo's first microbrewer, which it took over in 2009. Mehana's Mauna Kea Pale Ale is the most popular, but don't miss the Hawai'i Nui's Southern Cross, a powerful Belgian ale that gives those Trappist monks a run for their money.

Bayfront Kava Bar Bar

(📞808-345-1698; www.bayfrontkava.com; 264 Keawe St; cup of kava $5; ⏰4-10pm Mon-Sat) If you're curious about kava ('awa in Hawaiian), try a cup at this minimalist bar.

Friendly bar staff serve freshly brewed, locally grown kava root in coconut shells. Get ready for tingling taste buds and a calm buzz. Live music and art exhibitions kick off on a regular basis.

Hilo Town Tavern   Bar
(www.hilotavern.com; 168 Keawe St; mains $9-11; 11:30am-2am) This super-casual, untrendy tavern has indoor and outdoor stages, a pool hall, lively music and a mixed crowd of locals and tourists. It's among the only spots for local-style bar food, cold beer and nightlife past midnight.

ENTERTAINMENT

Palace Theater   Theater
(808-934-7010; www.hilopalace.com; 38 Haili St; box office 10am-3pm) This historic theater is Hilo's cultural crown jewel. Its eclectic programming includes art-house and silent films (accompanied by the house organ), music and dance concerts, Broadway musicals and cultural festivals.

GETTING THERE & AWAY

The **Hilo International Airport** (p313) is located at the northeastern corner of Hilo, less than 3 miles from downtown. Almost all flights arriving here are interisland, mostly from Honolulu. Rental-car booths and taxis are located right outside the baggage-claim area.

The drive from Hilo to Kailua-Kona (via Waimea) along Hwy 19 is 95 miles and takes about 2½ hours. Driving along Saddle Road can cut travel time by about 15 minutes.

GETTING AROUND

Free parking is generally available around town. Downtown street parking is free for two hours (or more, since enforcement is slack); finding a spot is easy except when the Wednesday and Saturday farmers markets are on.

View into the crater, Haleakalā National Park

In Focus

Hawaii Today 278
Growing pains are par for the course in paradise, where self-reliance and sustainability paint the way forward.

History 280
From Polynesian wayfarers and Hawaiian royalty to missionaries, sugar barons and the US military, this is Hawaii's story.

People & Culture 289
Forget the myths and stereotypes about island life, far from 'da' mainland at this multicultural Pacific crossroads.

Hawaiian Arts & Crafts 293
Discover the island's soulful side: lilting Hawaiian music, sensuous hula dancing, artisan handicrafts and dramatic stories.

Outdoor Activities 297
The best part about hiking, surfing, kayaking and exploring the great outdoors? The stunning backdrops, from lush rainforests to lava coasts.

Cuisine 302
Go find fresh seafood shacks, plate-lunch trucks and chef's farm-to-table restaurants, then sip mai tais by the beach.

Hanauma Bay, O'ahu

Hawaii Today

The state motto, Ua Mau ke Ea o ka 'Āina i Ka Pono ('The life of the land is perpetuated in righteousness'), is not just an idealistic catchphrase. Hawaii's modern sovereignty movement, eco-sustainability initiatives and antidevelopment activism are rooted in aloha 'aina (literally, love and respect for the land), a traditional Hawaiian value that is deeply felt. This belief has helped nurture commitment to overcoming 21st-century challenges.

Hawaiian Renaissance

Evolving from ancient Polynesian traditions, Hawaiian culture was attacked and suppressed in the two centuries after first Western contact with Captain James Cook in 1778. But beginning with the Hawaiian Renaissance in the 1970s, a rebirth of Native Hawaiian cultural and artistic traditions, as well as the Hawaiian language, has taken hold. For over four decades, there have been Hawaiian-language immersion programs in public schools and Hawaiian-culture-focused charter schools.

Today, Hawaiian culture is about more than just melodic place names and luau shows. Traditional arts like *lauhala* (pandanus leaf) weaving, *kapa* (pounded-bark cloth) making, and gourd and wood carving are experiencing a revival. Healing arts like *lomilomi* ('loving touch') massage and *la'au lapa'au* (plant medicine) are being shared with students. Ancient heiau (temples) and

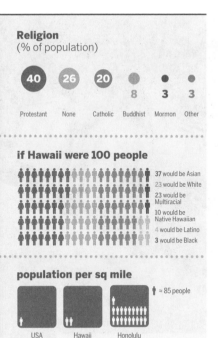

Religion
(% of population)

40 Protestant · 26 None · 20 Catholic · 8 Buddhist · 3 Mormon · 3 Other

if Hawaii were 100 people

37 would be Asian
23 would be White
23 would be Multiracial
10 would be Native Hawaiian
4 would be Latino
3 would be Black

population per sq mile

≈ 85 people

USA Hawaii Honolulu

fishponds are being restored, native forests replanted and endangered birds and marine mammals protected.

Being Hawaiian remains an important part of the identity of the islands. Although few island residents can agree on what shape the sovereignty movement should take (or if it should exist at all), its grassroots political activism has achieved results. Decades of protests and a federal lawsuit filed by sovereignty activists finally pressured the US military into returning the island of Kaho'olawe, which had been used for bombing practice since WWII, in 1994. From 2014 through 2016, sovereignty activists successfully protested against construction of the Thirty Meter Telescope (TMT) atop Mauna Kea, a sacred Hawaiian summit on the Big Island.

Seeking Sustainability

Before the 19th-century arrival of foreign whalers, traders and Christian missionaries, the population of the Hawaiian Islands was between 200,000 and a million people. As modern-day Hawaii's population swells, new housing developments sprawl, stretching the state's water resources, transportation systems, public schools and landfills.

Today, Hawaii's economy is less than stable because it has become dependent on the outside world. Despite being blessed with a wealth of natural energy sources, over 80% of Hawaii's power still comes from carbon-based fuels. However, Hawaii is striving to become a pioneer in clean energy. In 2015, Hawaii generated 35% of its electricity from solar power – more than any other state. Already Hawaii has the fourth-lowest per capita energy consumption in the nation. It is also the only state to set a legal deadline for sourcing 100% of its electricity from renewable energy, by 2045. The government and private industry are pursuing every renewable and clean energy option available – wind farms on Maui, for example.

Diversifying the Economy

After losing sugar and pineapple plantations to cheap imports from the developing world, Hawaii's economy was reliant on tourism. When a recession tanked the national economy in 2008, Hawaii's tourism went with it.

Since 2011 Hawaii's economy has slowly rebounded, though not entirely. Tourism will likely be Hawaii's bread and butter for the foreseeable future, but at a price. More than eight million travelers visit annually – over five times the resident population – overcrowding roads and driving up the price of real estate.

Today the islands stand at a crossroads. Hawaii can either continue to suffer the side effects of its dependence on tourism, imported goods and fossil fuels that hasten global climate change, or boldly move toward capturing a more secure, homegrown and eco-sustainable future.

Old sugar-plantation train

History

Hawaii's colonization is one of humanity's epic tales, starting with ancient Polynesians who found their way to these tiny islands – the world's most isolated – in the midst of Earth's largest ocean. Almost a millennium passed before Western explorers, missionaries and entrepreneurs arrived. During the tumultuous 19th century, immigrants came to work the plantations before the kingdom was overthrown, making way for US annexation.

30 million BC
The first Hawaiian island, Kure, rises from the sea, appearing where the Big Island is today.

AD 300–600
The first wave of Polynesians, most likely from the Marquesas Islands, voyage by canoe to the Hawaiian Islands.

1000–1300
Sailing from Tahiti, a second wave of Polynesians arrives.

Traditional Hawaiian wooden carvings

GEORGE BURBA/SHUTTERSTOCK ©

Polynesian Voyagers

To ancient Polynesians, the Pacific Ocean was a passageway, not a barrier, and the islands it contained were connected, not isolated. Between AD 300 and 600, they made their longest journey yet and discovered the Hawaiian Islands. This would mark the northern reach of their migrations, which were so astounding that Captain James Cook – the first Western explorer to take their full measure – could not conceive of how the Polynesians did it, settling 'in every quarter of the Pacific Ocean' and becoming one of the most widespread nations on earth.

Although the discovery of Hawai'i may have been accidental, subsequent journeys were not. Polynesians were highly skilled seafarers, navigating over thousands of miles of open ocean without maps, and with only the sun, stars, wind and waves to guide them. In double-hulled wooden canoes, they imported to the islands over two dozen food plants and domestic animals, along with their religious beliefs and social structures. What they

1778–79	1810	1820
Captain Cook visits Hawai'i twice. After being warmly welcomed, Cook loses his temper over a stolen boat and is killed by Hawaiians.	Kamehameha the Great negotiates to take control of Kaua'i, uniting the islands into one kingdom.	The first Christian missionaries arrive in Hawai'i at Kailua-Kona.

Ruins at Puʻukoholā Heiau National Historic Site

★ **Hawaiian Temples**

Puʻuhonua O Hōnaunau National Historical Park, Hawaiʻi (Big Island)

Piʻilanihale Heiau (p170), Maui

Puʻukoholā Heiau National Historic Site, Hawaiʻi (Big Island)

Ahuʻena Heiau (p244), Hawaiʻi (Big Island)

GEORGE BURBA/SHUTTERSTOCK ©

didn't possess is equally remarkable: no metals, no wheels, no alphabet or written language, and no clay to make pottery.

Ancient Hawaiʻi

When for unknown reasons trans-Pacific voyages from Polynesia stopped around AD 1300, ancient Hawaiian culture kept evolving in isolation, but retained a family resemblance to cultures found throughout Polynesia. Hawaiian society was highly stratified, ruled by a chiefly class called *aliʻi* whose power derived from their ancestry: they were believed to be descended from the gods. In ancient Hawaiʻi, clan loyalty trumped individuality, elaborate traditions of gifting and feasting conferred prestige, and a pantheon of shape-shifting gods animated the natural world.

Several ranks of *aliʻi* ruled each island, and life was marked by frequent warfare as they jockeyed for power. The largest geopolitical division was the *mokupuni* (island), presided over by a member of the *aliʻi nui* (kingly class). Each island was further divided into *moku* (districts), wedge-shaped areas of land running from the ridge of the mountains to the sea. Smaller, similarly wedge-shaped *ahupuaʻa* comprised each *moku;* they were mostly self-sustaining and had local chiefs.

A culture of mutuality and reciprocity infused what was essentially a feudal agricultural society. Chiefs were custodians of their people, and humans custodians of nature, all of which was sacred – the living expression of *mana* (spiritual essence). Everyone played a part through work and ritual to maintain the health of the community and its comity with the gods. Ancient Hawaiians also developed rich traditions in art, music, dance and competitive sports.

Captain Cook & First Western Contact

Captain Cook had spent a decade traversing the Pacific over the course of three voyages. He sought the fabled 'Northwest Passage' linking the Pacific and Atlantic, but his were

1846

A record 736 whaling ships stop over in the islands. Four of Hawaiʻi's 'Big Five' sugar plantation companies get started supplying whalers.

1852

The first indentured plantation laborers arrive from China; upon completing their contracts, most choose to stay.

1868

Japanese laborers arrive to work the plantations. Mauna Loa volcano erupts on the Big Island, causing an estimated magnitude-7.9 earthquake.

also voyages of discovery. He sailed with a complement of scientists and artists to document what they found. On the third voyage in 1778, and quite by accident, Cook sailed into the main Hawaiian Islands chain. Ending nearly half a millennium of isolation, his arrival irrevocably altered the course of Hawaiian history.

Cook dropped anchor off Oʻahu and, as he had elsewhere in the Pacific, bartered with the indigenous people for fresh water and food. When Cook returned the following year, he sailed around before eventually anchoring at Kealakekua Bay on the Big Island. Cook's ships were greeted by as many as a thousand canoes, and Hawaiian chiefs and priests honored him with rituals and deference. Cook had landed at an auspicious time during the *makahiki*, a time of festival and celebration in honor of the god Lono. The Hawaiians were so unrelentingly gracious, in fact, that Cook and his men felt safe to move about unarmed.

Cook set sail some weeks later, but storms forced him to turn back. The mood in Kealakekua had changed, however. The makahiki had ended: no canoes met the Europeans, and suspicion replaced welcome. A small series of minor conflicts, including the theft of a boat by some Hawaiians, provoked Cook into leading an armed party ashore to capture local chief Kalaniʻōpuʻu. When the Englishmen disembarked, they were surrounded by angry Hawaiians. In an uncharacteristic fit of pique, Cook shot and killed a Hawaiian man. Hawaiians immediately mobbed Cook, killing him on February 14, 1779.

A Place of Refuge

In ancient Hawaiʻi, a very strict code – called the kapu (taboo) system – governed daily life. If a commoner dared to eat *moi*, a type of fish reserved for *aliʻi* (royalty or chiefs), for example, it was a violation of kapu. Penalties for violations could be harsh, even including death. Furthermore, in a society based on mutual respect, slights to honor could not be abided.

Although ancient Hawaiʻi could be a fiercely uncompromising place, it offered forgiveness for errors. Anyone who had broken kapu or been defeated in battle could avoid the death penalty by fleeing to a *puʻuhonua* (a place of refuge). At the heiau (stone temple), a kahuna (priest) would perform purification rituals. Absolved of their transgressions, kapu breakers were free to return home in safety.

Kamehameha the Great

In the years following Cook's death, a steady number of exploring and trading ships sought out the Kingdom of Hawaiʻi as a resupply spot. For Hawaiian chiefs, the main items of interest were firearms, which the Europeans willingly traded.

Bolstered with muskets and cannons, Kamehameha, a chief from the Big Island, began a campaign in 1790 to conquer all of the Hawaiian Islands. Other chiefs had tried and failed, but Kamehameha had Western guns; not only that, he was prophesied to succeed and

1893	1895	1898
On January 17, the Hawaiian monarchy is overthrown by a group of US businessmen supported by military troops.	Robert Wilcox leads a failed counter-revolution to restore the monarchy. The queen is placed under house arrest at ʻIolani Palace.	On July 7, President McKinley signs the resolution annexing Hawaii as a US territory.

possessed an unyielding determination and exceptional personal charisma. Within five years he united – albeit bloodily – the main islands, except for Kaua'i (which eventually joined peacefully in 1810). The dramatic final skirmish in Kamehameha's major campaign, the Battle of Nu'uanu, took place on O'ahu in 1795.

Kamehameha was a singular figure who reigned over the most peaceful era in Hawaiian history. Most importantly, Kamehameha I absorbed growing foreign influences while fastidiously honoring Hawai'i's indigenous customs. He did the latter even despite widespread doubts among his people about the justice of Hawai'i's *kapu* (taboo) system and traditional Hawaiian ideas about a divine social hierarchy.

When Kamehameha died in 1819, he left the question of how to resolve these troubling issues to his son and heir, 22-year-old Liholiho. Within the year, Liholiho had broken with the traditional religion in one sweeping, stunning act of repudiation.

Missionaries & Whalers

After Cook's expedition sailed back to Britain, news of his 'discovery' of Hawai'i soon spread throughout Europe and the Americas, opening the floodgates to seafaring explorers and traders. By the 1820s, whaling ships began pulling into Hawai'i's harbors for fresh water and food, supplies, liquor and women. To meet their needs, ever more shops, taverns and brothels sprang up around busy ports, especially in Honolulu on O'ahu and Lahaina on Maui. By the 1840s, the islands had become the unofficial whaling capital of the Pacific.

To the ire of 'dirty-devil' whalers, Hawai'i's first Christian missionary ship sailed into Honolulu's harbor on April 14, 1820, carrying staunch Protestants who were set on saving the Hawaiians from their 'heathen ways.' Their timing could not have been more opportune, as Hawai'i's traditional religion had been abolished the year before, leaving Hawaiians in a spiritual vacuum. Both missionaries and the whalers hailed from New England, but soon were at odds: missionaries were intent on saving souls, while to many sailors there was 'no God west of the Horn.'

Because the missionaries' god seemed powerful, Christianity attracted Hawaiian converts, notably Queen Ka'ahumanu. But many of these conversions were not deeply felt; Hawaiians often quickly abandoned the church's teachings, reverting to their traditional lifestyles.

The missionaries found one thing that attracted avid, widespread interest: literacy. The missionaries formulated an alphabet for the Hawaiian language, and with this tool, Hawaiians learned to read with astonishing speed.

The Great Land Grab

Throughout the period of the monarchy, the ruling sovereigns of Hawai'i fought off continual efforts on the part of European and American settlers to gain control of the kingdom.

1909	**1916**	**1922**
7000 Japanese plantation workers strike to protest low pay and harsh treatment. The strike fails, winning no concessions.	The US National Park Service is created by Congress; Hawai'i National Park is established.	James Dole becomes the sole landowner of 98% of Lana'i. He starts a pineapple plantation that becomes the world's largest.

In 1848, under pressure from foreigners who wanted to own land, a sweeping land-reform act known as the Great Mahele was instituted. This act allowed, for the first time, the ownership of land, which had previously been held exclusively by monarchs and chiefs. The chiefs had not owned the land in the Western sense but were caretakers of both the land and the commoners who lived and worked on the land, giving their monarchs a portion of the harvest in return for the right to stay.

The reforms of the Great Mahele had far-reaching implications. For foreigners, who had money to buy land, it meant greater economic and political power. For Hawaiians, who had little or no money, it meant a loss of land-based self-sufficiency and enforced entry into the low-wage labor market, primarily run by Westerners.

When King David Kalakaua came to power in 1874, American businessmen had wrested substantial control over the economy and were bent on gaining control over the political scene as well. King Kalakaua was an impassioned Hawaiian revivalist, known as the 'Merrie Monarch.' He brought back the hula, reversing decades of missionary repression against the 'heathen dance,' and he composed 'Hawaii Ponoi', which is now the state song. The king also tried to ensure a degree of self-rule for Native Hawaiians, who had become a minority in their own land.

King Sugar & the Plantation Era

Kō (sugarcane) arrived in Hawai'i with the early Polynesian settlers. But it wasn't until 1835 that Bostonian William Hooper saw a business opportunity to establish Hawai'i's first sugar plantation. Hooper persuaded Honolulu investors to put up the money for his venture and then worked out a deal with Kamehameha III to lease agricultural land at Koloa on Kaua'i. The next order of business was finding an abundant supply of low-cost labor, which was needed to make sugar plantations profitable.

The natural first choice for plantation workers was Hawaiians, but even when willing, they were not enough. Due to introduced diseases like typhoid, influenza, smallpox and syphilis, the Hawaiian population had steadily and precipitously declined. By some estimates around 800,000 indigenous people lived on the islands before Western contact, but by 1800 that had dropped by two-thirds, to around 250,000. By 1860 Hawaiians numbered fewer than 70,000.

Wealthy plantation owners began to look overseas for a labor supply of immigrants accustomed to working long days in hot weather, and for whom the low wages would seem like an opportunity. In the 1850s, wealthy sugar-plantation owners began recruiting laborers from China, then Japan and Portugal. After annexing Hawaii in 1898, US restrictions on Chinese and Japanese immigration made O'ahu's plantation owners turn to Puerto Rico, Korea and the Philippines for laborers. Different immigrant groups, along with the shared pidgin language they developed, created a unique plantation community that ultimately transformed Hawaii into the multicultural, multiethnic society it is today.

1925	1941	1946
The first US military seaplane lands safely in Hawaii.	On December 7, Pearl Harbor is attacked by Japanese forces, catapulting the US into WWII.	On April 1, the most destructive tsunami in Hawaii history kills 159 people across the islands.

During California's Gold Rush and later the US Civil War, sugar exports to the mainland soared, making plantation owners wealthier and more powerful. Five sugar-related holding companies, known as the Big Five, came to dominate all aspects of the industry: Castle & Cooke, Alexander & Baldwin, C Brewer & Co, American Factors (today Amfac, Inc), and Theo H Davies & Co. All were run by haole (Caucasian) businessmen, many the sons and grandsons of missionaries, who eventually reached the same prejudicial conclusion as their forebears: Hawaiians could not be trusted to govern themselves. So, behind closed doors, the Big Five developed plans to relieve Hawaiians of the job.

The Merrie Monarch

King Kalakaua, who reigned from 1874 to 1891, fought to restore Hawaiian culture and indigenous pride. He resurrected hula and its attendant arts from near extinction. Along with his fondness for drinking, gambling and partying, this earned him the nickname 'the Merrie Monarch' – much to the dismay of Christian missionaries. Foreign businessmen considered his pastimes to be follies, but worse, Kalakaua was a mercurial decision-maker given to replacing his entire cabinet on a whim.

Kalakaua spent money lavishly, piling up massive debts. Wanting Hawai'i's monarchy to equal any in the world, he commissioned 'Iolani Palace, holding an extravagant coronation there in 1883. He also saw Hawai'i playing a role on the global stage, and in 1881 embarked on a trip to meet foreign heads of state and develop stronger ties with Japan especially. When he returned to Hawai'i later that year, he became the first king to have traveled around the world.

Even so the days of the Hawaiian monarchy were numbered. The Reciprocity Treaty of 1875, which had made Hawai'i-grown sugar profitable, had expired. Kalakaua refused to renew the treaty, as it now contained a provision giving the US a permanent naval base at Pearl Harbor – a provision that Native Hawaiians regarded as a threat to the sovereignty of the kingdom. A secret anti-monarchy group called the Hawaiian League, led by a committee of mostly American lawyers and businessmen, 'presented' Kalakaua with a new constitution in 1887.

This new constitution stripped the monarchy of most of its powers, reducing Kalakaua to a figurehead, and it changed the voting laws to exclude Asians and allow only those who met income and property requirements to vote – effectively disenfranchising all but wealthy, mostly white business owners. Kalakaua signed under threat of violence, earning the document the moniker the 'Bayonet Constitution.' Soon the US got its base at Pearl Harbor, and the foreign businessmen consolidated their power.

Overthrow of the Monarchy

When King Kalakaua died in 1891, his sister ascended the throne. Queen Lili'uokalani was a staunch supporter of her brother's efforts to maintain Hawaiian independence.

1959	1961	1971
On August 21, Hawaii becomes the 50th US State. Hawaii's Daniel Inouye is the first Japanese American elected to the US Congress.	Elvis Presley stars in the musical *Blue Hawaii*, kick-starting the mood for Hawaii's post-statehood tourism boom.	The Merrie Monarch hula festival, begun in 1964, holds its first hula competition, starting part of a Hawaiian cultural renaissance.

In January 1893, Queen Liliʻuokalani was preparing to proclaim a new Constitution to restore royal powers when a group of armed US businessmen occupied the Supreme Court and declared the monarchy overthrown. They announced a provisional government, led by Sanford B Dole, son of a pioneer missionary family.

After the monarchy's overthrow, the new government leaders pushed hard for annexation by the US, believing that it would bring greater stability to the islands, and more profits to Caucasian-run businesses. Although US law required that any entity petitioning for annexation must have the backing of the majority of its citizens through a public vote, no such vote was held in Hawaii.

Nonetheless on July 7, 1898, President William McKinley signed a joint congressional resolution approving annexation. Some historians feel that Hawaii would not have been annexed if it had not been for the outbreak of the Spanish–American War in April 1898, which sent thousands of US troops to the Philippines, making Hawaii a crucial Pacific staging point for the war.

World War II

On December 7, 1941, when Japanese warplanes appeared above the Pearl Harbor area, most residents thought they were mock aircraft being used in practice maneuvers. Of course, it *was* the real thing, and by the day's end hundreds of ships and airplanes had been destroyed, more than 1000 Americans had been killed and the war in the Pacific had begun.

The impact on Hawaii was dramatic. The army took control of the islands, martial law was declared and civil rights were suspended. Unlike on the mainland, Japanese Americans in Hawaii were not sent to internment camps because they made up most of the labor force in the cane fields in Hawaii's sugar-dependent economy. Thousands of Japanese Americans, many from Hawaii, eventually fought for the United States. Many were decorated for their bravery.

The War Department stationed the 4th Marine Division on Maui, where thousands of marines conducted training exercises for combat in the Pacific theater.

Statehood

Throughout the 20th century numerous Hawaiian statehood bills were introduced in Congress, only to be shot down. One reason for this lack of support was racial prejudice against Hawaii's multiethnic population. US congressmen from a still-segregated South were vocal in their belief that making Hawaii a state would open the doors to Asian immigration and the so-called 'Yellow Peril' threat that was so feared at the time. Others believed Hawaii's labor unions were hotbeds of communism.

However, the fame of the 442nd Regimental Combat Team in WWII went a long way toward reducing anti-Japanese sentiments. In March 1959 Congress voted again, this time

1976	1983	1993
Native Hawaiian sovereignty activists occupy the island of Kahoʻolawe.	Kilauea volcano begins its current eruption cycle, now the longest in recorded history.	President Clinton signs the 'Apology Resolution,' acknowledging the US government's role in the kingdom's illegal takeover.

admitting Hawaii into the Union. On August 21, President Eisenhower signed the admission bill that officially deemed Hawaii the 50th state.

Tourism & Development

Statehood had an immediate economic impact on Hawaii, most notably in boosting the tourism industry. Coupled with the advent of jet airplanes, which could transport thousands of people per week to the islands, tourism exploded, creating a hotel-building boom previously unmatched in the US.

Hawaiian Renaissance & Sovereignty

By the 1970s, Hawaii's rapid growth meant new residents (mostly mainland transplants) and tourists were crowding island beaches and roads. Runaway construction was rapidly transforming resorts almost beyond recognition, and the relentless peddling of 'aloha' had some islanders wondering what it meant to be Hawaiian. Some Native Hawaiians turned to *kapuna* (elders) and the past to recover their heritage, and by doing so became more politically assertive.

In 1976, a group of activists illegally occupied Kahoʻolawe, an island in Maui County dubbed 'Target Island.' The government had taken the island during WWII and used it for bombing practice until 1990. During another protest occupation attempt in 1977, two members of the Protect Kahoʻolawe ʻOhana (PKO) – George Helm and Kimo Mitchell – disappeared at sea, instantly becoming martyrs. Saving Kahoʻolawe became a rallying cry and it radicalized a nascent Native Hawaiian–rights movement.

When the state held its landmark Constitutional Convention in 1978, it passed a number of important amendments of special importance to Native Hawaiians. For example, it made Hawaiian the official state language (along with English) and mandated that Hawaiian culture be taught in public schools. At the grassroots level, the islands were experiencing a renaissance of Hawaiian culture, with a surge in residents – of all ethnicities – joining hula *halau* (schools), learning to play Hawaiian instruments and rediscovering traditional crafts like feather lei making.

In 2011, then-Governor Neil Abercrombie signed into law a bill recognizing Native Hawaiians as the state's only indigenous people and establishing a commission to create and maintain a list of qualifying Native Hawaiians. For those who qualified, this is the first step toward eventual self-governance.

2002	2008	2013
US mainland-born Linda Lingle is elected Hawaii's first Republican governor in 40 years. She is re-elected in 2006.	Born and raised in Honolulu on Oʻahu, Barack Obama is elected US President. He wins more than 70% of the vote in Hawaii.	Hawaii joins a growing number of US states to legalize same-sex marriage.

Performers in the Aloha Festivals

BRUCE C. MURRAY/SHUTTERSTOCK

People & Culture

Whatever your postcard tropical idyll might be — a paradise of white sandy beaches, emerald cliffs and azure seas; of falsetto-voiced ukulele strummers, bare-shouldered hula dancers and sun-bronzed surfers — it exists somewhere on these islands. But beyond its edges is a different version of Hawaii, a real place where a multicultural mixed plate of everyday people work and live.

Island Life Today

Hawaii may be a Polynesian paradise, but it's one with shopping malls, landfills and industrial parks, cookie-cutter housing developments and sprawling military bases. In many ways, it's much like the rest of the USA. A first-time visitor stepping off the plane may be surprised to find a thoroughly modern place where interstate highways and McDonald's look pretty much the same as back on 'da mainland.'

Underneath the veneer of consumer culture, the tourist industry is a different world, defined by — and proud of — its separateness, its geographic isolation and its unique blend of Polynesian, Asian and Western traditions. While those cultures don't always merge seamlessly in Hawaii, there are few places in the world where so many ethnicities, with no single group commanding a majority, get along.

Dos & Don'ts

o Don't try to speak pidgin.

o Do liberally wave the *shaka* (Hawaii's hand greeting sign).

o Do take off your shoes when entering a home.

o Do ask permission before picking fruit or flowers on private property.

o Don't overdress. Casual sportswear is the way to go.

o Do drive slowly. Locals rarely have far to go, and they drive that way. In fact, do everything slowly.

o Do try to correctly pronounce Hawaiian place names and words.

o Don't freak out at every gecko and cockroach. It's the tropics. There are critters.

o Don't collect (or even move) stones at sacred sites. If you're not sure whether something's sacred, consider that in Hawaiian thinking, everything is sacred, especially in nature.

Perhaps it's because they live on tiny islands in the middle of a vast ocean that Hawaii residents strive to treat one another with aloha, act politely and respectfully, and 'make no waves' (ie be cool). As the Hawaiian saying goes, 'We're all in the same canoe.' No matter their race or background, residents share a common bond: an awareness of living in one of the planet's most bewitchingly beautiful places.

Local vs Mainland Attitudes

Hawaii often seems overlooked by the other 49 states (except maybe by Alaska, the mainland's other oddball younger sibling), yet it's protective of its separateness. This has both advantages and disadvantages. On the upside, there's a genuine appreciation for Hawaii's uniqueness. On the downside, it reinforces an insider-outsider mentality that in its darkest moments manifests as exclusivity or, worse, blatant discrimination.

Island Identity

Honolulu is 'the city,' not only for those who live on O'ahu but for all of Hawaii. Far slower paced than New York City or Los Angeles, Hawaii's capital can still be surprisingly cosmopolitan, technologically savvy and fashion-conscious. Rightly or wrongly, Honoluluans see themselves at the center of everything; they have sports stadiums, the state's premier university and actual (if relatively tame) nightlife. Kaua'i, Maui, Hawai'i (the Big Island), Lana'i and especially Moloka'i are considered 'country.' That said, in a landscape as compressed as Hawaii, 'country' is a relative term. Rural areas tend not to be too far from the urban or suburban, and there are no vast swaths of uninterrupted wilderness like on the US mainland.

Neighbor Island residents tend to dress more casually and speak more pidgin. Status isn't measured by a Lexus but by a lifted pickup truck. *'Ohana* (extended family and friends) is important everywhere, but on the islands it's often the center of one's life. When locals first meet, they usually don't ask 'What do you do?' but 'Where you wen' grad?' (Where did you graduate from high school?). Like ancient Hawaiians comparing genealogies, locals often define themselves not by their accomplishments but by the communities to which they belong: island, town, high school.

Regardless of where they're from within the state, when two locals happen to meet each other outside Hawaii, there's often an automatic bond based on mutual affection and nostalgic longing for their island home – wherever they go, they belong to Hawaii's all-embracing *'ohana*.

Island Values, Multiculturalism & Diversity

During the 2012 US presidential election, island residents were thrilled that someone from Hawaii was re-elected president ('*Hana hou!*' read the front-page headline in the *Honolulu Star-Advertiser* newspaper, meaning 'bravo' or 'encore'). Barack Obama, who spent most of his boyhood in Honolulu, was embraced by local voters because his calm demeanor and respect for diversity represent Hawaii values. It also didn't hurt that he can bodysurf, and, more importantly, that he displayed true devotion to his *'ohana*. His grandmother, who lived in Honolulu, died one day before the 2008 election – Obama suspended his campaign to visit her before she passed. To many locals, these are the things that count.

What didn't matter to Hawaii is what the rest of the country seemed fixated on: his race. That Obama is of mixed-race parentage was barely worth mentioning. *Of course* he's mixed race – who in Hawaii isn't? One legacy of the plantation era is Hawaii's unselfconscious mixing of ethnicities. Cultural differences are freely acknowledged, even carefully maintained, but they don't normally divide people. For residents, the relaxed lifestyle and inclusive cultural values are probably the most defining, best-loved aspects of island life. Depending on your perspective, Honolulu is either America's most Asian city or Polynesia's most American city.

Among the older generation of locals, plantation-era stereotypes still inform social hierarchies and interactions. During plantation days, whites were the wealthy plantation owners, and for years after minorities would joke about the privileges that came with being a haole *luna* (Caucasian boss). But in a growing generational divide, Hawaii's youth often dismiss these distinctions even as they continue to speak pidgin. As intermarriage increases, racial distinctions become even more blurred. It's not uncommon nowadays to meet locals who can rattle off four or five different ethnicities in their ancestry – Hawaiian, Chinese, Portuguese, Filipino and Caucasian, for example.

Hawaii is as ethnically diverse as California, Texas or Florida – and more racially intermixed – but it's noticeably missing the significant African American and Latino populations that help define those other states and most multiculturalism on the mainland. Politically, the majority of Hawaii residents are middle-of-the-road Democrats who vote along party, racial/ethnic, seniority and local/nonlocal lines. As more mainland transplants arrive, conservative Republican candidates – such as Hawaii's former governor Linda Lingle – stand a better chance.

Who's Who

Hawaiian A person of Native Hawaiian ancestry. It's a faux pas to call just any Hawaii resident 'Hawaiian', thus semantically ignoring the islands' indigenous people.

Local A person who grew up in Hawaii. Locals who move away retain their local 'cred,' at least in part. Transplant residents never become local, even having lived in the islands for years.

Malihini 'Newcomer,' someone who's just moved to Hawaii and intends to stay.

Resident A person who lives, but might not have been born and raised, in Hawaii.

Haole White person (except local Portuguese people); further subdivided as 'mainland' or 'local' haole. Can be insulting or playful, depending on the context.

Hapa A person of mixed ancestry; *hapa* is Hawaiian for 'half.' A common racial designation is *hapa* haole (part white and part other, such as Hawaiian and/or Asian).

Kama'aina Literally a 'child of the land.' A person who is native to a particular place, eg a Hilo native, is a *kama'aina* of Hilo, not Kona. The term connotes a deep connection to a place.

Surfer tackling Hawaiian swell

Island Style

'On the islands, we do it island style,' sings local musician John Cruz in his slack key guitar anthem to life in Hawaii. While he doesn't say explicitly what 'island style' means, he doesn't have to; every local understands. Island style is easygoing, low-key, casual; even guitar strings are more relaxed here. Islanders take pride in being laid-back – that everything happens on 'island time' (a euphemism for taking things slow or being late), that aloha shirts are preferred over suits and that a *tutu* (grandmother) will hold up a line to chat with the checkout person at Longs Drugs (and that no one waiting seems to mind). 'Slow down! This ain't da mainland!' reads one popular bumper sticker.

Even in urban Honolulu, the 55th-largest US city, with a population of more than 350,000, there's something of a small-town vibe. Shave ice, surfing, 'talking story,' ukulele, hula, baby luau, pidgin, 'rubbah slippah' (flip-flops) and particularly *'ohana* – these are touchstones of everyday life, which tends to be family-oriented. School sporting events are packed with eager parents plus the gamut of aunties and uncles (whether they're actual relatives or not). Working overtime is uncommon, and weekends are saved for playing and potlucks at the beach.

Hawaiian woman playing the ukelele

ROBERT CRAVENS/SHUTTERSTOCK ©

Hawaiian Arts & Crafts

E komo mai *(welcome) to these unique Polynesian islands, where storytelling and slack key guitar are among the sounds of everyday life. Contemporary Hawaii is a vibrant mix of multicultural traditions. Underneath it all beats a Hawaiian heart, pounding with an ongoing revival of Hawaii's indigenous language, artisanal crafts, music and the hula.*

Hula

In ancient Hawai'i, hula sometimes was a solemn ritual, in which *mele* (songs, chants) were an offering to the gods or celebrated the accomplishments of *ali'i* (chiefs). At other times hula was lighthearted entertainment, in which chief and *kama'aina* (commoner) danced together, including at annual festivals such as the makahiki held during harvest season. Most importantly, hula embodied the community – telling stories of, and celebrating, itself.

Traditionally, dancers trained rigorously in *halau* (schools) under a *kumu* (teacher), so their hand gestures, facial expressions and synchronized movements were exact. In a culture without written language, chants were important, giving meaning to the movements and preserving Hawaii's oral history, anything from creation stories about gods to

★ Hawaiian Folktales, Proverbs & Poetry

Folktales of Hawai'i, illustrated by Sig Zane

'Olelo No'eau, illustrated by Dietrich Varez

Hānau ka Ua: Hawaiian Rain Names

Obake Files, by Glen Grant

royal genealogies. Songs often contained *kaona* (hidden meanings), which could be spiritual, but also slyly amorous, even sexual.

In hula competitions today, dancers vie in *kahiko* (ancient) and *'auana* (modern) categories. *Kahiko* performances are raw and elemental, accompanied only by chanting and thunderous gourd drums; costumes are traditional, with *ti*-leaf lei, *kapa* skirts or wraps, primary colors and sometimes lots of skin showing. Hawaii's Olympics of hula is the Big Island's Merrie Monarch Festival, but authentic hula competitions and celebrations happen year-round on all of the islands.

Island Music

Hawaiian music is rooted in ancient chants. Foreign missionaries and sugar-plantation workers introduced new melodies and instruments, which were incorporated and adapted to create a unique local musical style. *Leo ki'eki'e* (falsetto, or 'high voice') vocals, sometimes just referred to as soprano for women, employs a signature *ha'i* (vocal break, or split-note) style, with a singer moving abruptly from one register to another. Contemporary Hawaiian musical instruments include the steel guitar, slack key guitar and ukulele.

But if you tune your rental-car radio to today's island radio stations, you'll hear everything from US mainland hip-hop beats, country-and-western tunes and Asian pop hits to reggae-inspired 'Jawaiian' grooves. A few Hawaii-born singer-songwriters, most famously Jack Johnson, have achieved international stardom. To discover new hit-makers, check out this year's winners of the Na Hoku Hanohano Awards (www.nahokuhanohano. org), Hawaii's version of the Grammies.

Slackin' Sounds

Since the mid-20th century, the Hawaiian steel guitar has usually been played with slack key *(ki ho'alu)* tunings, in which the thumb plays the bass and rhythm chords, while the fingers play the melody and improvisations, in a picked style. Traditionally, slack key tunings were closely guarded secrets among *'ohana* (extended family and friends).

The legendary guitarist Gabby Pahinui launched the modern slack key guitar era with his first recording of 'Hi'ilawe' in 1946. In the 1960s, Gabby and his band the Sons of Hawaii embraced the traditional Hawaiian sound. Along with other influential slack key guitarists such as Sonny Chillingworth, they spurred a renaissance in Hawaiian music that continues to this day. The list of contemporary slack key masters is long and ever growing, including Keola Beamer, Ledward Ka'apana, Martin and Cyril Pahinui, Ozzie Kotani and George Kuo.

Traditional Crafts

In the 1970s, the Hawaiian renaissance sparked interest in artisan crafts. The most beloved traditional craft is lei-making, stringing garlands of flowers, leaves, berries, nuts or shells. More-lasting souvenirs include wood carvings, woven baskets and hats, and Hawaiian quilts. All of these have become so popular with tourists that cheap imitation imports from across the Pacific have flooded into Hawaii, so shop carefully and always buy local.

Lei hanging on Duke Kahanamoku statue (p78)

JEFF WHYTE/SHUTTERSTOCK ©

Lei

Greetings. Love. Honor. Respect. Peace.
Celebration. Spirituality. Good luck.
Farewell. A Hawaiian lei – a handcrafted
garland of fresh tropical flowers – can
signify all of these meanings and many
more. Lei-making may be Hawaii's most
sensuous and transitory art form. Fragrant
and ephemeral, lei embody the beauty of
nature and the embrace of 'ohana and the
community, freely given and freely shared.

In choosing their materials, lei makers
express emotions and tell a story, since
flowers and other plants may embody
Hawaiian places and myths. Traditional
lei makers may use feathers, nuts, shells,
seeds, seaweed, vines, leaves and fruit, in
addition to more familiar fragrant flowers.
The most common methods of making lei
are by knotting, braiding, winding, stringing or sewing the raw natural materials
together.

Lei Dos & Don'ts

o Do not wear a lei hanging directly
down around your neck. Instead, drape
a closed (circular) lei over your shoul-
ders, making sure equal lengths are
hanging over your front and back.

o Don't give a closed lei to a pregnant
woman for it may bring bad luck;
choose an open (untied) lei or *haku*
(head) lei instead.

o Resist the temptation to wear a lei
intended for someone else. That's bad
luck. Never refuse a lei, and do not take
one off in the presence of the giver.

o When you stop wearing your lei,
don't throw it away. Untie the string,
remove the bow and return the lei's
natural elements to the earth (eg
scatter flowers in the ocean, bury
seeds or nuts).

Traditional Hawaiian wood carving

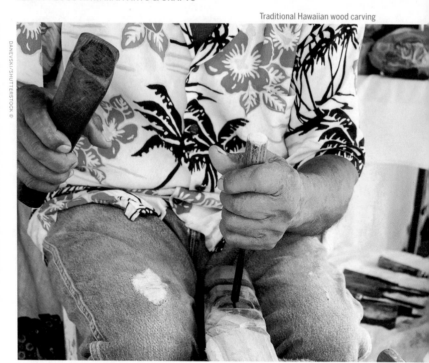

Worn daily, lei were integral to ancient Hawaiian society. In the islands' Polynesian past, they were part of sacred hula dances and given as special gifts to loved ones, as healing medicine to the sick and as offerings to the gods, all practices that continue today. So powerful a symbol were they that on ancient Hawaii's battlefields, a lei could bring peace to warring armies.

Today, locals wear lei for special events, such as weddings, birthdays, anniversaries and graduations. It's no longer common to make one's own lei, unless you belong to a hula *halau*. For ceremonial hula, performers are often required to make their own lei, even gathering raw materials by hand.

Woodworking

Ancient Hawaiians were expert woodworkers, carving canoes out of logs and hand-turning lustrous bowls from a variety of beautifully grained tropical hardwoods, such as koa and milo. *Ipu* (gourds) were also dried and used as containers and as drums for hula. Contemporary woodworkers take native woods to craft traditional bowls, exquisite furniture, jewelry and free-form sculptures. Traditionally, Hawaiian wooden bowls are not decorated or ornate, but are shaped to bring out the natural beauty of the wood. The thinner and lighter the bowl, the finer the artistry and greater the value – and the price. Don't be fooled into buying cheaper monkeypod bowls imported from the Philippines.

Green sea turtle

SHANE MYERS PHOTOGRAPHY/SHUTTERSTOCK ©

Outdoor Activities

Nature has given Hawaii such awesome scenery, you could simply do nothing here but lie on your beach towel. But you didn't come all this way to rest on your elbows. To find the outdoor adventures of a lifetime, the only real question is – how much time have you got?

In the Water

Beaches & Swimming

When it comes to swimming beaches, your options seem endless in Hawaii. Coastal strands come in a rainbow of hues and an infinite variety of textures – with sand that's a sparkling white, tan, black, charcoal, green or orange, or scattered with sea-glass, pebbles and boulders, and cratered with lava-rock tide pools.

By law, all beaches in Hawaii are open to the public below the high-tide line. Private land-owners can prevent access to their shoreline from land, but not by watercraft. Resort hotel

★ Top Island Adventures

Surfing Waikiki (p78), O'ahu.
Kayaking Na Pali Coast (p108), Kaua'i.
Hiking Haleakalā's summit
(p208), Maui.
Diving Cathedrals (p198), Lana'i.

beaches provide limited beach-access parking spots for the public, occasionally charging a small fee.

Most of Hawaii's hundreds of state and county beach parks have basic restrooms and outdoor cold-water showers; about half are patrolled by lifeguards. A few parks have gates that close during specified hours or they're signposted as off-limits from sunset until sunrise.

Nudity is legally prohibited on all public beaches in Hawaii. However, at a scant handful of beaches, going nude or topless sunbathing by women is grudgingly tolerated. Law enforcement at de facto nude beaches can vary, from absolutely nothing to a stern verbal warning to a written ticket with a mandatory fine and a possible court appearance.

Diving

Ocean temperatures in Hawaii are perfect for scuba diving, averaging 71°F to 83°F (22°C to 28°C) at the surface year-round. Even better than the bathwater temperature is the visibility, which is usually ideal for seeing the plethora of fish, coral and other sea creatures. November through March aren't the best months for diving, because winter rainstorms and winds bring rougher seas and higher waves to Hawaii.

Dive costs range widely depending on gear, dive length, location (especially shore versus boat dives) and so on. The average price for two-tank boat dives including all gear rental is $125 to $180. Remember to bring your dive certification card from home.

Some dive operators offer a beginners 'discover scuba' option, which includes brief instruction, and possibly swimming-pool practice, followed by a shallow beach or boat dive. No previous experience is necessary, but you must be a strong swimmer. These introductory dives generally cost $110 to $200, depending on your location and whether or not a boat is used.

If you don't already know how to dive, Hawaii is a great place to learn. **PADI** (Professional Association of Diving Instructors; www.padi.com) open-water certification courses can be completed in as few as three days, usually costing from $300 to $600 per person. Book classes ahead of your trip.

Kayaking

Sea kayakers will find heavenly bits of coastline and offshore islets beckoning across the archipelago. Indeed, there are many beaches, bays and valleys that can be reached in no other way but from the open ocean. If it's your first time out, consider taking a guided kayaking tour (from $50), which usually includes some basic paddling instruction. DIY kayak rentals are available near popular put-ins, typically for $40 to $75 per day.

Kitesurfing

Kitesurfing, also called kiteboarding, is a little like strapping on a snowboard, grabbing a parachute and sailing over the water. It's an impressive feat to watch, and if you already know how to windsurf, surf or wakeboard, there's a good chance you'll master it quickly. Any place that's good for windsurfing is also good for kitesurfing. The best winds usually blow in summer, but it varies depending on where you are on each island. Maui dominates the attention of kitesurfers, aspiring or otherwise.

Snorkeling

If you can swim, Hawaii's magnificent coral reefs are yours. In addition to more than 500 species of often neon-colored tropical fish, endangered sea turtles are sometimes spotted, and you may see manta rays, spinner dolphins, jacks, sharks and other impressive predators.

Every island has fantastic shoreline snorkeling spots, in addition to snorkel cruises that deliver you to places you can't swim to.

Stand Up Paddle Boarding (SUP)

For safety, always paddle with a buddy and use a leash. Carry enough water and a whistle or a cellphone in a waterproof case for emergencies. Don't forget about sun protection, including sunblock, sunglasses, a hat and a rash guard (surf shirt).

You'll see SUP fans paddling on all the main islands, anywhere from ocean beaches and calm bays to flat-water rivers, the latter on Kaua'i.

Some outdoor outfitters specialize in SUP, offering instruction (two-hour group lessons average $75 to $130), rentals (from $25 to $75 per day) and occasionally guided tours (from $120). Otherwise, ask at local surf shops and surf schools about SUP rentals and lessons.

Surfing

Ancient Hawaiians invented surfing (calling it *he'e nalu*, 'wave sliding'). In Hawaii today surfing is both its own intense subculture as well as a part of everyday island life. Hawaii's biggest waves roll in to the north shores of the islands from November through March. Summer swells, which break along the south shores, are smaller and more infrequent.

With its overwhelming variety and abundance of surf spots, O'ahu is where all the major pro surfing competitions happen; its North Shore is home to the **Triple Crown of Surfing** (http://vanstriplecrownofsurfing.com; ⊘Nov & Dec), which draws thousands of roadside spectators every November and December. All of the main islands have good, even great, surfing breaks. Surf lessons and board rentals are available at just about every tourist beach that has rideable waves.

Windsurfing

With warm waters and steady winds, Hawaii ranks as one of the world's premier spots for windsurfing. Generally, the best winds blow from June through September, but trade winds will keep windsurfers – somewhere, at least – happy all year.

As O'ahu's North Shore is to surfing, so Maui's **Ho'okipa Beach** (☏808-572-8122;

Reef-Safe Sunscreen

Remember to wear reef-safe sunscreen lotion before kicking off to snorkel. Many modern lotions are reef killers. Safe ingredients are titanium dioxide and zinc oxide. Avoid sunscreens with oxybenzone and other chemical UV-radiation filters.

www.mauicounty.gov/facilities; Hana Hwy, Mile 9; ⊘5:30am-7pm; P) is to windsurfing: a dangerous, fast arena where the top international windsurfing competitions sort out who's best. The other islands have windsurfing, but they don't reach Maui's pinnacle. Only Moloka'i, bracketed by wind-whipped ocean channels, provides an equivalent challenge for experts.

On Land

Caving

Funny thing, lava. As the top of a flow cools and hardens, the molten rock beneath keeps moving. When the eruption stops and the lava drains, what's left behind is an underground maze of tunnels like some colossal ant farm. Many of these lava tubes are cultural as well as ecological wonders, since ancient Hawaiians used them as burial chambers, water caches, temporary housing and more.

Being the youngest island and still volcanically active, Hawai'i (Big Island) is a caving hot spot, with six of the world's 10 longest lava tubes. Ka'u's Kanohina cave system, managed by the **Cave Conservancy of Hawai'i** (www.hawaiicaves.org) ✎, has 20 miles of complex tunnels – take a peek at **Kula Kai Caverns** (☏808-929-9725; www.kulakaicaverns. com; 92-8864 Lauhala Dr; tours adult/child 6-12yr from $20/10). Kea'au's **Kazumura Cave** (☏808-967-7208; www.kazumuracave.com; off Volcano Hwy, past Mile 22; from $30; ⊘Mon-Sat by appointment) is even longer.

Other islands have fewer caving opportunities. Maui's **Hana Lava Tube** (p173), also called Ka'eleku Caverns, is a short cave system that even kids can explore.

Best Islands for Hiking

For variety, **Hawai'i (Big Island)** wins by a nose. Hawai'i Volcanoes National Park contains an erupting volcano, plus steaming craters, lava deserts and rainforests. Then there are the two nearly 14,000ft mountains to scale – Mauna Loa and Mauna Kea.

On **Maui**, Haleakalā National Park provides awe-inspiring descents across the volcanic summit's eroded moonscape, while the Road to Hana tempts with short excursion hikes to waterfalls.

The legendary Kalalau Trail on **Kaua'i's** Na Pali Coast edges spectacularly fluted sea cliffs. An abundance of paths crisscross clifftop Koke'e State Park and cavernous Waimea Canyon.

On **O'ahu**, you can escape Honolulu in a hurry in the forests of the Manoa and Makiki Valleys around Mt Tantalus or lose the crowds entirely at Ka'ena Point.

Cycling & Mountain Biking

Quality trumps quantity when it comes to cycling and mountain biking in Hawaii. Cyclists will find the most bike-friendly roads and organizational support on O'ahu, but all of the main islands offer bicycle rentals, as well as trails and 4WD roads that double as two-wheel, pedal-powered adventures.

Hiking & Backpacking

Hikers will find that, mile for mile, these tiny islands almost cannot be topped for heart-stopping vistas and soulful beauty. Being small, even the most rugged spots are usually accessible as day hikes. Backpacking is rarely necessary, though when it is, the rewards so outstrip the effort it's almost ludicrous. Start exploring Hawaii's public trails online through the **Nā Ala Hele Trail & Access Program** (http://hawaiitrails.org/trails).

Trespassing on private land or government land not intended for public use is illegal, no matter how many people you see

MATT MUNRO/LONELY PLANET ©

Exploring lava caves, Hawaiian Volcanoes National Park (p251)

doing it. Show respect for all 'Kapu' or 'No Trespassing' signs – not just for legal reasons, but also for your own safety.

Stargazing

Astronomers are drawn to Hawaii's night sky the way surfers are drawn to the islands' big waves. The view from Mauna Kea volcano on Hawai'i, the Big Island, is unmatched in clarity. Mauna Kea has more astronomical observatories than any mountain on Earth. On Mauna Kea's summit road, the visitor information station (p235) hosts free public stargazing programs nightly (weather permitting). During the day, catch a family-friendly planetarium show at Hilo's educational 'Imiloa Astronomy Center (p266), also on the Big Island, or at Honolulu's Bishop Museum (p50) on O'ahu.

Astronomical observatories at **Science City** (Haleakalā Observatories; www.ifa.hawaii.edu) on Maui's Haleakalā volcano study the sun, not the stars, and they aren't open to the public. For do-it-yourself astronomy outings, Haleakalā National Park's summit visitor center stocks star maps and you can rent high-powered binoculars from island dive shops before you head up. Resort hotels, especially on Maui and the Big Island, occasionally offer stargazing programs for guests that use high-quality telescopes.

Spam *musubi* (rice balls)

Cuisine

We love the cuisine in Hawaii because of its tasty exuberance and no-worries embrace of foreign flavors. The plate lunch. Loco moco (rice, fried egg and hamburger patty with gravy). Even Spam musubi (rice ball) has a sassy – if salty – international charm. So join the fun, sample the unknown and savor the next bite.

Native Hawaiian Food

With its earthy flavors and Polynesian ingredients, Native Hawaiian cooking is a genre unique unto the culinary world. But it's not necessarily easy for visitors to find – look for it at roadside markets, plate-lunch kitchens, old-school delis and island diners.

Kalua pig is traditionally roasted whole underground in an imu, a pit of red-hot stones layered with banana and *ti* leaves. Cooked this way, the pork is smoky, salty and succulent. Nowadays *kalua* pork is typically oven-roasted and seasoned with salt and liquid smoke. At a commercial luau, a pig placed in an *imu* is usually only for show (it couldn't feed 300-plus guests anyway).

Poi – a purplish paste made of pounded taro root, often steamed and fermented – was sacred to ancient Hawaiians. Taro is highly nutritious, low in calories, easily digestible and versatile to prepare. Tasting bland to mildly tart or even sour, poi is usually not eaten by itself, but as a starchy counterpoint to strongly flavored dishes such as *lomilomi* salmon (minced, salted salmon with diced tomato and green onion). Fried or baked taro chips are sold at grocery stores, gas stations and the like.

★ **Best Restaurants**

Alan Wong's (p67)

Monkeypod Kitchen (p203)

Roy's Waikiki (p91)

Takenoko Sushi (p274)

Umekes (p247)

A popular main dish is *laulau*, a bundle of pork or chicken and salted butterfish wrapped in taro or *ti* leaves and steamed until it has a soft spinach-like texture. We find it a little bland, but locals swear by the stuff. Other traditional Hawaiian fare includes baked *'ulu* (breadfruit), with a mouthfeel similar to potato; *'opihi* (limpet), tiny mollusks picked off reefs at low tide; and *haupia*, a coconut-cream custard thickened with arrowroot or cornstarch.

In general, we'd characterize Native Hawaiian cuisine as extremely filling, if not the most flavorful – there's a lot of emphasis on starch and meat. If you've dined elsewhere in Polynesia, it has a very similar ingredient and flavor profile to sister cuisines located across the ocean.

Hawaii Regional Cuisine

Hawaii was considered a culinary backwater until the early 1990s, when a handful of island chefs – including Alan Wong, Roy Yamaguchi, Sam Choy and Peter Merriman, all of whom still have restaurants on the Big Island – created a new cuisine, borrowing liberally from Hawaii's multiethnic heritage. These chefs partnered with island farmers, ranchers and fishers to highlight fresh, local ingredients, and in doing so transformed childhood favorites into gourmet Pacific Rim masterpieces. Suddenly macadamia nut-crusted mahimahi, miso-glazed butterfish and *liliko'i* (passion fruit) anything were all the rage.

This culinary movement was dubbed 'Hawaii Regional Cuisine' and its 12 pioneering chefs became celebrities. At first, Hawaii Regional Cuisine was rather exclusive, found only at high-end dining rooms. Its hallmarks included Eurasian fusion flavors and gastronomic techniques with elaborate plating.

Upscale restaurants are still the mainstay for Hawaii's star chefs, but now you'll find neighborhood bistros and even plate-lunch food trucks serving dishes inspired by Hawaii Regional Cuisine, with island farms lauded like designer brands on menus.

Local Specialties

Cheap, tasty and filling, local '*grinds*' (food) is the stuff of cravings and comfort. There's no better example than that classic plate lunch: a fixed-plate meal of 'two scoop' rice, macaroni or potato salad and a hot protein dish, such as fried mahimahi, teriyaki chicken or *kalbi* short ribs. Often eaten with disposable chopsticks on disposable plates, these meals pack a flavor (and caloric) punch: fried, salty and meaty. Nowadays, healthier plates come with brown rice and salad greens, but in general, the backbone of the plate lunch are those two scoops of rice and potato/macaroni salad, a heaping mountain of carbohydrates that are Mauna Kea-esque in their proportions.

Sticky white rice is more than a side dish in Hawaii – it's a culinary building block, and an integral partner in everyday meals. Without rice, Spam *musubi* (rice balls) would just be a slice of canned meat. *Loco moco* would be nothing more than an egg-and-gravy covered

Saimin (noodle soup with dumplings)

HAPPYSARU/SHUTTERSTOCK ©

hamburger patty. Just so you know, sticky white rice means exactly that. Not fluffy rice. Not wild rice. And definitely not instant.

One must-try local *pupu* (snack or appetizer) is *poke* (pronounced 'poh-keh'), a savory dish of bite-sized raw fish (typically ahi), seasoned with *shōyu*, sesame oil, green onion, chili-pepper flakes, sea salt, *ogo* (crunchy seaweed) and *'inamona* (a condiment made of roasted, ground kukui – candlenut tree – nuts). Few foodstuffs we've tried short of a raw oyster can match *poke* when it comes to evoking the flavors of the ocean.

Another favorite local food is *saimin*, a soup of chewy Chinese egg noodles swimming in Japanese broth, garnished with green onion, dried nori (Japanese dried seaweed), *kamaboko* (steamed fish cake) and *char siu* (Chinese barbecued pork).

The traditional local sweet treat is Chinese crack seed. It's preserved fruit (typically plum, cherry, mango or lemon) that, like Coca-Cola or curry, is impossible to describe – it can be sweet, sour, salty or spicy. Sold prepackaged at supermarkets and Longs Drugs or scooped by the pound at specialty shops, crack seed is truly addictive.

They grow avocados here that look to be the size of your head, their size only out-stripped by their tastiness. With that said, don't measure an avocado strictly by its size; smaller ones can be just as delicious. Many avocado trees are marked with 'no spray' signs, especially in, shall we say, the 'crunchier' corners of the island (Puna, North Kohala and the South Kona Coast come to mind). The 'no spray' request is aimed at those spraying pesticides – there's a muscular no-pesticide, no-GMO movement on the island, and while Big Island folks are generally laid-back, the issue can provoke incredibly heated discussions.

There's beef, and then there's Big Island beef. The northern valleys of Hawai'i are carpeted in mile upon mile of grassy pastureland, all dotted with roaming herds of cattle. This enormous well of beef is often exported, but head to the right restaurants and you'll be dining on finely marbled steaks and juicy, locally sourced burgers that would be the envy of any Texas table. We're not sure what it is about the grasses these cows are dining on, but the beef here has a richness that is hard to both describe and match.

In parts of the Big Island, particularly Hilo and the South Kona Coast, a version of Japanese cuisine that has taken on island elements has become its own subgenre of native cuisine. In diners run by Japanese Americans, you may see hot dogs served alongside rice and *furikake* (a seasoning of dried fish, seaweed and other goodies), while most meals are preceded by a complimentary bowl of edamame (soybeans) and come with a bowl of miso soup

Coffee, Tea & Traditional Drinks

Hawaii was the first US state to grow coffee. World-famous Kona coffee wins raves for its mellow flavor with no bitter aftertaste. The upland slopes of Mauna Loa and Hualalai volcanoes in the Kona district offer an ideal climate (sunny mornings and afternoon clouds with light seasonal showers) for coffee cultivation.

While 100% Kona coffee has the most cachet, commanding $20 to $40 per pound, in recent years crops from the island's southernmost district of Ka'u have won accolades and impressed aficionados. Small coffee farms have also fruited in Puna and Honoka'a on the island's windward side. It's worth noting that the '100%' designation on real Kona coffee is more than marketing language; a lot of the 'Kona' coffee you see sold in larger chain grocery stores consists of cheaper beans laced with a smattering of the real stuff. True, 100% Kona coffee has an incredibly complex, multinote flavor, balancing bitterness with dark, caffeinated depths.

Ancient Hawaiians never got buzzed on coffee beans, which were first imported in the early 19th century. Hawaii's original intoxicants were plant-based Polynesian elixirs: *'awa* (a mild, mouth-numbing sedative made from the kava plant's roots) and *noni* (Indian mulberry), which some consider a cure-all. Both of these drinks are pungent in smell and taste, so they're often mixed with other juices, but it's not terribly tough to find drinkable kava. It pretty much tastes like the earth; some people think this speaks to kava's deep connections to Hawaiian terroir, and some people say, 'Hey, this stuff tastes like dirt. Yech.'

Tea-growing was introduced to Hawaii in the late 19th century, but never took hold as a commercial crop due to high labor and production costs. In 1999, University of Hawai'i researchers discovered that a particular cultivar of tea would thrive in volcanic soil and tropical climates, especially at higher elevations. Small, often organic, tea farms are now spreading around Volcano and along the Hamakua Coast.

Fruit trees also thrive here. Alas, most supermarket cartons contain imported purees or sugary 'juice drinks' like POG (passion fruit, orange and guava). Don't get us wrong, it's tasty, but it's also just fruity enough to fool you into thinking you're drinking something healthy – you're not. Look for real, freshly squeezed and blended juices at health food stores, farmers markets and roadside fruit stands. Don't assume that the fruit is local, though.

Na Pali Coast (p103)

MARC LEATHAM/500PX ©

Survival Guide

DIRECTORY A–Z   **307**

Accommodations   307
Electricity   307
Entry & Exit
Requirements   307
Customs Regulations   307
Food   309
Gay & Lesbian Travelers   309
Health   309

Insurance   309
Internet Access   310
Legal Matters   310
Money   310
Public Holidays   311
Telephone   311
Time   312
Tourist Information   312
Travelers with Disabilities   312

TRANSPORT   **313**

Getting There & Away   313
Getting Around   314

GLOSSARY   **315**

Directory A–Z

Accommodations

Advance booking is almost always necessary. If visiting at peak times, the sooner the better – up to a year ahead for Christmas and New Year's.

o **Hotels & Resorts** At popular beaches; expect daily resort and/or parking fees.

o **Condos** Plentiful on bigger islands, offering apartment-style amenities and often weekly discounts.

o **B&Bs & Vacation Rentals** Generally reliable, with more space and amenities than comparably priced hotels.

o **Hostels** For cheap rooms and dormitory beds.

o **Camping & Cabins** Bring your own camping gear.

Book Your Stay Online

For more accommodations reviews by Lonely Planet authors, check out http://hotels.lonelyplanet.com/Hawaii. You'll find independent reviews, as well as recommendations on the best places to stay. Best of all, you can book online.

Electricity

120V/60Hz

120V/60Hz

Entry & Exit Requirements

o Double-check current visa and passport requirements *before* coming to the USA.

o For current information about entry requirements and eligibility, check the visas section of the **US Department of State** (http://travel.state.gov) website and the travel section of the **US Customs and Border Protection** (CBP; www.cbp.gov) website.

o Upon arrival in the USA, most foreign citizens (excluding, for now, many Canadians, some Mexicans, all children under age 14 and seniors over age 79) must register with the **Department of Homeland Security** (www.dhs.gov), which entails having electronic (inkless) fingerprints and a digital photo taken.

Customs Regulations

Currently, each international visitor is allowed to bring into the USA duty-free:

o 1L of liquor (if you're over 21 years old)

o 200 cigarettes (1 carton) or 100 cigars (if you're over 18 years old)

Amounts higher than $10,000 in cash, traveler's checks, money orders and other cash equivalents must be declared. For more detailed, up-to-date information, check with

Etiquette

Island residents are mostly casual and informal in their everyday life, but there are some (unspoken) rules of etiquette you should follow:

o Take off your shoes when entering someone's home. Most residents wear 'rubbah slippah' (flip-flops) partly for this reason – easy to slip on and off, no socks required.

o Ask permission before you pick fruit or flowers or otherwise trespass private property.

o Drive slowly. Unless you're about to hit someone, don't honk your car horn.

o Try to correctly pronounce Hawaiian place names and words. Even if you fail, the attempt is appreciated.

o Don't collect (or even move) stones at sacred sites. If you're not sure whether something's sacred, consider that in Hawaiian thinking, everything is sacred, especially in nature.

o Don't stack rocks or wrap them in ti leaves at waterfalls, heiau (temples) etc. This bastardization of the ancient Hawaiian practice of leaving hoʻokupu (offerings) at sacred sites is littering.

US Customs and Border Protection (CBP; www.cbp.gov). Most fresh fruits and plants are restricted from entry into Hawaii (to prevent the spread of invasive species), and customs officials strictly enforce these regulations. Because Hawaii is a rabies-free state, the pet quarantine laws are draconian. Questions? Contact the **Hawaii Department of Agriculture** (http://hdoa. hawaii.gov).

All checked and carry-on bags leaving Hawaii for the US mainland, Alaska or Guam must be X-ray checked by an agricultural inspector at the airport. Make sure that any fresh food, produce or flowers in your baggage has been commercially packaged and approved for travel, or else you'll be forced to surrender those pineapples and orchids at the airport.

Passports

o A machine-readable passport (MRP) is required for all foreign citizens to enter the USA.

o Your passport must be valid for six months beyond your expected dates of stay in the USA.

o If your passport was issued/renewed after October 26, 2006, you need an 'e-passport' with a digital photo and an integrated chip containing biometric data.

Visas

o Currently, under the US Visa Waiver Program (VWP), visas are not required for citizens of 38 countries for stays up to 90 days (no extensions).

o Under the VWP program you must have a return ticket (or onward ticket to any foreign destination) that's nonrefundable in the USA.

o All VWP travelers must register online at least 72 hours before arrival with the **Electronic System for Travel Authorization** (ESTA; https:// esta.cbp.dhs.gov/esta/esta.html), which currently costs $14. Once approved, registration is valid for two years (or until your passport expires, whichever comes first).

o Canadian citizens are generally admitted visa-free for stays up to 182 days total during a 12-month period; they do not need to register with the ESTA.

o All other foreign visitors who don't qualify for the VWP and aren't Canadian citizens must apply for a tourist visa. The process costs a nonrefundable fee (minimum $160), involves a personal interview and can take several weeks, so apply early.

o www.usembassy.gov has links for all US embassies and consulates abroad. You're better off applying for a visa in your home country rather than while on the road.

Food

The following price ranges refer to an average main course at dinner in a restaurant (lunch is cheaper, usually half-price) or a meal at a casual takeout joint. Unless otherwise stated, taxes and tips are not included in the price.

$	Less than $12
$$	$12–30
$$$	More than $30

Gay & Lesbian Travelers

The state of Hawaii has strong minority protections and a constitutional guarantee of privacy that extends to sexual behavior between consenting adults. Same-sex couples have the right to marry.

Locals tend to be private about their personal lives, so you will not see much public hand-holding or open displays of affection, either same-sex or opposite-sex. Everyday LGBTQ life is low-key – it's more about picnics and potlucks, not nightclubs. Even in Waikiki, the laid-back gay scene comprises just a half dozen or so bars, clubs and restaurants.

That said, Hawaii is a popular destination for LGBTQ travelers, who are served by a small network of gay-owned and gay-friendly

B&Bs, guesthouses and hotels. For more information on recommended places to stay, beaches, events and more, check out the following resources:

Out Traveler (www.outtraveler.com/hawaii) LGBTQ-oriented Hawaii travel articles free online.
Pride Guide Hawaii (www.gogayhawaii.com) Free island visitor guides for gay-friendly activities, accommodations, dining, nightlife, shopping, festivals, weddings and more.
Hawai'i LGBT Legacy Foundation (http://hawaiilgbtlegacyfoundation.com) News, resources and a community calendar of LGBTQ events, mostly on O'ahu.
Gay Hawaii (http://gayhawaii.com) Short listings of LGBTQ-friendly businesses, beaches and community resources on O'ahu, Maui, Kaua'i and Hawai'i, the Big Island.
Purple Roofs (www.purpleroofs.com) Online directory of gay-owned and gay-friendly B&Bs, vacation rentals, guesthouses and hotels.

VOG

Vog, a visible haze or smog caused by volcanic emissions from the Big Island, is often (but not always) dispersed by trade winds before it reaches other islands. On the Big Island, vog can make sunny skies hazy in West Hawai'i, especially in the afternoons around Kailua-Kona.

Short-term exposure to vog is not generally hazardous; however, high sulfur-dioxide levels can create breathing problems for sensitive groups (eg anyone with respiratory or heart conditions, pregnant women, young children and infants). Avoid vigorous physical exertion outdoors on voggy days.

Health

o For emergency medical assistance anywhere in Hawaii, call 911 or go directly to the emergency room (ER) of the nearest hospital. For nonemergencies, consider an urgent-care center or walk-in medical clinic.

o Some insurance policies require you to get preauthorization for medical treatment from a call center before seeking help. Keep all medical receipts and documentation for claims reimbursement later.

Insurance

Getting travel insurance to cover theft, loss and medical problems is highly recommended. Some insurance policies do not cover 'risky' activities such as scuba diving, trekking and motorcycling, so read the fine print. Make sure your policy at least covers hospital stays and an emergency flight home.

Paying for your airline ticket or rental car with a credit card may provide limited travel accident insurance. If you already have private US health insurance or a homeowners or renters policy, find out what those policies cover and only get supplemental insurance. If you have prepaid a large portion of your vacation, trip cancellation insurance may be a worthwhile expense.

Worldwide travel insurance is available at www.lonelyplanet.com/bookings. You can buy, extend and claim online any time – even if you're already on the road.

Internet Access

○ Most accommodations, many coffee shops and a few bars, restaurants and other businesses offer public wi-fi hot spots (sometimes free only for paying customers). In-room internet access at Hawaii's hotels is increasingly wireless, not wired.

○ Cities and larger towns may have cybercafes or business centers like **FedEx Office** (☑800-463-3339; http://local.fedex.com/hi) offering pay-as-you-go internet terminals (typically $12 to $20 per hour) and

sometimes wi-fi (free or fee-based).

○ Hawaii's **public libraries** (☑808-586-3500; www.librarieshawaii.org) provide free internet access via computer terminals if you get a temporary nonresident library card ($10). A few library branches also offer free wi-fi (library card and PIN required).

Legal Matters

If you are arrested, you have the right to an attorney; if you can't afford one, a public defender will be provided for free. The **Hawaii State Bar Association** (☑808-537-9140; http://hawaiilawyerreferral.com; Suite 1000, 1100 Alakea St, Honolulu; ☺8:30am-4:30pm Mon-Fri) makes attorney referrals. International visitors may want to call their nearest consulate or embassy for advice; police will provide the telephone number upon request.

Money

ATMs are available in cities and larger towns. Credit cards are widely accepted (except at some lodgings) and are often required for reservations. Tipping is customary.

ATMS

○ ATMs are available 24/7 at banks, shopping malls, airports and grocery and convenience stores.

○ Expect a minimum surcharge of around $3 per transaction, in addition to any fees charged by your home bank.

○ Most ATMs are connected to international networks (Plus and Cirrus are common) and offer decent exchange rates.

Credit Cards

○ Credit cards are widely accepted and often required for car rentals, hotel reservations etc. Some B&Bs and vacation rentals refuse them (pay in US dollar traveler's checks, personal checks or cash instead) or else add a 3% surcharge.

○ Visa, MasterCard and American Express are most commonly accepted, followed by Discover and JTB.

Exchange Rates

Australia	A$1	$0.72
Canada	C$1	$0.74
China	Y10	$1.44
Euro zone	€1	$1.04
Japan	¥100	$0.85
New Zealand	NZ$1	$0.69
UK	UK£1	$1.22

For current exchange rates see www.xe.com

Money Changers

○ Exchange foreign currency at Honolulu International Airport or the main branches of bigger banks, such as the **Bank of Hawaii** (☏808-643-3888; www.boh.com) or **First Hawaiian Bank** (☏808-844-4444; www.fhb.com).

○ Outside of cities and larger towns, exchanging money may be impossible, so make sure you carry enough cash and/or a credit or debit card.

Public Holidays

On the following national holidays, banks, schools and government offices (including post offices) close, and museums, transportation and other services operate on a Sunday schedule. Holidays falling on a weekend are usually observed the following Monday.

New Year's Day January 1
Martin Luther King Jr Day Third Monday in January
Presidents' Day Third Monday in February
Prince Kuhio Day March 26
Good Friday Friday before Easter Sunday in March/April
Memorial Day Last Monday in May
King Kamehameha Day June 11
Independence Day July 4
Statehood Day Third Friday in August

Tipping

Tipping is *not* optional; only withhold tips in cases of outrageously bad service.
Airport and hotel porters $2 per bag, minimum $5 per cart.
Bartenders 15% to 20% per round, minimum $1 per drink.
Concierges Nothing for simple information, up to $20 for securing last-minute restaurant reservations etc.
Housekeeping staff $2 to $4 per night, left under the card provided; more if you're messy.
Parking valets At least $2 when your keys are returned.
Restaurant servers and room service 18% to 20%, unless a gratuity is already charged (common for groups of six or more).
Taxi drivers 10% to 15% of metered fare, rounded up to the next dollar.

Labor Day First Monday in September
Veterans Day November 11
Thanksgiving Fourth Thursday in November
Christmas Day December 25

Telephone

Cell Phones

International travelers need a multiband GSM phone in order to make calls in the USA. With an unlocked multiband phone, popping in a US prepaid rechargeable SIM card is usually cheaper than using your own network. SIM cards are available at any telecommunications or electronics store. If your phone doesn't work in the USA, these stores also sell inexpensive prepaid phones, including some airtime.

Otherwise, check with your service provider about using your cell phone in Hawaii. Among US providers, Verizon has the most extensive network. Cellular coverage is best on O'ahu, but sometimes spotty outside major towns (especially on the Neighbor Islands) and nonexistent in many rural areas, including on hiking trails and at remote beaches.

Payphones & Phonecards

○ Payphones are a dying breed, usually found at shopping centers, hotels and public places (eg beaches, parks).

○ Some payphones are coin-operated (local calls usually cost 50¢), while others only accept credit cards or phonecards.

○ Private prepaid phone cards are available from convenience stores, newsstands, supermarkets and pharmacies.

Dialing Codes

○ All Hawaii phone numbers consist of a three-digit area code (☏808) followed by a seven-digit local number.

○ To call long-distance from one Hawaiian Island to another, dial ☏1 + 808 + local number.

○ Always dial ☏1 before toll-free numbers (☏800, 888 etc). Some toll-free numbers only work within Hawaii or from the US mainland (and possibly Canada).

○ To call Canada from Hawaii, dial ☏1 + area code + local number (international rates still apply).

○ For all other international calls from Hawaii, dial ☏011 + country code + area code + local number.

○ To call Hawaii from abroad, the international country code for the USA is ☏1.

Useful Numbers

○ Emergency (police, fire, ambulance) ☏911

○ Local directory assistance ☏411

○ Long-distance directory assistance ☏1-808-555-1212

○ Toll-free directory assistance ☏1-800-555-1212

○ Operator ☏0

Time

○ Hawaii-Aleutian Standard Time (HAST) is GMT minus 10 hours.

○ Hawaii doesn't observe Daylight Saving Time (DST).

Tourist Information

There are staffed tourist information desks in the airport arrivals areas. While you're waiting for your bags to appear on the carousel, you can peruse racks of free tourist brochures and magazines, which contain discount coupons for activities, tours, restaurants etc.

For pretrip planning in several languages, browse the information-packed website of the **Hawaii Visitors & Convention Bureau** (www.gohawaii.com).

Travelers with Disabilities

○ Bigger, newer hotels and resorts in Hawaii have elevators, wheelchair-accessible rooms (reserve these well in advance) and TDD-capable phones.

○ Telephone companies provide relay operators (TTY/TDD dial ☏711) for the hearing-impaired.

○ Many banks provide ATM instructions in Braille.

○ Traffic intersections in cities and some towns have dropped curbs and audible crossing signals.

○ Guide and service dogs are not subject to the same quarantine requirements as other pets, but must enter the state at Honolulu International Airport. Contact the Department of Agriculture's **Animal Quarantine Station** (☏808-483-7151; http://hdoa.hawaii.gov/ai/aqs/animal-quarantine-information-page; ⊗8am-5pm) before arrival.

○ Search the **Disability & Communication Access Board** (☏808-586-8121; www.hawaii.gov/health/dcab) website for free, downloadable 'Traveler Tips' brochure guides to all islands except Lana'i.

○ **Access Aloha Travel** (☏808-545-1143, 800-480-1143; www.accessalohatravel.com), an O'ahu-based travel agency, can help book wheelchair-accessible accommodations, rental vans, cruises and tours.

Transport

Getting There & Away

Air

Hawaii is a competitive market for US domestic and international airfares, which vary tremendously by season, day of the week and demand. Competition is highest among airlines flying to Honolulu from major US mainland cities, especially between Hawaiian Airlines, Alaska Airlines and Virgin America.

The 'lowest fare' fluctuates constantly. In general, return fares from the US mainland to Hawaii cost from $400 (in low season from the West Coast) to $800 or more (in high season from the East Coast).
Pleasant Holidays (☏800-742-9244; www.pleasantholidays.com) offers competitive vacation packages from the US mainland. For discounted flights and vacation packages from Canada, check with low-cost carrier **WestJet** (☏888-937-8538; www.westjet.com).

All checked and carry-on bags leaving Hawaii for the US mainland, Alaska and Guam must be inspected by a US Department of Agricul-ture (USDA) x-ray machine at the airport.

Airports

The majority of incoming flights from overseas and the US mainland arrive at **Honolulu International Airport** (HNL; ☏808-836-6411; http://hawaii.gov/hnl; 300 Rodgers Blvd; ☏) on O'ahu. Flights to Lana'i and Moloka'i usually originate from Honolulu or Maui.

The main Neighbor Island airports include the following:

Hilo International Airport (ITO; ☏808-961-9300; www.hawaii.gov/ito; 2450 Kekuanaoa St), East Hawai'i (Big Island).
Kahului International Airport (OGG; ☏808-872-3830; http://hawaii.gov/ogg; 1 Kahului Airport Rd), Maui.
Kona International Airport (KOA; ☏808-327-9520; http://hawaii.gov/koa; 73-200 Kupipi St), at Keahole West Hawai'i (Big Island).

Lana'i Airport (LNY; ☏808-565-7942; http://hawaii.gov/lny; off Hwy 440), Lana'i.
Lihu'e Airport (LIH; ☏808-274-3800; http://hawaii.gov/lih; 3901 Mokulele Loop), Kaua'i.
Moloka'i Airport (MKK, Ho'olehua; ☏808-567-9660; http://hawaii.gov/mkk; Ho'olehua), Moloka'i.

Among the many domestic and international airlines serving the islands, the only Hawaii-based carrier is **Hawaiian Airlines** (☏800-367-5320; www.hawaiianairlines.com).

Sea

Most cruises to Hawaii include stopovers in Honolulu and on Maui, Kaua'i and Hawai'i, the Big Island. Cruises typically last two weeks, with fares starting around $120 per person per night, based on double occupancy; airfare to/from the departure point costs extra.

Climate Change & Travel

Every form of transport that relies on carbon-based fuel generates CO_2, the main cause of human-induced climate change. Modern travel is dependent on aeroplanes, which might use less fuel per kilometre per person than most cars but travel much greater distances. The altitude at which aircraft emit gases (including CO_2) and particles also contributes to their climate change impact. Many websites offer 'carbon calculators' that allow people to estimate the carbon emissions generated by their journey and, for those who wish to do so, to offset the impact of the greenhouse gases emitted with contributions to portfolios of climate-friendly initiatives throughout the world. Lonely Planet offsets the carbon footprint of all staff and author travel.

Popular cruise lines include the following:

Holland America (☎877-932-4259; www.hollandamerica.com) Departures from San Diego, Seattle and Vancouver, British Columbia.

Norwegian Cruise Line (NCL; ☎855-577-9489; www.ncl.com) Departures from Vancouver, British Columbia.

Princess Cruises (☎800-774-6237; www.princess.com) Departures from Los Angeles, San Francisco and Vancouver, British Columbia.

Royal Caribbean (☎866-562-7625; www.royalcaribbean.com) Departures from Vancouver, British Columbia.

Getting Around

Most interisland travel is by plane, while traveling around individual islands usually requires renting a car.

Air

Interisland flights are short, frequent and surprisingly expensive.

Hawaii's airports handling most interisland air traffic are Honolulu (Oʻahu), Kahului (Maui), Kona and Hilo on Hawaiʻi (Big Island) and Lihuʻe (Kauaʻi). Smaller regional airports served mainly by commuter airlines and charter flights include Lanaʻi City (Lanaʻi); Kaunakakai and Kalaupapa on Molokaʻi; Kapalua and Hana on Maui; and Kamuela (Waimea) on Hawaiʻi (Big Island).

Boat

Limited ferry services connect Maui with Lanaʻi.

Bus

Public buses run on the larger islands, but you'll probably find it time-consuming and difficult to get around by bus, except on Oʻahu.

Car

Most visitors to Hawaii rent their own vehicles, particularly on the Neighbor Islands. If you're just visiting Honolulu and Waikiki, a car may be more of a hindrance than a help. Free parking is usually plentiful outside of cities and major towns. Bigger hotels and resorts, especially in Waikiki, typically charge $10 to $40 or more for overnight parking, either self-parking or valet.

Glossary

'a'a – type of lava that is rough and jagged

ahu – stone cairns used to mark a trail; an altar or shrine

ahupua'a – traditional land division, usually in a wedge shape that extends from the mountains to the sea (smaller than a *moku*)

'aina – land

'akala – Hawaiian raspberry or thimbleberry

ali'i – chief, royalty

ali'i nui – high chiefs, kingly class

aloha – the traditional greeting meaning love, welcome, good-bye

aloha 'aina – love of the land

'amakihi – small, yellow-green honeycreeper; one of the more common native birds

anchialine pool – contains a mixture of seawater and freshwater

'apapane – bright red native Hawaiian honeycreeper

'aumakua – protective deity or guardian spirit, deified ancestor

'awa – see *kava*

e komo mai – welcome

ha'i – voiced register-break technique used by women singers

haku – head

hala – pandanus tree; the leaves (*lau*) are used in weaving mats and baskets

haole – Caucasian; literally, 'without breath'

hapa – portion or fragment; person of mixed blood

hapa haole – Hawaiian music with predominantly English lyrics

he'e nalu – wave sliding, or surfing

heiau – ancient stone temple; a place of worship in Hawaii

ho'okupu – offering

hula – Hawaiian dance form, either traditional or modern

hula halau – hula school or troupe

hula kahiko – traditional and sacred hula

'i'iwi – scarlet Hawaiian honeycreeper with a curved, salmon-colored beak

'iliahi – Hawaiian sandalwood

'ilima – native plant, a ground cover with delicate yellow-orange flowers; O'ahu's official flower

ipu – spherical, narrow-necked gourd used as a hula implement

kahuna – knowledgeable person in any field; commonly a priest, healer or sorcerer

kama'aina – person born and raised, or a longtime resident, in Hawaii; literally, 'child of the land'

kapa – see *tapa*

kapu – taboo, part of strict ancient Hawaiian social and religious system

kapuna – elders

kava – a mildly narcotic drink ('awa in Hawaiian) made from the roots of *Piper methysticum*, a pepper shrub

ki ho'alu – slack key

kiawe – a relative of the mesquite tree introduced to Hawaii in the 1820s

ki'i – see *tiki*

kilau – a stiff, weedy fern

ko – sugarcane

koa – native hardwood tree often used in making Native Hawaiian crafts and canoes

kukui – candlenut, the official state tree; its oily nuts were once burned in lamps

kumu – teacher

Kumulipo – Native Hawaiian creation story or chant

kupuna – grandparent, elder

la'au lapa'au – plant medicine

lanai – veranda; balcony

lauhala – leaves of the *hala* plant, used in weaving

lei – garland, usually of flowers, but also of leaves, vines, shells or nuts

leptospirosis – a disease acquired by exposure to water contaminated by the urine of infected animals, especially livestock

limu – seaweed

lomilomi – traditional Hawaiian massage; known as 'loving touch'

Lono – Polynesian god of harvest, agriculture, fertility and peace

loulu – native fan palms

luau – traditional Hawaiian feast

luna – supervisor or plantation boss

mahalo – thank you

mai ho'oka'awale – leprosy (Hansen's disease); literally, 'the separating sickness'

maile – native plant with twining habit and fragrant leaves; often used for lei

makahiki – traditional annual wet-season winter festival dedicated to the agricultural god Lono

makai – toward the sea; seaward

malihini – newcomer, visitor

mana – spiritual power

mauka – toward the mountains; inland

mele – song, chant

menehune – 'little people' who, according to legend, built many of Hawaii's fishponds, heiau and other stonework

milo – a native shade tree with beautiful hardwood

moku – wedge-shaped areas of land running from the ridge of the mountains to the sea

mokupuni – low, flat island or atoll

Neighbor Islands – the term used to refer to the main Hawaiian Islands except for O'ahu

nene – a native goose; Hawaii's state bird

niu – coconut palm

'ohana – family, extended family; close-knit group

'olelo Hawai'i – the Hawaiian language

'opihi – an edible limpet

pahoehoe – type of lava that is quick and smoothflowing

pali – cliff

paniolo – cowboy

pau – finished, no more

pau hana – 'stop work'; happy hour

Pele – goddess of fire and volcanoes; her home is in Kilauea Caldera

pidgin – distinct local language and dialect, originating from Hawaii's multiethnic plantation immigrants

piko – navel, umbilical cord

pohaku – rock

pono – righteous, respectful and proper

pukiawe – native plant with red and white berries and evergreen leaves

pulu – the silken clusters encasing the stems of tree ferns

pupu – snack or appetizer; also a type of shell

pu'u – hill, cinder cone

pu'uhonua – place of refuge

raku – a style of Japanese pottery characterized by a rough, handmade appearance

rubbah slippah – flip-flops

sansei – third-generation Japanese immigrants

shaka – hand gesture used in Hawaii as a greeting or sign of local pride

talk story – to strike up a conversation, make small talk

tapa – cloth made by pounding the bark of paper mulberry, used for Native Hawaiian clothing (*kapa* in Hawaiian)

ti – common native plant; its long shiny leaves are used for wrapping food and making hula skirts (*ki* in Hawaiian)

tiki – wood- or stone-carved statue, usually depicting a deity (*ki'i* in Hawaiian)

tutu – grandmother or grandfather; also term of respect for any member of that generation

ukulele – a stringed musical instrument derived from the *braguinha,* which was introduced to Hawaii in the 1800s by Portuguese immigrants

'ulu – breadfruit

Wakea – sky father

Behind the Scenes

Our Readers

Many thanks to the travelers who used the last edition and wrote to us with helpful hints, useful advice and interesting anecdotes:

Adam Keffen, Andzejs Neguliners, Brittany Dalziel, Christian Huss, David Barrett, Elena Hidalgo, Femke Vinkx, Mark Galeck, Nikki Leeuwrik, Richard Larking, Sara Legato

Acknowledgements

Climate map data adapted from Peel MC, Finlayson BL & McMahon TA (2007) 'Updated World Map of the Köppen-Geiger Climate Classification', Hydrology and Earth System Sciences, 11, 163344.

Cover photograph: Overview of island in lagoon, Hawaii, Sandy Kelly ©

This Book

This 1st edition of Lonely Planet's *Best of Hawaii* guidebook was researched and written by Amy Balfour, Sara Benson, Greg Benchwick, Adam Skolnick, Ryan Ver Berkmoes, Craig McLachlan, Jade Bremner, Adam Karlin, Luci Yamamoto and Loren Bell. This guidebook was produced by the following:

Destination Editor Alexander Howard

Product Editor Shona Gray

Senior Cartographer Corey Hutchison

Book Designer Jessica Rose

Assisting Editors Katie Connolly, Carly Hall

Cover Researcher Naomi Parker

Thanks to William Allen, Joel Cotterell, Bruce Evans, Liz Heynes, Kate Mathews, Anne Mulvaney, Claire Naylor, Karyn Noble, Susan Paterson, Kirsten Rawlings, Alison Ridgway, Tony Wheeler

---

Send Us Your Feedback

We love to hear from travelers – your comments keep us on our toes and help make our books better. Our well-traveled team reads every word on what you loved or loathed about this book. Although we cannot reply individually to postal submissions, we always guarantee that your feedback goes straight to the appropriate authors, in time for the next edition. Each person who sends us information is thanked in the next edition, the most useful submissions are rewarded with a selection of digital PDF chapters.

Visit lonelyplanet.com/contact to submit your updates and suggestions or to ask for help. Our award-winning website also features inspirational travel stories, news and discussions.

Note: We may edit, reproduce and incorporate your comments in Lonely Planet products such as guidebooks, websites and digital products, so let us know if you don't want your comments reproduced or your name acknowledged. For a copy of our privacy policy visit lonelyplanet.com/privacy.

Index

A

accommodations 307, *see also* individual locations
activities 22-4, *see also* individual activities
air tours
  Hana 181
  Honolulu 63-4
  Kona 247
air travel 313-14
Aloha Tower 58
area codes 312
art galleries, *see* museums & galleries
arts 20, 293-6
ATMs 310

B

Battleship Missouri Memorial 49
beaches 297-8
  Hawai'i (Big Island) 244, 266-7
  Kaua'i 111-2, 118-9, 126-8, 196
  Lana'i 201-3
  Maui 12, 180-1, 196-7, 200
  Moloka'i 154
  O'ahu 6, 59, 85-7
birds 127, 140, 148, 177, 209, 218, 261
Big Island *see* Hawai'i (Big Island)
Bishop Museum 50-1
boat tours
  Hanalei Bay 130
  Kona 244
  Lana'i 201

Moloka'i 163
Na Pali Coast 106-9
Waikiki 89
Waimea Canyon 145-6
boat travel 314
books 25
bus travel 314
business hours 17

C

camping 307 *see also* individual locations
Canyon Trail 142
car travel 314, *see also* driving tours
caves
  Hana Lava Tube 173
  Maniniholo Dry Cave 119
  Thurston Lava Tube 264-5
  Waikanaloa Wet Cave 115
  Waikapala'e Wet Cave 115
caving 300
cell phones 311
children, travel with 32-3
Chinatown (Honolulu) 38-43, **56-7**
  itineraries 42-3, **42**
  markets 38-9
churches, *see also* temples & shrines
  Ke'anae Congregational Church 176
  Waimea Hawaiian Church 145
  Wai'oli Hui'ia Church 126-7
climate 16, 22-4
costs 17
crafts 294-6
credit cards 310
culture, *see* Hawaiian culture
currency 16, 310
customs regulations 307-8
cycling 300

Honoka'a 228
Moloka'i 163
Waimea Canyon 146

D

Damien Tours 158
demographics 279
dialing codes 312
Diamond Head 85
disabilities, travelers with 312
diving & snorkeling 298
  Hana Hwy 183
  Hilo 270
  Twenty Mile Beach 161
  Waikiki 88
driving 314
driving tours
  Chain of Craters Rd 265
  Crater Rim Drive 254. 262-5
  Hana Hwy 166-85
  Tantalus Round-Top Scenic Drive 62
  Waimea Canyon 138-9

E

economy 279
electricity 307
emergency services 309, 312
environmental issues 279
etiquette 308
events 22-4, 309, *see also* Hawaiian culture
exchange rates 310

F

family travel 32-3
festivals 22-4
films 25
fish, *see* sea life

food 21, 192-5, 302-5, 309
see also festivals, *individual locations*
Foster Botanical Garden 40

G

galleries, see *museums & galleries*
gardens, *see* parks & gardens
gay travelers 309
glossaries 315-16
golf 88-9

H

Ha'ena 118
Ha'ena State Park 114-17
Halawa Tropical Flower Farm 155
Halawa Valley 152-5
Haleakalā National Park 13, 204-19, **207**
  hiking 208-11
  itineraries 206
  travel to/from 207, 219
  travel within 219
Haleakalā summit **206-9, 219, 216**
Halema'uma'u Trail 261
Halema'uma'u Viewpoint 256-7, 264
Halemau'u Trail 209
Hana 180-5, **181**
Hana Hwy 11, 166-85, **169, 182, 184**
  activities 181-3
  drinking & nightlife 185
  food 183-5
  itineraries 168
  shopping 183
  tours 181
  travel to/from 169, 185
  travel within 185
Hana Lava Tube 173
Hanakoa Valley 112

Hanalei 126, **128**
Hanalei Bay 8, 120-31, **123**
  activities 129
  drinking & nightlife 131
  food 130-1
  itineraries 122
  tours 129-30
  travel to/from 123, 131
  travel within 131
Hansen's disease 158-9
Hawai'i (Big Island) 220-275, **223, 233, 244, 253**, see also Waipi'o Valley, Hawai'i Volcanoes National Park, Mauna Kea
Hawaii Theater 41, 71
Hawai'i Volcanoes National Park 15, 250-75, **253**
  itineraries 252
  travel to/from 253
Hawaiian culture 278-9, 289-92, 308
  Aloha Festivals 24
  Eo e Emalani I Alaka'i 143
  Honolulu Festival 22-3
  Kaua'i Mokihana Festival 24
  Koloa Plantation Days Celebration 24
  Merrie Monarch Festival 23
  Native Books/Nā Mea Hawaii 65
  Waimea Town Celebration 22, 147
Hawaiian Islands Humpback Whale National Marine Sanctuary 190-1
Hawaiian people 289-92
health 309
hiking 300-1, *see also* volcano hiking
  Hawai'i 224-7, 270
  Kaua'i 110-3, 129, 139-43
  Lana'i 203
  Maui 174-5, 183, 197-8, 207-11
  Moloka'i 155-9
  O'ahu 52-3, 64-5, 88

Hilo 266-75, **267, 268-9**
  activities 267
  drinking & nightlife 274-5
  entertainment 275
  food 271
  shopping 270-1
  travel to/from 275
  travel within 275
  walking tours 42-3, 65
history 280-8
holidays 311
Honoka'a 228-9
  activities 228
  entertainment 229
  food 228-9
  tours 228
  travel to/from 229
  travel within 229
Honolulu 4, 35-71, **36, 56-7, 60**
  activities 63-5
  drinking & nightlife 70
  entertainment 71
  food 66-9
  itineraries 36
  shopping 66
  tours 65
  travel to/from 37, 71
  travel within 71
Hosmer Grove Trail 209
hula 293-4
  Kaua'i Mokihana Festival 24
  Moloka'i Ka Hula Piko 23-4
Hulihe 'Ie Palace 244
Humu'ula-Mauna Kea Summit Trail 238-9

I

immigration 307-9
insurance 309-10
internet access 310
internet resources 17
'Iolani Palace 44-5
itineraries 26-31, *see also*

individual regions
Izumo Taishakyo Mission 41

J

Jaggar Museum 263-4

K

Kahanamoku, Duke 78, 86
Kahanu Garden 172
Kaiulani, Princess 85
Kalalau Trail 110-13
Kalakaua, King David 44-5, 80-1, 285
Kalaupapa Peninsula 156-7
Kalaupapa Trail 156-9
Kamehameha the Great 245, 283-4
Kapi'olani, Queen 84-5
Kaua'i 102-147, **105**, **123**, **128**, **135**, **144** see also Hanalei Bay, Na Pali Coast Wilderness State Park, Waimea Canyon
Kaulu Paoa Heiau 115
Kaunakakai 160-6, **160**
kayaking 298
    Hana Hwy 183
    Hanalei Bay 129
    Moloka'i 155, 163
    Na Pali Coast Wilderness State Park 108
Ke'anae Peninsula & Valley 176-7, **184**
Keonehe'ehe'e (Sliding Sands) Trail 208-9
Kihei 12, 188-203
    drinking & nightlife 199
    food 198
    itineraries 188
    travel to/from 199
    travel within 199
Kilauea Iki Overlook & Trail 254-5
Kilauea Overlook 263
Kilauea Visitor Center & Museum 254

Kipahulu 210-11
Kipuka Puaulu 261
kitesurfing, see surfing
Koai'e Canyon Trail 139
Koke'e Resource Conservation Program 143
Koke'e Museum 140-1
Koke'e State Park 140-3
Kona 245-9, **246**
    activities 244-5
    drinking & nightlife 249
    food 247-9
    shopping 247
    tours 247
    travel to/from 249
    travel within 249
Kuan Yin Temple 40-1
Kuhio Beach Park 76-7
Kula 217-19
Kuloa Point Trail 211

L

Lana'i 200-3
languages 16, 315-16
lavafields, see volcanoes & lava fields
legal matters 310
leprosy 158-9
lesbian travelers 309
LGBTI travelers 309
Lili'uokalani, Queen 55, 286-7
Luahiwa Petroglyphs 202
luau 99-100

M

Makiki Valley Trails 53, 64-5
Manoa Cliffs Trail 64-5
Manoa Falls Trail 52-3
Maui 166-219, **169**, **182**, **184**, **189**, **207**
Mauna Iki Trail 258
Mauna Kea 15, 230-49, **233**, **244**
    itineraries 232

Summit Area 234-7
    travel to/from 233
Mauna Loa Observatory Trail 242-3
medical serices 309
mobile phones 311
Moloka'i 10, 148-65, **151**, **162**
    activities 161-3
    drinking & nightlife 165
    food 164-5
    itineraries 150
    shopping 163-4
    travel to/from 151, 165
    travel within 165
money 16, 17, 310-11
Muliwai Trail 224-7
museums & galleries
    Bishop Museum 50-1
    Hawaii Army Museum 85-6
    Hawai'i State Art Museum 54
    Hawaiian Mission Houses Historic Site 58
    Honolulu Museum of Art 59-61
    'Imiloa Astronomy Center of Hawai'i 267
    Jaggar Museum 263-4
    Koke'e Museum 140-1
    Pacific Aviation Museum 49
    Pacific Tsunami Museum 267
    Spalding House 62-3
    USS Bowfin Submarine Museum & Park 49
    Volcano Arts Center 262
    West Kaua'i Technology & Visitor Center 144
music 25, 294, see also slack key guitar

N

Na Pali Coast Wilderness State Park 6, 102-19, **105**
    activities 119
    food 119

itineraries 104
shopping 119
travel to/from 105, 119
Napau Crater Trail 259
national parks & reserves
Ha'ena State Park 114-17,
204-19, **207**
Haleakalā National Park 13,
204-19, **207**
Hawai'i Volcanoes National
Park 15, 15, 250-75, **253**
Koke'e State Park 140-3
Pua'a Ka'a State Wayside
Park 179
Wai'anapanapa State Park
173, 182
nene 218
Nu'alolo Trail 141-2
Nu'uanu Valley Lookout 53

O

O'ahu 34-101, **36**, **56-7**, **60**
see also Honolulu, Waikiki
Obama, Barack 59
opening hours 17

P

Pacific Aviation Museum 49
paddleboarding
Kona 246
Moloka'i 163
paragliding 217
parks & gardens
Ali'i Kula Lavender 217
Foster Botanical Garden 40
Kahanu Garden 172
Kapi'olani Regional Park 85
Limahuli Garden 118
Lyon Arboretum 62
USS Bowfin Submarine
Museum & Park 49
passports 308
payphones 311-12
Pearl Harbor 46-9

people 289-92
petroglyophs
Luahiwa Petroglyphs 202
Pu'u Loa Petroglyphs 258-9
phonecards 311-12
Pihea Trail 143
Pi'ilanihale Heiau 170-3
Pi'ilani Trail 174-5
Pipiwai Trail 210-11
planning
itineraries 26-31
travel with children 32-3
politics 279
Polynesians 281, 289, 296
Pua'a Ka'a State
Wayside Park 179
public holidays 311
Pu'u Huluhulu Trail 259-60
Pu'u Loa Petroglyphs 258-9

R

religions 279, 284
Road to Hana, see Hana Hwy
running 24, 89

S

scuba diving, see diving &
snorkeling
sea life 299, see also diving &
snorkeling, whale-watching
seals 81, 178
sea turtles 20, 201, 267
sharks 117
sharks 117
shopping 20, see also individual
locations
slack key guitar 24, 25,
292, 294
snorkeling, see diving
& snorkeling
South Maui 186-203
activities 197-8
food 198-9

stargazing 301
Mauna Kea 240-1
Planetarium 51
Steaming Bluff 263
Subaru Telescope 236-7
surfing 299-300
Ha'ena 119
Halawa Valley 154
Hana Hwy 181
Hanalei Bay 125
Hilo 270
Honolulu 65
Kona 244-5
Triple Crown of Surfing 24
Waikiki 78-9, 88
Waimea Rivermouth 146
swimming 76, 297-8, see also
beaches, diving & snorkeling,
individual locations
swimming holes 178-9,
198-9, 226

T

telephone services 311-12
temples & shrines
Ahu'ena Heiau 244
Izumo Taishakyo Mission 41
Kaulu Paoa Heiau 115
Kuan Yin Temple 40-1
Pi'ilanihale Heiau 170-3
tennis 89
Thurston Lava Tube 264-5
time 312
tipping 311
tourist information 312
travel to/from Hawaii 313
travel within Hawaii 314

U

USS Arizona Memorial 49
USS Bowfin Submarine
Museum & Park 49

V

vacations 311
viewpoints
  Diamond Head Lookout 85
  Haleakalā 212-15
  Halemaʻumaʻu Viewpoint
    256-7, 264
  Kilauea Iki Overlook 254-5
  Kilauea Overlook 263
  Nuʻuanu Valley Lookout 53
  Puʻu ʻUalakaʻa State
    Wayside 62
  Waipiʻo Valley Lookout 229
visas 308
Volcano Arts Center 262
volcano hiking
  Halemaʻumaʻu Trail 261
  Halemauʻu Trail 209
  Hosmer Grove Trail 209
  Humuʻula-Mauna Kea
    Summit Trail 238-9
  Keonehe'ehe'e (Sliding
    Sands) Trail 208-9
  Kilauea Iki Trail 254-5
  Kipuka Puaulu 261
  Mauna Iki Trail 258
  Mauna Loa Observatory Trail
    242-3
  Napau Crater Trail 259
  Puʻu Huluhulu Trail 259-60
volcanoes & lava fields
  Haleakalā 208-9, 212-15, **216**
  Halemaʻumaʻu 256-7, 264
  Hawaiʻi Volcanoes National

  Park 250-63
  Kilauea 263
  Kilauea Iki 254-5
  Mauna Iki 258
  Mauna Kea 230-43
  Mauna Loa 242-3
  Puʻu Loa 258-9
  Thurston Lava Tube 264-5

W

Waiʻanapanapa State
  Park 173, **182**
Waikiki 6, 72-101, **75**, **82-3**
  accommodations 101, **101**
  activities 88-9
  drinking & nightlife 96-8
  entertainment 98-100
  food 91-6
  itineraries 74
  shopping 89-90
  tours 89
  travel to/from 75, 100
  travel within 100
Wailea 12, 189-200, **189**
  itineraries 188
  travel to/from 189
Wailua **182**
Waimea 144-7, **144**
Waimea Canyon 9, 132-47, **135**
  activities 145-6
  entertainment 147
  food 147
  itineraries 134

  shopping 146-7
  travel to/from 135, 147
  travel within 147
Waimea Canyon Trail 139
Waipiʻo Valley 14, 220-9, **223**
  itineraries 222
  travel to/from 223
walking see hiking
walking tours
  Chinatown (Honolulu) 42-3,
    42
  Hilo 268-9, **268-9**
war memorials 48-9
waterfalls
  Hanakapiʻai Falls 111
  Hipuapua Falls 155
  Manoa Falls Trail 52-3
  Moaʻula Falls 155
  Three Bears Falls 178-9
  Twin Falls 178, **184**
  Wailua Falls 179
weather 16, 22-4
whale-watching
  Honolulu 63
  Molokaʻi 163
  South Maui 190-1
wi-fi 310
windsurfing, see surfing
WM Keck Observatory 237
WWII Valor in the Pacific Na-
  tional Monument 48-9

Z

ziplining 217

Symbols & Map Key

Look for these symbols to quickly identify listings:

◉ Sights
✪ Activities
✪ Courses
✪ Tours
✪ Festivals & Events

✪ Eating
✪ Drinking
✪ Entertainment
✪ Shopping
ⓘ Information & Transport

These symbols and abbreviations give vital information for each listing:

🌿 Sustainable or green recommendation

FREE No payment required

☎ Telephone number
🕓 Opening hours
Ⓟ Parking
⊘ Nonsmoking
❄ Air-conditioning
@ Internet access
🛜 Wi-fi access
🏊 Swimming pool

🚌 Bus
⛴ Ferry
🚊 Tram
🚆 Train
📖 English-language menu
🌱 Vegetarian selection
👪 Family-friendly

Find your best experiences with these Great For... icons.

Art & Culture
Beaches
Budget
Cafe/Coffee
Cycling
Detour
Drinking
Entertainment
Events
Family Travel
Food & Drink

History
Local Life
Nature & Wildlife
Photo Op
Scenery
Shopping
Short Trip
Sport
Walking
Winter Travel

Sights

◉ Beach
◉ Bird Sanctuary
◉ Buddhist
◉ Castle/Palace
◉ Christian
◉ Confucian
◉ Hindu
◉ Islamic
◉ Jain
◉ Jewish
◉ Monument
◉ Museum/Gallery/ Historic Building
◉ Ruin
◉ Shinto
◉ Sikh
◉ Taoist
◉ Winery/Vineyard
◉ Zoo/Wildlife Sanctuary
◉ Other Sight

Points of Interest

◉ Bodysurfing
◉ Camping
◉ Cafe
◉ Canoeing/Kayaking
◉ Course/Tour
◉ Diving
◉ Drinking & Nightlife
◉ Eating
◉ Entertainment
◉ Sento Hot Baths/ Onsen
◉ Shopping
◉ Skiing
◉ Sleeping
◉ Snorkelling
◉ Surfing
◉ Swimming/Pool
◉ Walking
◉ Windsurfing
◉ Other Activity

Information

◉ Bank
◉ Embassy/Consulate
◉ Hospital/Medical
@ Internet
◉ Police
◉ Post Office
◉ Telephone
◉ Toilet
◉ Tourist Information
● Other Information

Geographic

◉ Beach
◉ Gate
◉ Hut/Shelter
◉ Lighthouse
◉ Lookout
▲ Mountain/Volcano
◉ Oasis
◉ Park
)(Pass
◉ Picnic Area
◉ Waterfall

Transport

◉ Airport
Ⓑ BART station
◉ Border crossing
Ⓣ Boston T station
◉ Bus
Cable car/Funicular
Cycling
Ferry
Metro/MRT station
Monorail
Ⓟ Parking
◉ Petrol station
◉ Subway/S-Bahn/ Skytrain station
◉ Taxi
Train station/Railway
Tram
◉ Tube Station
Ⓤ Underground/ U-Bahn station
● Other Transport

Our Story

A beat-up old car, a few dollars in the pocket and a sense of adventure. In 1972 that's all Tony and Maureen Wheeler needed for the trip of a lifetime – across Europe and Asia overland to Australia. It took several months, and at the end – broke but inspired – they sat at their kitchen table writing and stapling together their first travel guide, Across Asia on the Cheap. Within a week they'd sold 1500 copies. Lonely Planet was born.

Today, Lonely Planet has offices in Franklin, London, Melbourne, Oakland, Dublin, Beijing, and Delhi, with more than 600 staff and writers. We share Tony's belief that 'a great guidebook should do three things: inform, educate and amuse'.

Our Writers

Amy Balfour

Amy practiced law in Virginia before moving to Los Angeles to try to break in as a screenwriter. If you listen carefully, you can still hear the horrified screams of her parents echoing through the space-time continuum. After a stint as a writer's assistant on *Law & Order*, she jumped into freelance writing, focusing on travel, food, and the outdoors. She has hiked, biked, and paddled across Southern California and the Southwest. She recently criss-crossed the Great Plains in search of the region's best burgers and barbecue.

Sara Benson

After graduating from college in Chicago, Sara jumped on a plane to California with one suitcase and just $100 in her pocket. She landed in San Francisco, and today she makes her home in Oakland, just across the Bay. She also spent three years of living in Japan, after which she followed her wanderlust around Asia and the Pacific before returning to the USA, where she has worked as a teacher, a journalist, a nurse, and a national park ranger. To keep up with Sara's latest travel adventures, read her blog, The Indie Traveler (indietraveler.blogspot.com), and follow her on Twitter (@indie_traveler) and Instagram (indietraveler).

Contributing Writers

Loren Bell, Greg Benchwick, Jade Bremner, Adam Karlin, Craig McLachlan, Adam Skolnik, Ryan Ver Berkmoes, Luci Yamamato.

STAY IN TOUCH LONELYPLANET.COM/CONTACT

AUSTRALIA The Malt Store, Level 3, 551 Swanston St, Carlton, Victoria 3053
☏ 03 8379 8000,
fax 03 8379 8111

IRELAND Unit E, Digital Court. The Digital Hub, Rainsford St, Dublin 8, Ireland

USA 124 Linden Street, Oakland, CA 94607
☏ 510 250 6400,
toll free 800 275 8555,
fax 510 893 8572

UK 240 Blackfriars Road, London SE1 8NW
☏ 020 3771 5100,
fax 020 3771 5101

 twitter.com/lonelyplanet
 facebook.com/lonelyplanet
 instagram.com/lonelyplanet
 youtube.com/lonelyplanet
 lonelyplanet.com/newsletter